D0272532

Selected Poems of Alfred Lord Tennyson

Selected Poems of Alfred Lord Tennyson

Alfred Lord Tennyson

THORNDIKE
CHIVERS

This Large Print edition is published by Thorndike Press®, Waterville, Maine USA and by BBC Audiobooks Ltd, Bath, England.

Originally published in 1892 and is now in Public Domain in the United States and the United Kingdom.

U.S. Hardcover	0-7862-8691-1	(Classics)
U.K. Hardcover 10:	1 4056 3816 8	(Chivers Large Print)
U.K. Hardcover 13:	978 1 405 63816 6	
U.K. Softcover 10:	1 4056 3817 6	(Camden Large Print)
U.K. Softcover 13:	978 1 405 63817 3	

The text of this Large Print edition is unabridged.
Other aspects of the book may vary from the original edition.

Set in 16 pt. Plantin by Christina S. Huff.

Printed in the United States on permanent paper.

British Library Cataloguing-in-Publication Data available

Library of Congress Cataloging-in-Publication Data

Tennyson, Alfred Tennyson, Baron, 1809–1892
[Poems. Selections]
Selected poems of Alfred Lord Tennyson / by Alfred Lord Tennyson.
p. cm. — (Thorndike Press large print classics)
Originally published: Wordsworth Poetry Library, 1892.
ISBN 0-7862-8691-1 (lg. print : hc : alk. paper)
1. Large type books. I. Title. II. Series.
PR5551 2006
821′.8—dc22 2006007805

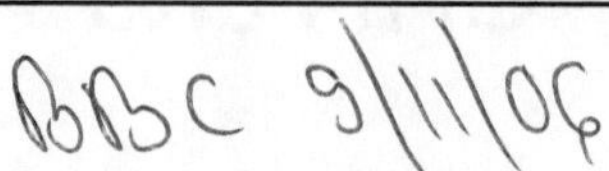

Selected Poems of Alfred Lord Tennyson

Contents

POEMS

To The Queen

Revered, beloved — O you that hold
  A nobler office upon earth
  Than arms, or power of brain, or birth
Could give the warrior kings of old,

Victoria, — since your Royal grace
  To one of less desert allows
  This laurel greener from the brows
Of him that utter'd nothing base;

And should your greatness, and the care
  That yokes with empire, yield you time
  To make demand of modern rhyme
If aught of ancient worth be there;

Then — while a sweeter music wakes,
  And thro' wild March the throstle calls,
  Where all about your palace-walls
The sun-lit almond-blossom shakes —

Take, Madam, this poor book of song,
  For tho' the faults were thick as dust
  In vacant chambers, I could trust
Your kindness, May you rule us long,

And leave us rulers of your blood
  As noble till the latest day!
  May children of our children say,
'She wrought her people lasting good;

'Her court was pure; her life serene;
  God gave her peace; her land reposed;
  A thousand claims to reverence closed
In her as Mother, Wife and Queen;

'And statesmen at her council met
  Who knew the seasons when to take
  Occasion by the hand, and make
The bounds of freedom wider yet

'By shaping some august decree,
  Which kept her throne unshaken still,
  Broad-based upon her people's will,
And compass'd by the inviolate sea.'

March 1851

POEMS, CHIEFLY LYRICAL

Claribel

A Melody

I

Where Claribel low-lieth
  The breezes pause and die,
    Letting the rose-leaves fall:
But the solemn oak-tree sigheth
    Thick-leaved, ambrosial,
  With an ancient melody
  Of an inward agony,
Where Claribel low-lieth.

II

At eve the beetle boometh
  Athwart the thicket lone:
At noon the wild bee hummeth
  About the moss'd headstone:
At midnight the moon cometh,
  And looketh down alone.
Her song the lintwhite swelleth,

The clear-voiced mavis dwelleth,
  The callow throstle lispeth,
The slumbrous wave outwelleth,
  The babbling runnel crispeth,
The hollow grot replieth
Where Claribel low-lieth.

Lilian

I

  Airy, fairy Lilian,
  Flitting, fairy Lilian,
When I ask her if she love me
Claps her tiny hands above me,
  Laughing all she can;
She'll not tell me if she love me,
  Cruel little Lilian.

II

    When my passion seeks
    Pleasance in love-sighs
She, looking thro' and thro' me
Thoroughly to undo me,
    Smiling, never speaks:
So innocent-arch, so cunning-simple,
From beneath her gather'd wimple

Glancing with black-beaded eyes,
Till the lightning laughters dimple
The baby-roses in her cheeks;
Then away she flies.

III

Prythee weep, May Lilian!
Gaiety without eclipse
Wearieth me, May Lilian:
Thro' my very heart it thrilleth,
When from crimson-threaded lips
Silver-treble laughter trilleth:
Prythee weep, May Lilian.

IV

Praying all I can
If prayers will not hush thee,
Airy Lilian
Like a rose-leaf I will crush thee,
Fairy Lilian.

Isabel

I

Eyes not down-dropt nor over-bright,
but fed
With the clear-pointed flame of chastity,
Clear, without heat, undying, tended by
Pure vestal thoughts in the translucent
fane
Of her still spirit; locks not wide-dispread,
Madonna-wise on either side her head;
Sweet lips whereon perpetually did
reign
The summer calm of golden charity,
Were fixed shadows of thy fixed mood,
Revered Isabel, the crown and head,
The stately flower of female fortitude,
Of perfect wifehood and pure
lowlihead.

II

The intuitive decision of a bright
And thorough-edged intellect to part
Error from crime a prudence to with-
hold;
The laws of marriage character'd in
gold

Upon the blanched tablets of her heart;
A love still burning upward, giving light
To read those laws; an accent very low
In blandishment, but a most silver flow
Of subtle-paced counsel in distress,
Right to the heart and brain, tho' undescried,
Winning its way with extreme gentleness
Thro' all the outworks of suspicious pride;
A courage to endure and to obey,
A hate of gossip parlance, and of sway,
Crown'd Isabel, thro' all her placid life,
The queen of marriage, a most perfect wife.

III

The mellow'd reflex of a winter moon;
A clear stream flowing with a muddy one,
Till in its onward current it absorbs
With swifter movement and in purer light
The vexed eddies of its wayward brother:
A leaning and upbearing parasite,
Clothing the stem, which else had fallen quite,
With cluster'd flower-bells and ambrosial orbs

Of rich fruit-bunches leaning on each
other —
Shadow forth thee: — the world hath
not another
(Tho' all her fairest forms are types of thee,
And thou of God in thy great charity)
Of such a finish'd chasten'd purity.

Elegiacs

Low-flowing breezes are roaming the broad
valley dimm'd in the gloaming:
Thoro' the black-stemm'd pines only the far
river shines.
Creeping through blossomy rushes and
bowers of rose-blowing bushes,
Down by the poplar tall rivulets babble
and fall.
Barketh the shepherd-dog cheerly;
the grasshopper carolleth clearly;
Deeply the turtle coos; shrilly the owlet
halloos;
Winds creep; dews fall chilly: in her first
sleep earth breathes stilly:
Over the pools in the burn water-gnats
murmur and mourn.
Sadly the far kine loweth:
the glimmering water outfloweth:
Twin peaks shadow'd with pine slope

to the dark hyaline.
Low-throned Hesper is stayed between
the two peaks; but the Naiad
Throbbing in mild unrest holds him
beneath in her breast.
The ancient poetess singeth,
that Hesperus all things bringeth,
Smoothing the wearied mind:
bring me my love, Rosalind.
Thou comest morning and even;
she cometh not morning or even.
False-eyed Hesper, unkind,
where is my sweet Rosalind?

Mariana

'Mariana in the moated grange'
— *Measure for Measure*

With blackest moss the flower-plots
Were thickly crusted, one and all:
The rusted nails fell from the knots
That held the pear to the garden-wall.
The broken sheds look'd sad and strange:
Unlifted was the clinking latch;
Weeded and worn the ancient thatch
Upon the lonely moated grange.
She only said, 'My life is dreary,
He cometh not,' she said;

She said, 'I am aweary, aweary,
  I would that I were dead!'

Her tears fell with the dews at even;
  Her tears fell ere the dews were dried;
She could not look on the sweet heaven,
  Either at morn or eventide.
After the flitting of the bats,
  When thickest dark did trance the sky,
  She drew her casement-curtain by,
And glanced athwart the glooming flats.
  She only said, 'The night is dreary,
    He cometh not,' she said;
  She said, 'I am aweary, aweary,
    I would that I were dead!'

Upon the middle of the night,
  Waking she heard the night-fowl crow:
The cock sung out an hour ere light:
  From the dark fen the oxen's low
Came to her: without hope of change,
  In sleep she seem'd to walk forlorn,
  Till cold winds woke the grey-eyed morn
About the lonely moated grange.
  She only said, 'The day is dreary,
    He cometh not,' she said;
  She said, 'I am aweary, aweary,
    I would that I were dead!'

About a stone-cast from the wall

A sluice with blacken'd waters slept,
And o'er it many, round and small,
The cluster'd marish-mosses crept.
Hard by a poplar shook alway,
All silver-green with gnarled bark:
For leagues no other tree did mark
The level waste, the rounding grey.
She only said, 'My life is dreary,
He cometh not,' she said;
She said, 'I am aweary, aweary,
I would that I were dead!'

And ever when the moon was low,
And the shrill winds were up and away,
In the white curtain, to and fro,
She saw the gusty shadow sway.
But when the moon was very low,
And wild winds bound within their cell,
The shadow of the poplar fell
Upon her bed, across her brow.
She only said, 'The night is dreary,
He cometh not,' she said;
She said, 'I am aweary, aweary,
I would that I were dead!'

All day within the dreamy house,
The doors upon their hinges creak'd;
The blue fly sung in the pane; the mouse
Behind the mouldering wainscot shriek'd,
Or from the crevice peer'd about.

Old faces glimmer'd thro' the doors,
Old footsteps trod the upper floors,
Old voices called her from without.
She only said, 'My life is dreary,
He cometh not,' she said;
She said, 'I am aweary, aweary,
I would that I were dead!'

The sparrow's chirrup on the roof,
The slow clock ticking, and the sound
Which to the wooing wind aloof
The poplar made, did all confound
Her sense; but most she loathed the hour
When the thick-moted sunbeam lay
Athwart the chambers, and the day
Was sloping toward his western bower.
Then, said she, 'I am very dreary,
He will not come,' she said;
She wept, 'I am aweary, aweary,
Oh God, that I were dead!'

To —

I

Clear-headed friend, whose joyful scorn,
Edged with sharp laughter, cuts atwain
The knots that tangle human creeds,
The wounding cords that bind and strain

The heart until it bleeds,
Ray-fringed eyelids of the morn
Roof not a glance so keen as thine:
If aught of prophecy be mine,
Thou wilt not live in vain.

II

Low-cowering shall the Sophist sit;
Falsehood shall bare her plaited brow:
Fair-fronted Truth shall droop not now
With shrilling shafts of subtle wit.
Nor martyr-flames, nor trenchant swords
Can do away that ancient lie;
A gentler death shall Falsehood die
Shot thro' and thro' with cunning words.

III

Weak Truth a-leaning on her crutch
Wan, wasted Truth in her utmost need,
Thy kingly intellect shall feed,
Until she be an athlete bold,
And weary with a finger's touch
Those writhed limbs of lightning speed;
Like that strange angel which of old,
Until the breaking of the light,
Wrestled with wandering Israel
Past Yabbok brook the livelong night,

And heaven's mazed signs stood still
In the dim tract of Penuel.

Madeline

I

Thou art not steep'd in golden languors,
   No tranced summer calm is thine,
      Ever varying Madeline.
   Thro' light and shadow thou dost range,
   Sudden glances, sweet and strange,
Delicious spites and darling angers,
   And airy forms of flitting change.

II

Smiling, frowning, evermore,
Thou art perfect in love-lore.
Revealings deep and clear are thine
Of wealthy smiles: but who may know
Whether smile or frown be fleeter?
Whether smile or frown be sweeter,
      Who may know?
Frowns perfect-sweet along the brow
Light-glooming over eyes divine,
Like little clouds sun-fringed, are thine,
      Ever varying Madeline.

Thy smile and frown are not aloof
From one another
Each to each is dearest brother;
Hues of the silken sheeny woof
Momently shot into each other.
All the mystery is thine;
Smiling, frowning, evermore,
Thou art perfect in love-lore,
Ever varying Madeline.

III

A subtle, sudden flame,
By veering passion fann'd,
About thee breaks and dances;
When I would kiss thy hand,
The flush of anger'd shame
O'erflows thy calmer glances,
And o'er black brows drops down
A sudden-curved frown:
But when I turn away,
Thou, willing me to stay,
Wooest not, nor vainly wranglest;
But, looking fixedly the while,
All my bounding heart entanglest
In a golden-netted smile;
Then in madness and in bliss,
If my lips should dare to kiss
Thy taper fingers amorously,

Again thou blushest angerly;
And o'er black brows drops down
A sudden-curved frown.

The Merman

I

Who would be
A merman bold,
Sitting alone,
Singing alone
Under the sea,
With a crown of gold,
On a throne?

II

I would be a merman bold;
I would sit and sing the whole of the
day;
I would fill the sea-halls with a voice of
power:
But at night I would roam abroad and play
With the mermaids in and out of the
rocks,
Dressing their hair with the white sea-
flower;

And holding them back by their flowing
locks
I would kiss them often under the sea,
And kiss them again till they kiss'd me
Laughingly, laughingly;
And then we would wander away, away
To the pale-green sea-groves straight and
high,
Chasing each other merrily.

III

There would be neither moon nor star;
But the wave would make music above us
afar —
Low thunder and light in the magic
night —
Neither moon nor star.
We would call aloud in the dreamy dells,
Call to each other and whoop and cry
All night, merrily, merrily;
They would pelt me with starry spangles
and shells,
Laughing and clapping their hands
between,
All night, merrily, merrily:
But I would throw to them back in
mine
Turkis and agate and almondine:
Then leaping out upon them unseen

I would kiss them often under the sea,
And kiss them again till they kiss'd me
  Laughingly, laughingly.
Oh! what a happy life were mine
Under the hollow-hung ocean green!
Soft are the moss-beds under the sea;
We would live merrily, merrily.

The Mermaid

I

Who would be
A mermaid fair,
Singing alone,
Combing her hair
Under the sea
In a golden curl
With a comb of pearl,
On a throne?

II

  I would be a mermaid fair;
I would sing to myself the whole of the day;
With a comb of pearl I would comb my hair;
And still as I comb'd I would sing and say,
'Who is it loves me? who loves not me?'

I would comb my hair till my ringlets would
fall,
Low adown, low adown,
From under my starry sea-bud crown
Low adown and around,
And I should look like a fountain of gold
Springing alone
With a shrill inner sound,
Over the throne
In the midst of the hall;
Till that great sea-snake under the sea
From his coiled sleeps in the central deeps
Would slowly trail himself sevenfold
Round the hall where I sate, and look in at
the gate
With his large calm eyes for the love of me.
And all the mermen under the sea
Would feel their immortality
Die in their hearts for the love of me.

III

But at night I would wander away, away
I would fling on each side my low-flowing
locks,
And lightly vault from the throne and play
With the mermen in and out of the
rocks;
We would run to and fro, and hide and seek,

On the broad sea-wolds in the crimson
shells,
Whose silvery spikes are nighest the sea.
But if any came near I would call, and shriek,
And adown the steep like a wave I would
leap
From the diamond-ledges that jut from
the dells
For I would not be kiss'd by all who would
list
Of the bold merry mermen under the sea;
They would sue me, and woo me, and flatter
me,
In the purple twilights under the sea;
But the king of them all would carry me,
Woo me, and win me, and marry me,
In the branching jaspers under the sea;
Then all the dry pied things that be
In the hueless mosses under the sea
Would curl round my silver feet silently,
All looking up for the love of me.
And if I should carol aloud, from aloft
All things that are forked, and horned, and
soft
Would lean out from the hollow sphere of
the sea,
All looking down for the love of me.

Supposed Confessions

of a second-rate sensitive mind not in unity with itself

Oh God! my God! have mercy now.
I faint, I fall. Men say that
Thou Did'st die for me, for such as *me,*
Patient of ill, and death, and scorn,
And that my sin was as a thorn
Among the thorns that girt Thy brow,
Wounding Thy soul. — That even now,
In this extremest misery
Of ignorance, I should require
A sign! and if a bolt of fire
Would rive the slumbrous summer noon
While I do pray to Thee alone,
Think my belief would stronger grow!
Is not my human pride brought low?
The boastings of my spirit still?
The joy I had in my freewill
  All cold, and dead, and corpse-like
    grown?
And what is left to me, but Thou,
And faith in Thee? Men pass me by;
Christians with happy countenances —
And children all seem full of Thee!
And women smile with saint-like glances
Like Thine own mother's when she bow'd
Above Thee, on that happy morn

When angels spake to men aloud,
And Thou and peace to earth were born.
Goodwill to me as well as all —
  I one of them: my brothers they:
Brothers in Christ — a world of peace
  And confidence, day after day;
And trust and hope till things should
    cease,
  And then one Heaven receive us all.

How sweet to have a common faith!
To hold a common scorn of death!
And at a burial to hear
  The creaking cords which wound and
    eat
Into my human heart, whene'er
Earth goes to earth, with grief, not fear,
  With hopeful grief, were passing sweet!
A grief not uninformed, and dull,
Hearted with hope, of hope as full
As is the blood with life, or night
And a dark cloud with rich moonlight.
To stand beside a grave, and see
The red small atoms wherewith we
Are built, and smile in calm, and say —
  'These little motes and grains shall be
  Clothed on with immortality
  More glorious than the noon of day.
    All that is pass'd into the flowers,
And into beasts, and other men,

And all the Norland whirlwind
showers
From open vaults, and all the sea
O'erwashes with sharp salts, again
Shall fleet together all, and be
Indued with immortality.'

Thrice happy state again to be
The trustful infant on the knee!
Who lets his waxen fingers play
About his mother's neck, and knows
Nothing beyond his mother's eyes.
They comfort him by night and day;
They light his little life alway;
He hath no thought of coming woes;
He hath no care of life or death,
Scarce outward signs of joy arise,
Because the Spirit of happiness
And perfect rest so inward is;
And loveth so his innocent heart,
Her temple and her place of birth,
Where she would ever wish to dwell,
Life of the fountain there, beneath
Its salient springs, and far apart,
Hating to wander out on earth,
Or breathe into the hollow air
Whose chillness would make visible
Her subtil, warm, and golden breath,
Which mixing with the infant's blood,
Fulfils him with beatitude.

Oh! sure it is a special care
Of God, to fortify from doubt,
To arm in proof, and guard about
With ttiple-mailèd trust, and clear
Delight, the infant's dawning year.

Would that my gloomed fancy were
As thine, my mother, when with brows
Propped on thy knees, my hands upheld
In thine, I listen'd to thy vows,
For me outpour'd in holiest prayer —
For me unworthy! — and beheld
Thy mild deep eyes upraised, that knew
The beauty and repose of faith,
And the clear spirit shining through.
Oh! wherefore do we grow awry
From roots which strike so deep? why
dare
Paths in the desert? Could not I
Bow myself down, where thou hast knelt,
To th' earth — until the ice would melt
Here, and I feel as thou hast felt?
What Devil had the heart to scathe
Flowers thou had'st reared — to brush the
dew
From thine own lily, when thy grave
Was deep, my mother, in the clay?
Myself? Is it thus? Myself? Had I
So little love for thee? But why
Prevail'd not thy pure prayers? Why pray

To one who heeds not, who can save
But will not? Great in faith, and strong
Against the grief of circumstance
Wert thou, and yet unheard. What if
Thou pleadest still, and seest me drive
Through utter dark a full-sail'd skiff,
Unpiloted i' the echoing dance
Of reboant whirlwinds, stooping low
Unto the death, not sunk! I know
At matins and at evensong,
That thou, if thou wert yet alive
In deep and daily prayers would'st strive
To reconcile me with thy God.
Albeit, my hope is grey, and cold
At heart, thou wouldest murmur still —
'Bring this lamb back into Thy fold,
My Lord, if so it be Thy will.'
Would'st tell me I must brook the rod,
And chastisement of human pride;
That pride, the sin of devils, stood
Betwixt me and the light of God!
That hitherto I had defied,
And had rejected God — that grace
Would drop from his o'erbrimming love,
As manna on my wilderness,
If I would pray — that God would move
And strike the hard hard rock, and
    thence,
Sweet in their utmost bitterness,
Would issue tears of penitence

Which would keep green hope's life.
Alas! I think that pride hath now no place
Nor sojourn in me. I am void,
Dark, formless, utterly destroyed.

Why not believe then? Why not yet
Anchor thy frailty there, where man
Hath moor'd and rested? Ask the sea
At midnight, when the crisp slope waves
After a tempest, rib and fret
The broad-imbased beach, why he
Slumbers not like a mountain tarn?
Wherefore his ridges are not curls
And ripples of an inland mere?
Wherefore he moaneth thus, nor can
Draw down into his vexed pools
All that blue heaven which hues and paves
The other? I am too forlorn,
Too shaken: my own weakness fools
My judgement, and my spirit whirls
Moved from beneath with doubt and fear.

'Yet,' said I, in my morn of youth,
The unsunn'd freshness of my strength,
When I went forth in quest of truth,
'It is man's privilege to doubt,
If so be that from doubt at length,
Truth may stand forth unmoved of change,
An image with profulgent brows,
And perfect limbs, as from the storm

Of running fires and fluid range
Of lawless airs, at last stood out
This excellence and solid form
Of constant beauty. For the Ox
Feeds in the herb, and sleeps, or fills
The horned valleys all about,
And hollows of the fringed hills
In summer heats, with placid lows
Unfeating, till his own blood flows
About his hoof. And in the flocks
The lamb rejoiceth in the year,
And raceth freely with his fere
And answers to his mother's calls
From the flower'd furrow. In a time,
Of which he wots not, run short pains
Through his warm heart; and then, from
whence
He knows not, on his light there falls
A shadow; and his native slope,
Where he was wont to leap and climb,
Floats from his sick and filmed eyes,
And something in the darkness draws
His forehead earthward, and he dies.
Shall man live thus, in joy and hope
As a young lamb, who cannot dream,
Living, but that he shall live on?
Shall we not look into the laws
Of life and death, and things that seem,
And things that be, and analyse
Our double nature, and compare

All creeds till we have found the one,
If one there be?' Ay me! I fear
All may not doubt, but everywhere
Some must clasp Idols. Yet, my God,
Whom call I Idol? Let Thy dove
Shadow me over, and my sins
Be unremember'd, and Thy love
Enlighten me. Oh teach me yet
Somewhat before the heavy clod
Weighs on me, and the busy fret
Of that sharp-headed worm begins
In the gross blackness underneath.
Oh weary life! oh weary death!
Oh spirit and heart made desolate!
Oh damned vacillating state!'

Song. The Owl

I

When cats run home and light is come,
  And dew is cold upon the ground,
And the far-off stream is dumb,
  And the whirring sail goes round,
  And the whirring sail goes round;
    Alone and warming his five wits,
    The white owl in the belfry sits.

II

When merry milkmaids click the latch,
  And rarely smells the new-mown hay,
And the cock hath sung beneath the
    thatch
  Twice or thrice his roundelay,
  Twice or thrice his roundelay;
    Alone and warming his five wits,
    The white owl in the belfry sits.

Second Song to the Owl

I

Thy tuwhits are lull'd I wot,
  Thy tuwhoos of yesternight,
Which upon the dark afloat,
  So took echo with delight,
  So took echo with delight,
    That her voice untuneful grown,
    Wears all day a fainter tone.

II

I would mock thy chaunt anew;
  But I cannot mimick it;
Not a whit of thy tuwhoo,

Thee to woo to thy tuwhit,
Thee to woo to thy tuwhit,
With a lengthen'd loud halloo,
Tuwhoo, tuwhit, tuwhit, tuwhoo-o-o.

Recollections of the Arabian Nights

When the breeze of a joyful dawn blew free
In the silken sail of infancy,
The tide of time flow'd back with me,
The forward-flowing tide of time;
And many a sheeny summer-morn,
Adown the Tigris I was borne,
By Bagdat's shrines of fretted gold,
High-walled gardens green and old;
True Mussulman was I and sworn,
For it was in the golden prime
Of good Haroun Alraschid.

Anight my shallop, rustling thro'
The low and bloomed foliage, drove
The fragrant, glistening deeps, and clove
The citron-shadows in the blue:
By garden porches on the brim,
The costly doors flung open wide,
Gold glittering thro' lamplight dim,
And broider'd sofas on each side:
In sooth it was a goodly time,

For it was in the golden prime
Of good Haroun Alraschid.

Often, where clear-stemm'd platans guard
The outlet, did I turn away
The boat-head down a broad canal
From the main river sluiced, where all
The sloping of the moon-lit sward
Was damask-work, and deep inlay
Of braided blooms unmown, which crept
Adown to where the water slept.
A goodly place, a goodly time,
For it was in the golden prime
Of good Haroun Alraschid.

A motion from the river won
Ridged the smooth level, beating on
My shallop thro' the star-strown calm,
Until another night in night
I enter'd, from the clearer light,
Imbower'd vaults of pillar'd palm,
Imprisoning sweets, which, as they clomb
Heavenward, were stay'd beneath the dome
Of hollow boughs. — A goodly time,
For it was in the golden prime
Of good Haroun Alraschid.

Still onward; and the clear canal

Is rounded to as clear a lake.
From the green rivage many a fall
Of diamond rillets musical
Thro' little crystal arches low
Down from the central fountain's flow
Fall'n silver-chiming, seem'd to shake
The sparkling flints beneath the prow.
  A goodly place, a goodly time,
  For it was in the golden prime
    Of good Haroun Alraschid.

Above thro' many a bowery turn
A walk with vary-colour'd shells
Wander'd engrain'd. On either side
All round about the fragrant marge
From fluted vase, and brazen urn
In order, eastern flowers large,
Some dropping low their crimson bells
Half-closed, and others studded wide
  With disks and tiars, fed the time
  With odour in the golden prime
    Of good Haroun Alraschid.

Far off, and where the lemon-grove
In closest coverture upsprung
The living airs of middle night
Died round the bulbul as he sung;
Not he: but something which possess'd
The darkness of the world, delight,
Life, anguish, death, immortal love,

Ceasing not, mingled, unrepress'd,
Apart from place, withholding time
But flattering the golden prime
Of good Haroun Alraschid.

Black the garden-bowers and grots
Slumber'd: the solemn palms were ranged
Above, unwoo'd of summer wind:
A sudden splendour from behind
Flush'd all the leaves with rich gold-green,
And, flowing rapidly between
Their interspaces, counterchanged
The level lake with diamond-plots
Of dark and bright. A lovely time
For it was in the golden prime
Of good Haroun Alraschid.

Dark-blue the deep sphere overhead,
Distinct with vivid stars inlaid
Grew darker from that under-flame:
So, leaping lightly from the boat,
With silver anchor left afloat,
In marvel whence that glory came
Upon me, as in sleep I sank
In cool soft turf upon the bank,
Entranced with that place and time,
So worthy of the golden prime
Of good Haroun Alraschid.

Thence thro' the garden I was drawn —

A realm of pleasance, many a mound,
And many a shadow-chequer'd lawn
Full of the city's stilly sound,
And deep myrrh-thickets blowing round
The stately cedar, tamarisks,
Thick rosaries of scented thorn,
Tall orient shrubs, and obelisks
  Graven with emblems of the time,
  In honour of the golden prime
    Of good Haroun Alraschid.

With dazed vision unawares
From the long alley's latticed shade
Emerged, I came upon the great
Pavilion of the Caliphat.
Right to the carven cedarn doors,
Flung inward over spangled floors,
Broad-based flights of marble stairs
Ran up with golden balustrade,
  After the fashion of the time,
  And humour of the golden prime
    Of good Haroun Alraschid.

The fourscore windows all alight
As with the quintessence of flame,
A million tapers flaring bright
From twisted silvers look'd to shame
The hollow-vaulted dark, and stream'd
Upon the mooned domes aloof
In inmost Bagdat, till there seem'd

Hundreds of crescents on the roof
Of night new-risen, that marvellous
time,
To celebrate the golden prime
Of good Haroun Alraschid.

Then stole I up, and trancedly
Gazed on the Persian girl alone,
Serene with argent-lidded eyes
Amorous, and lashes like to rays
Of darkness, and a brow of pearl
Tressed with redolent ebony,
In many a dark delicious curl,
Flowing beneath her rose-hued zone;
The sweetest lady of the time,
Well worthy of the golden prime
Of good Haroun Alraschid.

Six columns, three on either side,
Pure silver, underpropt a rich
Throne of the massive ore, from which
Down-droop'd, in many a floating fold,
Engarlanded and diaper'd
With inwrought flowers, a cloth of gold.
Thereon, his deep eye laughter-stirr'd
With merriment of kingly pride,
Sole star of all that place and time,
I saw him — in his golden prime,
THE GOOD HAROUN ALRASCHID!

Ode to Memory

I

Thou who stealest fire,
From the fountains of the past,
To glorify the present; oh, haste
Visit my low desire!
Strengthen me, enlighten me!
I faint in this obscurity,
Thou dewy dawn of memory.

II

Come not as thou camest of late,
Flinging the gloom of yesternight
On the white day; but robed in soften'd light
Of orient state.
Whilome thou camest with the morning mist,
Even as a maid, whose stately brow
The dew-impearled winds of dawn have kiss'd,
When she, as thou,
Stays on her floating locks the lovely freight
Of overflowing blooms, and earliest shoots
Of orient green, giving safe pledge of fruits,
Which in wintertide shall star
The black earth with brilliance rare.

III

Whilome thou camest with the morning mist,
And with the evening cloud,
Showering thy gleaned wealth into my open breast
(Those peerless flowers which in the rudest wind
Never grow sere,
When rooted in the garden of the mind,
Because they are the earliest of the year).
Nor was the night thy shroud.
In sweet dreams softer than unbroken rest
Thou leddest by the hand thine infant Hope.
The eddying of her garments caught from thee
The light of thy great presence; and the cope
Of the half-attain'd futurity,
Though deep not fathomless,
Was cloven with the million stars which tremble
O'er the deep mind of dauntless infancy.
Small thought was there of life's distress;
For sure she deem'd no mist of earth could dull
Those spirit-thrilling eyes so keen and beautiful:
Sure she was nigher to heaven's spheres,

Listening the lordly music flowing from
The illimitable years.
O strengthen me, enlighten me!
I faint in this obscurity,
Thou dewy dawn of memory.

IV

Come forth I charge thee, arise,
Thou of the many tongues, the myriad eyes!
Thou comest not with shows of flaunting vines
Unto mine inner eye,
Divinest Memory!
Thou wert not nursed by the waterfall
Which ever sounds and shines
A pillar of white light upon the wall
Of purple cliffs, aloof descried:
Come from the woods that belt the grey hill-side,
The seven elms, the poplars four
That stand beside my father's door,
And chiefly from the brook that loves
To purl o'er matted cress and ribbed sand,
Or dimple in the dark of rushy coves,
Drawing into his narrow earthen urn,
In every elbow and turn,
The filter'd tribute of the rough woodland.
O! hither lead thy feet!

Pour round mine ears the livelong bleat
Of the thick-fleeced sheep from wattled
    folds,
        Upon the ridged wolds,
When the first matin-song hath waken'd
    loud
Over the dark dewy earth forlorn,
What time the amber morn
Forth gushes from beneath a low-hung cloud.

V

Large dowries doth the raptured eye
  To the young spirit present
    When first she is wed;
      And like a bride of old
    In triumph led,
        With music and sweet showers
        Of festal flowers,
  Unto the dwelling she must sway.
Well hast thou done, great artist Memory,
  In setting round thy first experiment
      With royal frame-work of wrought
          gold;
Needs must thou dearly love thy first essay,
And foremost in thy various gallery
  Place it, where sweetest sunlight falls
  Upon the storied walls;
        For the discovery

And newness of thine art so pleased thee,
That all which thou hast drawn of fairest
  Or boldest since, but lightly weighs
With thee unto the love thou bearest
The first-born of thy genius. Artist-like,
Ever retiring thou dost gaze
On the prime labour of thine early days:
No matter what the sketch might be;
Whether the high field on the bushless Pike,
Or even a sand-built ridge
Of heaped hills that mound the sea,
Overblown with murmurs harsh,
Or even a lowly cottage whence we see
Stretch'd wide and wild the waste enormous
    marsh,
Where from the frequent bridge,
Like emblems of infinity,
The trenched waters run from sky to sky;
Or a garden bower'd close
With plaited alleys of the trailing rose,
Long alleys falling down to twilight grots,
Or opening upon level plots
Of crowned lilies, standing near
Purple-spiked lavender:
Whither in after life retired
From brawling storms,
From weary wind,
With youthful fancy reinspired,
We may hold converse with all forms
Of the many-sided mind,

And those whom passion hath not blinded,
Subtle-thoughted, myriad-minded.
My friend, with you to live alone,
Were how much better than to own
A crown, a sceptre, and a throne!
O strengthen me, enlighten me!
I faint in this obscurity,
Thou dewy dawn of memory.

Song

I

A spirit haunts the year's last hours
Dwelling amid these yellowing bowers:
        To himself he talks;
For at eventide, listening earnestly,
At his work you may hear him sob and sigh
        In the walks;
        Earthward he boweth the heavy stalks
Of the mouldering flowers:
    Heavily hangs the broad sunflower
        Over its grave i' the earth so chilly;
    Heavily hangs the hollyhock,
        Heavily hangs the tiger-lily.

II

The air is damp, and hush'd, and close,
As a sick man's room when he taketh
  repose
   An hour before death;
My very heart faints and my whole soul
  grieves
At the moist rich smell of the rotting leaves,
   And the breath
   Of the fading edges of box beneath,
And the year's last rose.
  Heavily hangs the broad sunflower
   Over its grave i' the earth so chilly;
  Heavily hangs the hollyhock,
   Heavily hangs the tiger-lily.

Adeline

I

Mystery of mysteries,
 Faintly smiling Adeline,
 Scarce of earth nor all divine,
  Nor unhappy, nor at rest,
   But beyond expression fair
   With thy floating flaxen hair;
Thy rose-lips and full blue eyes
  Take the heart from out my breast.

Wherefore those dim looks of thine,
Shadowy, dreaming Adeline?

II

Whence that aery bloom of thine,
Like a lily which the sun
Looks thro' in his sad decline,
And a rose-bush leans upon,
Thou that faintly smilest still,
As a Naiad in a well,
Looking at the set of day,
Or a phantom two hours old
Of a maiden past away,
Ere the placid lips be cold?
Wherefore those faint smiles of thine,
Spiritual Adeline?

III

What hope or fear or joy is thine?
Who talketh with thee, Adeline?
For sure thou art not all alone:
Do beating hearts of salient springs
Keep measure with thine own?
Hast thou heard the butterflies
What they say betwixt their wings?
Or in stillest evenings

With what voice the violet woos
To his heart the silver dews?
Or when little airs arise,
How the merry bluebell rings
To the mosses underneath?
Hast thou look'd upon the breath
Of the lilies at sunrise?
Wherefore that faint smile of thine,
Shadowy, dreaming Adeline?

IV

Some honey-converse feeds thy mind
Some spirit of a crimson rose
In love with thee forgets to close
His curtains, wasting odorous sighs
All night long on darkness blind.
What aileth thee? whom waitest thou
With thy soften'd, shadow'd brow,
And those dew-lit eyes of thine,
Thou faint smiler, Adeline?

V

Lovest thou the doleful wind
When thou gazest at the skies?
Doth the low-tongued Orient
Wander from the side of the morn,

Dripping with Sabaean spice
On thy pillow, lowly bent
With melodious airs lovelorn
Breathing Light against thy face,
While his locks a-dropping twined
Round thy neck in subtle ring
Make a carcanet of rays,
And ye talk together still,
In the language wherewith Spring
Letters cowslips on the hill?
Hence that look and smile of thine,
Spiritual Adeline.

A Character

With a half-glance upon the sky
At night he said, 'The wanderings
Of this most intricate Universe
Teach me the nothingness of things.'
Yet could not all creation pierce
Beyond the bottom of his eye.

He spake of beauty: that the dull
Saw no divinity in grass,
Life in dead stones, or spirit in air;
Then looking as 'twere in a glass,
He smooth'd his chin and sleek'd his hair,
And said the earth was beautiful.

He spake of virtue: not the gods
More purely, when they wish to charm
Pallas and Juno sitting by:
And with a sweeping of the arm,
And a lack-lustre dead-blue eye,
Devolved his rounded periods.

Most delicately hour by hour
He canvass'd human mysteries
And trod on silk, as if the winds
Blew his own praises in his eyes,
And stood aloof from other minds
In impotence of fancied power.

With lips depress'd as he were meek,
Himself unto himself he sold:
Upon himself himself did feed:
Quiet, dispassionate, and cold,
And other than his form of creed,
With chisell'd features clear and sleek.

The Poet

The poet in a golden clime was born,
With golden stars above;
Dower'd with the hate of hate, the scorn of scorn,
The love of love.

He saw thro' life and death, thro' good and ill,
He saw thro' his own soul.
The marvel of the everlasting will,
An open scroll,

Before him lay: with echoing feet he threaded
The secretest walks of fame:
The viewless arrows of his thoughts were headed
And wing'd with flame,

Like Indian reeds blown from his silver tongue,
And of so fierce a flight,
From Calpe unto Caucasus they sung,
Filling with light

And vagrant melodies the winds which bore
Them earthward till they lit;
Then, like the arrow-seeds of the field flower,
The fruitful wit

Cleaving, took root, and springing forth anew
Where'er they fell, behold,
Like to the mother plant in semblance, grew
A flower all gold,

And bravely furnish'd all abroad to fling
The winged shafts of truth,
To throng with stately blooms the breathing spring
Of Hope and Youth.

So many minds did gird their orbs with beams,
Tho' one did fling the fire.
Heaven flow'd upon the soul in many dreams
Of high desire.

Thus truth was multiplied on truth, the world
Like one great garden show'd
And thro' the wreaths of floating dark upcurl'd,
Rare sunrise flow'd.

And Freedom rear'd in that august sunrise
Her beautiful bold brow,
When rites and forms before his burning eyes
Melted like snow.

There was no blood upon her maiden robes
Sunn'd by those orient skies;
But round about the circles of the globes
Of her keen eyes

And in her raiment's hem was traced in
flame
WISDOM, a name to shake
All evil dreams of power — a sacred name.
And when she spake,

Her words did gather thunder as they ran,
And as the lightning to the thunder
Which follows it, riving the spirit of man,
Making earth wonder,

So was their meaning to her words.
No sword
Of wrath her right arm whirl'd,
But one poor poet's scroll, and with *his* word
She shook the world.

The Poet's Mind

I

Vex not thou the poet's mind
With thy shallow wit:
Vex not thou the poet's mind;
For thou canst not fathom it.
Clear and bright it should be ever,
Flowing like a crystal river;
Bright as light, and clear as wind.

II

Dark-brow'd sophist, come not anear;
All the place is holy ground;
Hollow smile and frozen sneer
Come not here.
Holy water kill I pour
Into every spicy flower
Of the laurel-shrubs that hedge it around.
The flowers would faint at your cruel cheer.
In your eye there is death,
There is frost in your breath
Which would blight the plants.
Where you stand you cannot hear
From the groves within
The wild-bird's din.
In the heart of the garden the merry bird
chants,
It would fall to the ground if you came in.
In the middle leaps a fountain
Like sheet lightning,
Ever brightening
With a low melodious thunder;
All day and all night it is ever drawn
From the brain of the purple mountain
Which stands in the distance yonder:
It springs on a level of bowery lawn,
And the mountain draws it from Heaven
above,
And it sings a song of undying love;

And yet, tho' its voice be so clear and full,
You never would hear it; your ears are so
dull,
So keep where you are: you are foul with sin;
It would shrink to the earth if you came in.

Nothing Will Die

When will the stream be aweary of flowing
Under my eye?
When will the wind be aweary of blowing
Over the sky?
When will the clouds be aweary of fleeting?
When will the heart be aweary of beating?
And nature die?
Never, oh! never, nothing will die;
The stream flows,
The wind blows,
The cloud fleets,
The heart beats,
Nothing will die.

Nothing will die;
All things will change
Through eternity.
'Tis the world's winter;
Autumn and summer
Are gone long ago.
Earth is dry to the centre,

But spring a new comer —
A spring rich and strange,
Shall make the winds blow
Round and round,
Through and through,
Here and there,
Till the air
And the ground
Shall be filled with life anew.

The world was never made;
It will change, but it will not fade.
So let the wind range;
For even and morn
Ever will be
Through eternity.
Nothing was born;
Nothing will die,
All things will change.

All Things Will Die

Clearly the blue river chimes in its flowing
Under my eye;
Warmly and broadly the south winds are blowing
Over the sky.
One after another the white clouds are fleeting;

Every heart this May morning in joyance is beating
Full merrily;
Yet all things must die.
The stream will cease to flow;
The wind will cease to blow;
The clouds will cease to fleet;
The heart will cease to beat;
For all things must die.

All things must die.
Spring will come never more.
Oh! vanity!
Death waits at the door.
See! our friends are all forsaking
The wine and the merrymaking.
We are called — we must go.
Laid low, very low,
In the dark we must lie.
The merry glees are still;
The voice of the bird
Shall no more be heard,
Nor the wind on the hill.
Oh! misery!
Hark! death is calling
While I speak to ye,
The jaw is falling,
The red cheek paling,
The strong limbs failing;
Ice with the warm blood mixing,

The eyeballs fixing.
Nine times goes the passing bell:
Ye merry souls, farewell.

The old earth
Had a birth,
As all men know
  Long ago.
And the old earth must die.
So let the warm winds range,
And the blue wave beat the shore;
For even and morn
Ye will never see
Through eternity.
All things were born.
Ye will come never more,
For all things must die.

The Dying Swan

I

The plain was grassy, wild and bare,
Wide, wild, and open to the air,
Which had built up everywhere
  An under-roof of doleful grey.
With an inner voice the river ran,
Adown it floated a dying swan,
    And loudly did lament.

It was the middle of the day.
Ever the weary wind went on,
And took the reed-tops as it went.

II

Some blue peaks in the distance rose,
And white against the cold-white sky,
Shone out their crowning snows.
One willow over the river wept,
And shook the wave as the wind did sigh;
Above in the wind was the swallow,
Chasing itself at its own wild will
And far thro' the marish green and still
The tangled water-courses slept,
Shot over with purple, and green, and yellow.

III

The wild swan's death-hymn took the soul
Of that waste place with joy
Hidden in sorrow: at first to the ear
The warble was low, and full and clear;
And floating about the under-sky,
Prevailing in weakness, the coronach stole
Sometimes afar, and sometimes anear
But anon her awful jubilant voice,
With a music strange and manifold,

Flow'd forth on a carol free and bold;
As when a mighty people rejoice
With shawms, and with cymbals, and harps
of gold,
And the tumult of their acclaim is roll'd
Thro' the open gates of the city afar,
To the shepherd who watcheth the evening
star.
And the creeping mosses and clambering
weeds,
And the willow-branches hoar and dank,
And the wavy swell of the soughing reeds,
And the wave-worn horns of the echoing
bank,
And the silvery marish-flowers that throng
The desolate creeks and pools among,
Were flooded over with eddying song.

A Dirge

I

Now is done thy long day's work;
Fold thy palms across thy breast,
Fold thine arms, turn to thy rest.
Let them rave.
Shadows of the silver birk
Sweep the green that folds thy grave
Let them rave.

II

Thee nor carketh care nor slander;
Nothing but the small cold worm
Fretteth thine enshrouded form.
        Let them rave.
Light and shadow ever wander
O'er the green that folds thy grave.
        Let them rave.

III

Thou wilt not turn upon thy bed;
Chaunteth not the brooding bee
Sweeter tones than calumny?
        Let them rave.
Thou wilt never raise thine head
From the green that folds thy grave.
        Let them rave.

IV

Crocodiles wept tears for thee;
The woodbine and eglatere
Drip sweeter dews than traitor's
    tear.
        Let them rave.
Rain makes music in the tree

O'er the green that folds thy grave.
        Let them rave.

V

Round thee blow, self-pleached deep,
Bramble-roses, faint and pale,
And long purples of the dale.
        Let them rave.
These in every shower creep
Thro' the green that folds thy grave.
        Let them rave.

VI

The gold-eyed kingcups fine;
The frail bluebell peereth over
Rare broidry of the purple clover.
        Let them rave.
Kings have no such couch as thine,
As the green that folds thy grave.
        Let them rave.

VII

Wild words wander here and there;
God's great gift of speech abused

Makes thy memory confused:
But let them rave.
The balm-cricket carols clear
In the green that folds thy grave
Let them rave.

The Deserted House

I

Life and Thought have gone away
Side by side,
Leaving door and windows wide:
Careless tenants they!

II

All within is dark as night:
In the windows is no light;
And no murmur at the door,
So frequent on its hinge before.

III

Close the door, the shutters close,
Or thro' the windows we shall see
The nakedness and vacancy

Of the dark deserted house.

IV

Come away: no more of mirth
Is here or merry-making sound.
The house was builded of the earth
And shall fall again to ground.

V

Come away: for Life and Thought
Here no longer dwell;
But in a city glorious —
A great and distant city — have bought
A mansion incorruptible.
Would they could have stayed with us!

Love and Death

What time the mighty moon was gathering light
Love paced the thymy plots of Paradise,
And all about him roll'd his lustrous eyes;
When, turning round a cassia, full in view

Death, walking all alone beneath a yew,
And talking to himself, first met his sight:
'You must begone,' said Death, 'these walks
 are mine.'
Love wept and spread his sheeny vans for
 flight;
Yet ere he parted said, 'This hour is thine:
Thou art the shadow of life, and as the tree
Stands in the sun and shadows all beneath,
So in the light of great eternity
Life eminent creates the shade of death;
The shadow passeth when the tree shall fall,
But I shall reign for ever over all. '

The Kraken

Below the thunders of the upper deep;
Far far beneath in the abysmal sea,
His ancient, dreamless, uninvaded sleep
The Kraken sleepeth: faintest sunlights flee
About his shadowy sides: above him swell
Huge sponges of millennial growth and
 height;
And far away into the sickly light,
From many a wondrous grot and secret cell
Unnumber'd and enormous polypi
Winnow with giant fins the slumbering green.
There hath he lain for ages and will lie
Battening upon huge seaworms in his sleep,

Until the latter fire shall heat the deep;
Then once by men and angels to be seen
In roaring he shall rise and on the surface
    die.

The Ballad of Oriana

My heart is wasted with my woe,
        Oriana.
There is no rest for me below,
        Oriana.
When the long dun wolds are ribb'd with
    snow,
And loud the Norland whirlwinds blow,
        Oriana,
Alone I wander to and fro,
        Oriana.

Ere the light on dark was growing,
        Oriana,
At midnight the cock was crowing,
        Oriana:
Winds were blowing, waters flowing,
We heard the steeds to battle going,
        Oriana;
Aloud the hollow bugle blowing,
        Oriana.

In the yew-wood black as night,

Oriana,
Ere I rode into the fight,
Oriana
While blissful tears blinded my sight
By star-shine and by moonlight,
Oriana
I to thee my troth did plight,
Oriana.

She stood upon the castle wall,
Oriana:
She watch'd my crest among them all,
Oriana:
She saw me fight, she heard me call,
When forth there stept a foeman tall,
Oriana
Atween me and the castle wall,
Oriana.

The bitter arrow went aside,
Oriana:
The false, false arrow went aside,
Oriana:
The damned arrow glanced aside,
And pierced thy heart, my love, my bride,
Oriana!
Thy heart, my life, my love, my bride,
Oriana!

Oh! narrow, narrow was the space,

Oriana.
Loud, loud rung out the bugle's brays,
Oriana.
Oh! deathful stabs were dealt apace,
The battle deepen'd in its place,
Oriana
But I was down upon my face,
Oriana.
They should have stabb'd me where I lay
Oriana!
How could I rise and come away,
Oriana?
How could I look upon the day?

They should have stabb'd me where I lay
Oriana —
They should have trod me into clay,
Oriana.
O breaking heart that will not break,
Oriana!
O pale, pale face so sweet and meek,
Oriana!
Thou smilest, but thou dost not speak,
And then the tears run down my cheek,
Oriana:
What wantest thou? whom dost thou seek,
Oriana?

I cry aloud: none hear my cries,
Oriana.

Thou comest atween me and the skies,
Oriana.
I feel the tears of blood arise
Up from my heart unto my eyes,
Oriana.
Within thy heart my arrow lies,
Oriana.
O cursed hand! O cursed blow!
Oriana!
O happy thou that liest low,
Oriana!
All night the silence seems to flow
Beside me in my utter woe,
Oriana.
A weary, weary way I go,
Oriana.

When Norland winds pipe down the sea,
Oriana,
I walk, I dare not think of thee,
Oriana.
Thou liest beneath the greenwood true,
I dare not die and come to thee,
Oriana.
I hear the roaring of the sea,
Oriana.

Circumstance

Two children in two neighbour villages
Playing mad pranks along the heathy leas;
Two strangers meeting at a festival
Two lovers whispering by an orchard wall;
Two lives bound fast in one with golden
    ease;
Two graves grass-green beside a grey
    church-tower,
Wash'd with still rains and daisy-blossomed;
Two children in one hamlet born and bred;
So runs the round of life from hour to
    hour.

We Are Free

The winds, as at their hour of birth,
  Leaning upon the ridged sea,
Breathed low around the rolling earth
  With mellow preludes, 'We are free,'
The streams through many a lilied row
  Down-carolling to the crisped sea,
Low-tinkled with a bell-like flow
  Atween the blossoms, 'We are free.'

The Sea-Fairies

Slow sail'd the weary mariners and saw,
Betwixt the green brink and the running foam,
Sweet faces, rounded arms, and bosoms prest
To little harps of gold; and while they mused,
Whispering to each other half in fear,
Shrill music reach'd them on the middle sea

Whither away, whither away, whither away? fly no more.
Whither away from the high green field, and the happy blossoming shore?
Day and night to the billow the fountain calls;
Down shower the gambolling waterfalls
From wandering over the lea:
Out of the live-green heart of the dells
They freshen the silvery-crimson shells,
And thick with white bells the clover-hill swells
High over the full-toned sea:
O hither, come hither and furl your sails,
Come hither to me and to me:
Either, come hither and frolic and play;
Here it is only the mew that wails;

We will sing to you all the day:
Mariner, mariner, furl your sails
For here are the blissful downs and dales,
And merrily merrily carol the gales,
And the spangle dances in bight and bay
And the rainbow forms and flies on the land
Over the islands free;
And the rainbow lives in the curve of the sand;
Hither, come hither and see;
And the rainbow hangs on the poising wave,
And sweet is the colour of cove and cave
And sweet shall your welcome be:
O hither, come hither, and be our lords,
For merry brides are we:
We will kiss sweet kisses, and speak sweet words:
O listen, listen, your eyes shall glisten
With pleasure and love and jubilee:
O listen, listen, your eyes shall glisten
When the sharp clear twang of the golden chords
Runs up the ridged sea.
Who can light on as happy a shore
All the world o'er, all the world o'er?
Whither away? listen and stay: mariner, mariner, fly no more.

Sonnet to J. M. K.

My hope and heart is with thee —
thou wilt be
A latter Luther, and a soldier-priest
To scare church-harpies from the master's
feast;
Our dusted velvets have much need of thee:
Thou art no sabbath-drawler of old saws
Distill'd from some worm-canker'd homily;
But spurr'd at heart with fieriest energy
To embattail and to wall about thy cause
With iron-worded proof, hating to hark
The humming of the drowsy pulpit-drone
Half God's good sabbath, while the
worn-out clerk
Brow-beats his desk below. Thou from a
throne
Mounted in heaven wilt shoot into the dark
Arrows of lightnings. I will stand and mark.

POEMS

Sonnet

Mine be the strength of spirit fierce and
free,
Like some broad river rushing down alone,
With the selfsame impulse wherewith he

was thrown
From his loud fount upon the echoing lea:—
Which with increasing might doth forward
flee
By town, and tower, and hill, and cape, and
isle,
And in the middle of the green salt sea
Keeps his blue waters fresh for many a mile.
Mine be the Power which ever to its sway
Will win the wise at once, and by degrees
May into uncongenial spirits flow;
Even as the great gulf-stream of Florida
Floats far away into the Northern seas
The lavish growths of southern Mexico.

To —

I

My life is full of weary days
  But good things have not kept aloof,
Nor wander'd into other ways:
  I have not lack'd thy mild reproof,
Nor golden largess of thy praise.

II

And now shake hands across the brink

Of that deep grave to which I go:
Shake hands once more: I cannot sink
So far — far down, but I shall know
Thy voice, and answer from below.

III

When in the darkness over me,
The four-handed mole shall scrape,
Plant thou no dusky cypress-tree,
Nor wreathe thy cap with doleful crape,
But pledge me in the flowing grape.

IV

And when the sappy field and wood
Grow green beneath the showery grey,
And rugged barks begin to bud
And through damp holts, new-flush'd with may
Ring sudden laughters of the Jay;

V

Then let wise Nature work her will
And on my clay her darnels grow.
Come only, when the days are still,

And at my headstone whisper low,
And tell me if the woodbines blow,

VII

If thou art blest, my mother's smile
Undimmed, if bees are on the wing:
Then cease, my friend, a little while,
That I may hear the throstle sing
His bridal song, the boast of spring.

VII

Sweet as the noise in parchèd plains
Of bubbling wells that fret the stones,
(If any sense in me remains)
Thy words will be; thy cheerful tones
As welcome to my crumbling bones.

Buonaparte

He thought to quell the stubborn hearts of oak,
Madman! — to chain with chains, and bind with bands
That island queen that sways the floods and lands

From Ind to Ind, but in fair daylight woke,
When from her wooden walls, lit by sure
hands,
With thunders, and with lightnings, and
with smoke,
Peal after peal, the British battle broke,
Lulling the brine against the Coptic sands.
We taught him lowlier moods, when
Elsinore
Heard the war moan along the distant sea,
Rocking with shattered spars, with sudden
fires
Flamed over: at Trafalgar yet once more
We taught him: late he learned humility
Perforce, like those whom Gideon school'd
with briers.

Sonnet

But were I loved, as I desire to be
What is there in the great sphere of the earth
And range of evil between death and birth,
That I should fear, — if I were loved by
thee?
All the inner, all the outer world of pain
Clear Love would pierce and cleave, if thou
wert mine,
As I have heard that, somewhere in the
main,

Fresh-water springs come up through bitter brine.
'Twere joy, not fear, clasped hand-in-hand with thee,
To wait for death — mute — careless of all ills,
Apart upon a mountain, tho' the surge
Of some new deluge from a thousand hills
Flung leagues of roaring foam into the gorge
Below us, as far on as eye could see.

The Lady of Shalott

Part 1

On either side the river lie
Long fields of barley and of rye,
That clothe the wold and meet the sky;
And thro' the field the road runs by
To many-tower'd Camelot;
And up and down the people go,
Gazing where the lilies blow
Round an island there below,
The island of Shalott.

Willows whiten, aspens quiver,
Little breezes dusk and shiver
Thro' the wave that runs for ever
By the island in the river

Flowing down to Camelot.
Four grey walls, and four grey towers,
Overlook a space of flowers,
And the silent isle imbowers
The Lady of Shalott.

By the margin, willow-veil'd,
Slide the heavy barges trail'd
By slow horses; and unhail'd
The shallop flitteth silken-sail'd
Skimming down to Camelot:

But who hath seen her wave her hand?
Or at the casement seen her stand?
Or is she known in all the land
The Lady of Shalott?

Only reapers, reaping early
In among the bearded barley,
Hear a song that echoes cheerly
From the river winding clearly,
Down to towered Camelot:
And by the moon the reaper weary,
Piling sheaves in uplands airy,
Listening, whispers
' 'Tis the fairy
Lady of Shalott.'

Part 2

There she weaves by night and day
A magic web with colours gay.
She has heard a whisper say,
A curse is on her if she stay
To look down to Camelot.
She knows not what the curse may be,
And so she weaveth steadily,
And little other care hath she,
The Lady of Shalott.
And moving thro' a mirror clear
That hangs before her all the year
Shadows of the world appear.
There she sees the highway near
Winding down to Camelot:
There the river eddy whirls
And there the surly village-churls,
And the red cloaks of market girls
Pass onward from Shalott.

Sometimes a troop of damsels glad,
An abbot on an ambling pad,
Sometimes a curly shepherd-lad,
Or long-hair'd page in crimson clad,
Goes by to tower'd Camelot;
And sometimes thro' the mirror blue
The knights come riding two and two:
She hath no loyal knight and true,
The Lady of Shalott.

But in her web she still delights
To weave the mirror's magic sights,
For often thro' the silent nights
A funeral, with plumes and lights,
            And music, went to Camelot:
Or when the moon was overhead,
Came two young lovers lately wed.
'I am half sick of shadows,' said
            The Lady of Shalott.

Part 3

A bow shot from her bower-eaves,
He rode between the barley-sheaves,
The sun came dazzling thro' the leaves
And flamed upon the brazen greaves
            Of bold Sir Lancelot.
A red-cross knight for ever kneel'd
To a lady in his shield
That sparkled on the yellow field,
            Beside remote Shalott.

The gemmy bridle glitter'd free,
Like to some branch of stars we see
Hung in the golden Galaxy.
The bridle bells rang merrily
            As he rode down to Camelot:
And from his blazon'd baldric slung
A mighty silver bugle hung,

And as he rode his armour rung,
Beside remote Shalott.

All in the blue unclouded weather
Thick-jewell'd shone the saddle-leather,
The helmet and the helmet-feather
Burn'd like one burning flame together,
As he rode down to Camelot.
As often thro' the purple night,
Below the starry clusters bright,
Some bearded meteor, trailing light,
Moves over still Shalott.

His broad clear brow in sunlight glow'd;
On burnish'd hooves his war-horse trode;
From underneath his helmet flow'd
His coal-black curls as on he rode
As he rode down to Camelot.
From the bank and from the river
He flash'd into the crystal mirror,
'Tirra lirra,' by the river
Sang Sir Lancelot.

She left the web, she left the loom,
She made three paces thro' the room,
She saw the water-lily bloom,
She saw the helmet and the plume,
She look'd down to Camelot.
Out flew the web and floated wide;
The mirror crack'd from side to side;

'The curse is come upon me,' cried
The Lady of Shalott.

Part 4

In the stormy east-wind straining,
The pale yellow woods were waning,
The broad stream in his banks complaining,
Heavily the low sky raining
Over tower'd Camelot;
Down she came and found a boat
Beneath a willow left afloat,
And round about the prow she wrote
The Lady of Shalott.

And down the river's dim expanse —
Like some bold seër in a trance,
Seeing all his own mischance —
With a glassy countenance
Did she look to Camelot.
And at the closing of the day
She loosed the chain, and down she lay;
The broad stream bore her far away,
The Lady of Shalott.

Lying robed in snowy white
That loosely flew to left and right —
The leaves upon her falling light —
Thro' the noises of the night

She floated down to Camelot:
And as the boat-head wound along
The willowy hills and fields among,
They heard her singing her last song,
The Lady of Shalott.

Heard a carol, mournful, holy
Chanted loudly, chanted lowly,
Till her blood was frozen slowly,
And her eyes were darken'd wholly,
Turn'd to tower'd Camelot.
For ere she reach'd upon the tide
The first house by the water-side,
Singing in her song she died,
The Lady of Shalott.

Under tower and balcony,
By garden-wall and gallery,
A gleaming shape she floated by,
Dead-pale between the houses high,
Silent into Camelot.
Out upon the wharfs they came,
Knight and burgher, lord and dame,
And round the prow they read her name,
The Lady of Shalott.

Who is this? and what is here?
And in the lighted palace near
Died the sound of royal cheer;
And they cross'd themselves for fear,

All the knights at Camelot:
But Lancelot mused a little space;
He said, 'She has a lovely face;
God in his mercy lend her grace,
The Lady of Shalott.'

Mariana in the South

With one black shadow at its feet,
The house thro' all the level shines,
Close-latticed to the brooding heat,
And silent in its dusty vines:
A faint-blue ridge upon the right,
An empty river-bed before,
And shallows on a distant shore,
In glaring sand and inlets bright.
But 'Ave Mary,' made she moan,
And 'Ave Mary,' night and morn,
And 'Ah,' she sang, 'to be all alone,
To live forgotten, and love forlorn.'
She, as her carol sadder grew,
From brow and bosom slowly down
Thro' rosy taper fingers drew
Her streaming curls of deepest brown
To left and right, and made appear,
Still-lighted in a secret shrine,
Her melancholy eyes divine,
The home of woe without a tear.
And 'Ave Mary,' was her moan,

'Madonna, sad is night and morn;'
And 'Ah,' she sang, 'to be all alone,'
To live forgotten, and love forlorn.'

Till all the crimson changed, and past
Into deep orange o'er the sea,
Low on her knees herself she cast,
Before Our Lady murmur'd she;
Complaining, 'Mother, give me grace
To help me of my weary load.'
And on the liquid mirror glow'd
The clear perfection of her face.
'Is this the form,' she made her moan,
'That won his praises night and morn?'
And 'Ah,' she said, 'but I wake alone,
I sleep forgotten, I wake forlorn.'

Nor bird would sing, nor lamb would bleat,
Nor any cloud would cross the vault,
But day increased from heat to heat,
On stony drought and steaming salt;
Till now at noon she slept again,
And seem'd knee-deep in mountain grass,
And heard her native breezes pass
And runlets babbling down the glen.
She breathed in sleep a lower moan,
And murmuring, as at night and morn,
She thought, 'My spirit is here alone,
Walks forgotten, and is forlorn.'

Dreaming, she knew it was a dream:
  She felt he was and was not there.
She woke: the babble of the stream
  Fell, and, without, the steady glare
Shrank one sick willow sere and small.
  The river-bed was dusty-white;
  And all the furnace of the light
Struck up against the blinding wall.
  She whisper'd, with a stifled moan
More inward than at night or morn,
  'Sweet Mother, let me not here alone
Live forgotten and die forlorn.'

And, rising, from her bosom drew
  Old letters, breathing of her worth,
For 'Love' they said, 'must needs be true,
  To what is loveliest upon earth.'
An image seem'd to pass the door,
  To look at her with slight, and say
  'But now thy beauty flows away,
So be alone for evermore.'
  'O cruel heart,' she changed her tone,
    'And cruel love, whose end is scorn,
  Is this the end to be left alone,
    To live forgotten, and die forlorn?'

But sometimes in the falling day
  An image seem'd to pass the door,
To look into her eyes and say,
  'But thou shalt be alone no more.'

And flaming downward over all
  From heat to heat the day decreased,
And slowly rounded to the east
The one black shadow from the wall.
  'The day to night,' she made her moan,
    'The day to night, the night to morn,
  And day and night I am left alone
    To live forgotten, and love forlorn.'

At eve a dry cicala sung,
  There came a sound as of the sea;
Backward the lattice-blind she flung,
  And lean'd upon the balcony.
There all in spaces rosy-bright
  Large Hesper glitter'd on her tears,
  And deepening thro' the silent spheres,
Heaven over Heaven rose the night.
    And weeping then she made her moan,
      'The night comes on that knows not morn
    When I shall cease to be all alone,
      To live forgotten, and love forlorn.'

Eleänore

I

Thy dark eyes open'd not,
Nor first reveal'd themselves to English air,
For there is nothing here,
Which, from the outward to the inward brought,
Moulded thy baby thought.
Far off from human neighbourhood,
Thou wert born, on a summer morn,
A mile beneath the cedar-wood.
Thy bounteous forehead was not fann'd
With breezes from our oaken glades
But thou wert nursed in some delicious land
Of lavish lights, and floating shades:
And fluttering thy childish thought
The oriental fairy brought,
At the moment of thy birth,
From old well-heads of haunted rills,
And the hearts of purple hills,
And shadow'd coves on a sunny shore,
The choicest wealth of all the earth,
Jewel or shell, or starry ore,
To deck thy cradle, Eleänor.

II

Or the yellow-banded bees,
Thro' half-open lattices
Coming in the scented breeze,
        Fed thee, a child, lying alone,
            With whitest honey in fairy
                gardens cull'd —
        A glorious child, dreaming alone,
        In silk-soft folds, upon yielding
                down,
With the hum of swarming bees
            Into dreamful slumber lull'd.

III

Who may minister to thee?
Summer herself should minister
        To thee, with fruitage golden-rinded
        On golden salvers, or it may be,
Youngest Autumn, in a bower
Grape-thicken'd from the light, and blinded
        With many a deep-hued bell-like
                flower
Of fragrant trailers, when the air
        Sleepeth over all the heaven,
        And the crag that fronts the Even,
            All along the shadowing shore,
Crimsons over an inland mere,
                Eleänor!

IV

How may full-sail'd verse express,
How may measured words adore
The full-flowing harmony
Of thy swan-like stateliness,
Eleänor?
The luxuriant symmetry
Of thy floating gracefulness,
Eleänor?
Every turn and glance of thine,
Every lineament divine,
Eleänor,
And the steady sunset glow,
That stays upon thee? For in thee
Is nothing sudden, nothing
single;
Like two streams of incense free
From one censer, in one
shrine,
Thought and motion mingle,
Mingle ever. Motions flow
To one another, even as tho'
They were modulated so
To an unheard melody,
Which lives about thee, and a sweep
Of richest pauses, evermore
Drawn from each other mellow-deep;
Who may express thee, Eleänor?

V

I stand before thee, Eleänor;
    I see thy beauty gradually unfold,
Daily and hourly, more and more.
I muse, as in a trance, the while
    Slowly, as from a cloud of gold,
Comes out thy deep ambrosial smile.
I muse, as in a trance, whene'er
    The languors of thy love-deep eyes
Float on to me. I would I were
    So tranced, so rapt in ecstasies,
To stand apart, and to adore,
Gazing on thee for evermore,
Serene, imperial Eleänor!

VI

Sometimes, with most intensity
Gazing, I seem to see
Thought folded over thought, smiling asleep,
Slowly awaken'd, grow so full and deep
In thy large eyes, that, overpower'd quite.
I cannot veil, or droop my sight,
But am as nothing in its light:
As tho' a star, in inmost heaven set,
Ev'n while we gaze on it,
Should slowly round his orb, and slowly
    grow

To a full face, there like a sun remain
Fix'd — then as slowly fade again,
        And draw itself to what it was before;
            So full, so deep, so slow,
            Thought seems to come and go
        In thy large eyes, imperial Eleänor.

VII

As thunder-clouds that, hung on high,
        Roof'd the world with doubt and fear,
Floating thro' an evening atmosphere,
Grow golden all about the sky;
In thee all passion becomes passionless
Touch'd by thy spirit's mellowness,
Losing his fire and active might
        In a silent meditation,
Falling into a still delight,
        And luxury of contemplation
As waves that up a quiet cove
        Rolling slide, and lying still
            Shadow forth the banks at will:
Or sometimes they swell and move,
        Pressing up against the land,
        With motions of the outer sea:
            And the self-same influence
            Controlleth all the soul and sense
        Of Passion gazing upon thee.
His bow-string slacken'd, languid Love

Leaning his cheek upon his hand,
Droops both his wings, regarding thee,
And so would languish evermore,
Serene, imperial Eleänor.

VIII

But when I see thee roam, with tresses unconfined,
While the amorous, odorous wind
Breathes low between the sunset and the moon;
Or, in a shadowy saloon,
On silken cushions half reclined;
I watch thy grace; and in its place
My heart a charmed slumber keeps,
While I muse upon thy face;
And a languid fire creeps
Thro' my veins to all my frame,
Dissolvingly and slowly: soon
From thy rose-red lips MY name
Floweth; and then, as in a swoon,
With dinning sound my ears are rife,
My tremulous tongue faltereth,
I lose my colour, I lose my breath,
I drink the cup of a costly death,
Brimm'd with delirious draughts of warmest life.
I die with my delight, before

I hear what I would hear from thee;
Yet tell my name again to me,
I *would* be dying evermore,
So dying ever, Eleänor.

The Miller's Daughter

I see the wealthy miller yet,
His double chin, his portly size,
And who that knew him could forget
The busy wrinkles round his eyes?
The slow wise smile that, round about
His dusty forehead dryly curl'd,
Seem'd half-within and half-without,
And full of dealings with the world?

In yonder chair I see him sit,
Three fingers round the old silver cup —
I see his grey eyes twinkle yet
At his own jest — grey eyes lit up
With summer lightnings of a soul
So full of summer warmth, so glad,
So healthy, sound, and clear and whole,
His memory scarce can make me sad.

Yet fill my glass: give me one kiss:
My own sweet Alice, we must die.
There's somewhat in this world amiss
Shall be unriddled by and by.

There's somewhat flows to us in life,
  But more is taken quite away.
Pray, Alice, pray, my darling wife,
  That we may die the self-same day.

Have I not found a happy earth?
  I least should breathe a thought of pain.
Would God renew me from my birth
  I'd almost live my life again.
So sweet it seems with thee to walk,
  And once again to woo thee mine —
It seems in after-dinner talk
  Across the walnuts and the wine —

To be the long and listless boy
  Late-left an orphan of the squire,
Where this old mansion mounted high
  Looks down upon the village spire:
For even here, where I and you
  Have lived and loved alone so long,
Each morn my sleep was broken thro'
  By some wild skylark's matin song.

And oft I heard the tender dove
  In firry woodlands making moan;
But ere I saw your eyes, my love,
  I had no motion of my own.
For scarce my life with fancy play'd
  Before I dream'd that pleasant dream —
Still hither thither idly sway'd

Like those long mosses in the stream.

Or from the bridge I lean'd to hear
The milldam rushing down with noise,
And see the minnows everywhere
In crystal eddies glance and poise,
The tall flag-flowers when they sprung
Below the range of stepping-stones,
Or those three chestnuts near, that hung
In masses thick with milky cones.

But, Alice, what an hour was that,
When after roving in the woods
('Twas April then), I came and sat
Below the chestnuts, when their buds
Were glistening to the breezy blue;
And on the slope, an absent fool,
I cast me down, nor thought of you,
But angled in the higher pool.

A love-song I had somewhere read,
An echo from a measured strain,
Beat time to nothing in my head
From some odd corner of the brain.
It haunted me, the morning long,
With weary sameness in the rhymes,
The phantom of a silent song,
That went and came a thousand times.

Then leapt a trout. In lazy mood

I watch'd the little circles die;
They past into the level flood,
And there a vision caught my eye;
The reflex of a beauteous form,
A glowing arm, a gleaming neck,
As when a sunbeam wavers warm
Within the dark and dimpled beck.
For you remember, you had set,
That morning, on the casement's edge
A long green box of mignonette,
And you were leaning from the ledge:
And when I raised my eyes, above
They met with two so full and bright —
Such eyes! I swear to you, my love,
That these have never lost their light.

I loved, and love dispell'd the fear
That I should die an early death:
For love possess'd the atmosphere,
And fill'd the breast with purer breath.
My mother thought, What ails the boy?
For I war alter'd, and began
To move about the house with joy,
And with the certain step of man.

I loved the brimming wave that swam
Thro' quiet meadows, round the mill,
The sleepy pool above the dam,
The pool beneath it never still,
The meal-sacks, on the whiten'd floor,

The dark round of the dripping wheel,
The very air about the door
Made misty with the floating meal.

And oft in ramblings on the wold,
When April nights began to blow,
And April's crescent glimmer'd cold,
I saw the village lights below;
I knew your taper far away,
And full at heart of trembling hope
From off the wold I came, and lay
Upon the freshly-flower'd slope.

The deep brook groan'd beneath the mill;
And 'by that lamp,' I thought, 'she sits!'
The white chalk-quarry from the hill
Gleam'd to the flying moon by fits.
'O that I were beside her now!
O will she answer if I call?
O would she give me vow for vow,
Sweet Alice, if I told her all?'

Sometimes I saw you sit and spin;
And, in the pauses of the wind,
Sometimes I heard you sing within;
Sometimes your shadow cross'd the
blind.
At last you rose and moved the light,'
And the long shadow of the chair
Flitted across into the night,

And all the casement darken'd there.

But when at last I dared to speak,
The lanes, you know, were white with may,
Your ripe lips moved not, but your cheek
Flush'd like the coming of the day;
And so it was — half-sly, half-shy,
You would, and would not, little one!
Although I pleaded tenderly,
And you and I were all alone.

And slowly was my mother brought
To yield consent to my desire:
She wish'd me happy, but she thought
I might have look'd a little higher;
And I was young — too young to wed:
'Yet must I love her for your sake;
Go fetch your Alice here,' she said:
Her eyelid quiver'd as she spake.

And down I went to fetch my bride:
But, Alice, you were ill at ease;
This dress and that by turns you tried,
Too fearful that you should not please.
I loved you better for your fears,
I knew you could not look but well;
And dews, that would have fall'n in tears,
I kiss'd away before they fell.

I watch'd the little flutterings,
  The doubt my mother would not see;
She spoke at large of many things,
And at the last she spoke of me;
And turning look'd upon your face,
As near this door you sat apart,
And rose, and, with a silent grace
Approaching, press'd you heart to heart.

Ah, well — but sing the foolish song
I gave you, Alice, on the day
When, arm in arm, we went along,
A pensive pair, and you were gay
With bridal flowers — that I may seem,
As in the nights of old, to lie
Beside the mill-wheel in the stream
While those full chestnuts whisper by.

It is the miller's daughter,
  And she is grown so dear, so dear,
That I would be the jewel
  That trembles at her ear:
For hid in ringlets day and night,
  I'd touch her neck so warm and white.

And I would be the girdle
  About her dainty dainty waist,
And her heart would beat against me,
  In sorrow and in rest:
And I should know if it beat right,

I'd clasp it round so close and tight.

And I would be the necklace,
And all day long to fall and rise
Upon her balmy bosom,
With her laughter or her sighs,
And I would lie so light, so light,
I scarce should be unclasp'd at night.

A trifle, sweet! which true love spells —
True love interprets — right alone.
His light upon the letter dwells,
For all the spirit is his own.
So, if I waste words now, in truth
You must blame Love. His early rage
Had force to make me rhyme in youth,
And makes me talk too much in age.

And now those vivid hours are gone,
Like mine own life to me thou art,
Where Past and Present, wound in one,
Do make a garland for the heart:
So sing that other song I made,
Half-anger'd with my happy lot,
The day, when in the chestnut shade
I found the blue Forget-me-not.

Love that hath as in the net,
Can he pass, and we forget?
Many suns arise and set.

Many a chance the years beget.
Love the gift is Love the debt.
Even so.
Love is hurt with jar and fret.
Love is made a vague regret.
Eyes with idle tears are wet.
Idle habit links us yet.
What is love? for we forget:
Ah, no! no!

Look thro' mine eyes with thine. True wife,
Round my true heart thine arms entwine;
My other dearer life in life,
Look thro' my very soul with thine!
Untouch'd with any shade of years,
May those kind eyes for ever dwell!
They have not shed a many tears,
Dear eyes, since first I knew them well.
Yet tears they shed: they had their part
Of sorrow: for when time was ripe,
The still affection of the heart
Became an outward breathing type,
That into stillness past again,
And left a want unknown before;
Although the loss that brought us pain,
That loss but made us love the more,

With farther lookings on. The kiss,
The woven arms, seem but to be
Weak symbols of the settled bliss,

The comfort, I have found in thee:
But that God bless thee, dear —
who wrought
Two spirits to one equal mind —
With blessings beyond hope or thought,
With blessings which no words can find.
Arise, and let us wander forth,
To yon old mill across the wolds;
For look, the sunset, south and north,
Winds all the vale in rosy folds,
And fires your narrow casement glass,
Touching the sullen pool below:
On the chalk-hill the bearded grass
Is dry and dewless. Let us go.

Fatima

O Love, Love, Love! O withering might!
O sun, that from thy noonday height
Shudderest when I strain my sight,
Throbbing thro' all thy heat and light,
Lo, falling from my constant mind,
Lo, parch'd and wither'd, deaf and blind,
I whirl like leaves in roaring wind.

Last night I wasted hateful hours
Below the city's eastern towers:
I thirsted for the brooks, the showers:
I roll'd among the tender flowers:

I crush'd them on my breast, my mouth:
I look'd athwart the burning drouth
Of that long desert to the south.

Last night, when some one spoke his name,
From my swift blood that went and came
A thousand little shafts of flame
Were shiver'd in my narrow frame.
O Love, O fire! once he drew
With one long kiss my whole soul thro'
My lips, as sunlight drinketh dew.

Before he mounts the hill, I know
He cometh quickly: from below
Sweet gales, as from deep gardens, blow
Before him, striking on my brow.
In my dry brain my spirit soon,
Down-deepening from swoon to swoon,
Faints like a dazzled morning moon.

The wind sounds like a silver wire,
And from beyond the noon a fire
Is pour'd upon the hills, and nigher
The skies stoop down in their desire;
And, isled in sudden seas of light,
My heart, pierced thro' with fierce
delight,
Bursts into blossom in his sight.

My whole soul waiting silently,

All naked in a sultry sky,
Droops blinded with his shining eye:
  I *will* possess him or will die.
  I will grow round him in his place,
  Grow, live, die looking on his face,
Die, dying clasp'd in his embrace.

Oenone

There lies a vale in Ida, lovelier
Than all the valleys of Ionian hills.
The swimming vapour slopes athwart the
    glen,
Puts forth an arm, and creeps from pine to
    pine,
And loiters, slowly drawn. On either hand
The lawns and meadow-ledges midway
    down
Hang rich in flowers, and far below them
    roars
The long brook falling thro' the clov'n
    ravine
In cataract after cataract to the sea.
Behind the valley topmost Gargarus
Stands up and takes the morning: but in
    front
The gorges, opening wide apart, reveal
Troas and Ilion's column'd citadel,
The crown of Troas.

Hither came at noon
Mournful Oenone, wandering forlorn
Of Paris, once her playmate on the hills.
Her cheek had lost the rose, and round her
neck
Floated her hair or seem'd to float in rest.
She, leaning on a fragment twined with
vine,
Sang to the stillness, till the mountain shade
Sloped downward to her seat from the
upper cliff.

'O mother Ida, many-fountain'd Ida,
Dear mother Ida, hearken ere I die.
For now the noonday quiet holds the hill:
The grasshopper is silent in the grass:
The lizard, with his shadow on the stone,
Rests like a shadow, and the cicala sleeps.
The purple flowers droop: the golden bee
Is lily-cradled: I alone awake.
My eyes are full of tears, my heart of love,
My heart is breaking, and my eyes are dim,
And I am all aweary of my life.

'O mother Ida, many-fountain'd Ida,
Dear mother Ida, hearken ere I die.
Hear me O Earth, hear me O Hills, O Caves
That house the cold crown'd snake!
O mountain brooks
I am the daughter of a River-God

Hear me, for I will speak, and build up all
My sorrow with my song, as yonder walls
Rose slowly to a music slowly breathed,
A cloud that gather'd shape: for it may be
That, while I speak of it, a little while
My heart may wander from its deeper woe.

'O mother Ida, many-fountain'd Ida,
Dear mother Ida, hearken ere I die.
I waited underneath the dawning hills,
Aloft the mountain lawn was dewy-dark,
And dewy-dark aloft the mountain pine:
Beautiful Paris, evil-hearted Paris,
Leading a jet-black goat white-horn'd,
    white-hooved,
Came up from reedy Simois all alone.

'O mother Ida, hearken ere I die.
Far-off the torrent call'd me from the cleft:
Far up the solitary morning smote
The streaks of virgin snow.
    With down-dropt eyes
I sat alone: white-breasted like a star
Fronting the dawn he moved; a leopard skin
Droop'd from his shoulder, but his sunny hair
Cluster'd about his temples like a God's;
And his cheek brighten'd as the foam-bow
    brightens
When the wind blows the foam, and all my
    heart

Went forth to embrace him coming ere he
came.

'Dear mother Ida, hearken ere I die.
He smiled, and opening out his milk-white
palm
Disclosed a fruit of pure Hesperian gold,
That smelt ambrosially, and while I look'd
And listen'd, the full-flowing river of speech
Came down upon my heart.

' "My own Oenone,
Beautiful-brow'd Oenone, my own soul,
Behold this fruit, whose gleaming rind
ingrav'n
'For the most fair,' would seem to award it
thine,
As lovelier than whatever Oread haunt
The knolls of Ida, loveliest in all grace
Of movement, and the charm of married
brows."

'Dear mother Ida, hearken ere I die.
He prest the blossom of his lips to mine,
And added "This was cast upon the board,
When all the full-faced presence of the Gods
Ranged in the halls of Peleus; whereupon
Rose feud, with question unto whom 'twere
due:
But light-foot Iris brought it yester-eve,

Delivering, that to me, by common voice
Elected umpire, Herè comes to-day,
Pallas and Aphrodite, claiming each
This meed of fairest. Thou, within the cave
Behind yon whispering tuft of oldest pine,
Mayst well behold them unbeheld, unheard
Hear all, and see thy Paris judge of Gods."
'Dear mother Ida, hearken ere I die.
It was the deep midnoon: one silvery cloud
Had lost his way between the piney sides
Of this long glen. Then to the bower they came,
Naked they came to that smooth-swarded bower,
And at their feet the crocus brake like fire,
Violet, amaracus, and asphodel,
Lotos and lilies: and a wind arose,
And overhead the wandering ivy and vine
This way and that, in many a wild festoon
Ran riot, garlanding the gnarled boughs
With bunch and berry and flower thro' and thro'.

'O mother Ida, hearken ere I die.
On the tree-tops a crested peacock lit,
And o'er him flow'd a golden cloud, and lean'd
Upon him, slowly dropping fragrant dew.
Then first I heard the voice of her, to whom

Coming thro' Heaven, like a light that grows
Larger and clearer, with one mind the Gods
Rise up for reverence. She to Paris made
Proffer of royal power, ample rule
Unquestion'd, overflowing revenue
Wherewith to embellish state, "from many a
vale
And river-sunder'd champaign clothed with
corn,
Or labour'd mines undrainable of ore.
Honour," she said, "and homage, tax and
toll,
From many an inland town and haven large,
Mast-throng'd beneath her shadowing
citadel
In glassy bays among her tallest towers."

'O mother Ida, hearken ere I die.
Still she spake on and still she spake of
power,
"Which in all action is the end of all;
Power fitted to the season; wisdom-bred
And throned of wisdom — from all
neighbour crowns
Alliance and allegiance, till thy hand Fail
Fail from the sceptre-staff. Such
boon from me,
From me, Heaven's Queen, Paris, to thee
king-born,
A shepherd all thy life but yet king-born,

Should come most welcome, seeing men, in
power
Only, are likest gods, who have attain'd
Rest in a happy place and quiet seats
Above the thunder, with undying bliss
In knowledge of their own supremacy."

'Dear mother Ida, hearken ere I die.
She ceased, and Paris held the costly fruit
Out at arm's-length, so much the thought of
power
Flatter'd his spirit; but Pallas where she
stood
Somewhat apart, her clear and bared limbs
O'erthwarted with the brazen-headed spear
Upon her pearly shoulder leaning cold,
The while, above, her full and earnest eye
Over her snow-cold breast and angry cheek
Kept watch, waiting decision, made reply.

' "Self-reverence, self-knowledge,
self-control,
These three alone lead life to sovereign
power.
Yet not for power (power of herself
Would come uncall'd for), but to live by law,
Acting the law we live by without fear;
And, because right is right, to follow right
Were wisdom in the scorn of consequence."

'Dear mother Ida, hearken ere I die.
Again she said: "I woo thee not with gifts.
Sequel of guerdon could not alter me
To fairer. Judge thou me by what I am,
So shalt thou find me fairest.
Yet, indeed,
If gazing on divinity disrobed
Thy mortal eyes are frail to judge of fair,
Unbiass'd by self-profit, oh! rest thee sure
That I shall love thee well and cleave to thee,
So that my vigour, wedded to thy blood
Shall strike within thy pulses, like a God's,
To push thee forward thro' a life of shocks,
Dangers, and deeds, until endurance grow
Sinew'd with action, and the full-grown will,
Circled thro' all experiences, pure law,
Commeasure perfect freedom."
'Here she ceased,
And Paris ponder'd, and I cried, "O Paris,
Give it to Pallas!" but he heard me not,
Or hearing would not hear me, woe is me!

'O mother Ida, many-fountain'd Ida,
Dear mother Ida, hearken ere I die.
Idalian Aphrodite beautiful,
Fresh as the foam, new-bathed in Paphian wells,
With rosy slender fingers backward drew
From her warm brows and bosom her deep hair

Ambrosial, golden round her lucid throat
And shoulder: from the violets her light foot
Shone rosy-white, and o'er her rounded form
Between the shadows of the vine-bunches
Floated the glowing sunlights, as she moved.
'Dear mother Ida, hearken ere I die.
She with a subtle smile in her mild eyes,
The herald of her triumph, drawing nigh
Half-whisper'd in his ear, "I promise thee
The fairest and most loving wife in Greece,"
She spoke and laugh'd: I shut my sight for fear:
But when I look'd, Paris had raised his arm
And I beheld great Herè's angry eyes,
As she withdrew into the golden cloud,
And I was left alone within the bower;
And from that time to this I am alone,
And I shall be alone until I die.

'Yet, mother Ida, hearken ere I die.
Fairest — why fairest wife? am I not fair?
My love hath told me so a thousand times,
Methinks I must be fair, for yesterday,
When I past by, a wild and wanton pard,
Eyed like the evening star, with playful tail
Crouch'd fawning in the weed. Most loving is she?
Ah me, my mountain shepherd, that my arms

Were wound about thee, and my hot lips
prest
Close, close to thine in that quick-falling
dew
Of fruitful kisses, thick as Autumn rains
Flash in the pools of whirling Simois.
'O mother, hear me yet before I die.
They came, they cut away my tallest pines,
My dark tall pines, that plumed the craggy
ledge
High over the blue gorge, and all between
The snowy peak and snow-white cataract
Foster'd the callow eaglet — from beneath
Whose thick mysterious boughs in the dark
morn
The panther's roar came muffled, while I sat
Low in the valley, Never, never more
Shall lone Oenone see the morning mist
Sweep thro' them; never see them overlaid
With narrow moon-lit slips of silver cloud,
Between the loud stream and the trembling
stars.

'O mother, hear me yet before I die.
I wish that somewhere in the ruin'd folds,
Among the fragments tumbled from the
glens,
Or the dry thickets, I could meet with her,
The Abominable, that uninvited came
Into the fair Peleïan banquet-hall,

And cast the golden fruit upon the board,
And bred this change; that I might speak my
mind,
And tell her to her face how much I hate
Her presence, hated both of Gods and men.

'O mother, hear me yet before I die.
Hath he not sworn his love a thousand
times,
In this green valley, under this green hill,
Ev'n on this hand, and sitting on this stone?
Seal'd it with kisses? water'd it with tears?
O happy tears, and how unlike to these!
O happy Heaven, how canst thou see my
face?
O happy earth, how canst thou bear my
weight?
O death, death, death, thou ever-floating
cloud,
There are enough unhappy on this earth,
Pass by the happy souls, that love to live:
I pray thee, pass before my light of life,
And shadow all my soul, that I may die.
Thou weighest heavy on the heart within,
Weigh heavy on my eyelids: let me die.

'O mother, hear me yet before I die.
I will not die alone, for fiery thoughts
Do shape themselves within me, more and
more,

Whereof I catch the issue, as I hear
Dead sounds at night come from the inmost
    hills,
Like footsteps upon wool. I dimly see
My far-off doubtful purpose, as a mother
Conjectures of the features of her child
Ere it is born: her child! — a shudder comes
Across me: never child be born of me,
Unblest, to vex me with his father's eyes!

'O mother, hear me yet before I die.
Hear me O earth. I will not die alone,
Lest their shrill happy laughter come to me
Walking the cold and starless road of Death
Uncomforted, leaving my ancient love
With the Greek woman. I will rise and go
Down into Troy, and ere the stars come
    forth
Talk with the wild Cassandra, for she says
A fire dances before her, and a sound
Rings ever in her ears of armed men.
What this may be I know not, but I know
That, wheresoe'er I am by night and day,
All earth and air seem only burning fire.'

The Sisters

We were two daughters of one race:
She was the fairest in the face:

The wind is blowing in turret and tree.
They were together, and she fell;
Therefore revenge became me well.
O the Earl was fair to see!

She died: she went to burning flame:
She mix'd her ancient blood with shame.
The wind is howling in turret and tree.
Whole weeks and months, and early and late,
To win his love I lay in wait:
O the Earl was fair to see!
I made a feast; I bad him come;
I won his love, I brought him home.
The wind is roaring in turret and tree.
And after supper, on a bed,
Upon my lap he laid his head:
O the Earl was fair to see!

I kiss'd his eyelids into rest:
His ruddy cheek upon my breast.
The wind is raging in turret and tree.
I hated him with the hate of hell,
But I loved his beauty passing well.
O the Earl was fair to see!

I rose up in the silent night:
I made my dagger sharp and bright.
The wind is raving in turret and tree.
As half-asleep his breath he drew,
Three times I stabb'd him thro' and thro'.

O the Earl was fair to see!

I curl'd and comb'd his comely head.
He look'd so grand when he was dead.
The wind is blowing in turret and tree.
I wrapt his body in the sheet,
And laid him at his mother's feet.
O the Earl was fair to see!

To —

with the following poem

I send you here a sort of allegory,
(For you will understand it) of a soul,
A sinful soul possess'd of many gifts,
A spacious garden full of flowering weeds,
A glorious Devil, large in heart and brain,
That did love Beauty only, (Beauty seen
In all varieties of mould and mind)
And Knowledge for its beauty; or if Good,
Good only for its beauty, seeing not
That Beauty, Good, and Knowledge, are three sisters
That doat upon each other, friends to man,
Living together under the same roof,
And never can be sunder'd without tears.
And he that shuts Love out, in turn shall be
Shut out from Love, and on her threshold lie

Howling in outer darkness. Not for this
Was common clay ta'en from the common
  earth,
Moulded by God, and temper'd with the tears
Of angels to the perfect shape of man.

The Palace of Art

I built my soul a lordly pleasure-house,
  Wherein at ease for ay to dwell.
I said, 'O Soul, make merry and carouse,
    Dear soul, for all is well.'

A huge crag-platform, smooth as burnish'd
    brass,
  I chose. The ranged ramparts bright
From level meadow-bases of deep grass
    Suddenly scaled the light.

Thereon I built it firm. Of ledge or shelf
  The rock rose clear, or winding stair.
My soul would live alone unto herself
    In her high palace there.

And 'while the world runs round and
    round,' I said,
'Reign thou apart, a quiet king
Still as, while Saturn whirls, his steadfast
    shade

Sleeps on his luminous ring.'

To which my soul made answer readily.
  'Trust me, in bliss I shall abide
In this great mansion, that is built for me,
    So royal-rich and wide.'

★

Four courts I made, East, West and South
    and North,
  In each a squared lawn, wherefrom
The golden gorge of dragons spouted forth
    A flood of fountain-foam.

And round the cool green courts there ran a
    row
  Of cloisters, branch'd like mighty woods,
Echoing all night to that sonorous flow
    Of spouted fountain-floods.

And round the roofs a gilded gallery
  That lent broad verge to distant lands,
Far as the wild swan wings, to where the sky
    Dipt down to sea and sands.

From those four jets four currents in one swell
Across the mountain stream'd below
In misty folds, that floating as they fell
    Lit up a torrent-bow.

And high on every peak a statue seem'd
  To hang on tiptoe, tossing up
A cloud of incense of all odour steam'd
    From out a golden cup.

So that she thought, 'And who shall gaze
    upon
  My palace with unblinded eyes,
While this great bow will waver in the sun
    And that sweet incense rise?'

For that sweet incense rose and never fail'd,
  And, while day sank or mounted higher,
The light aërial gallery, golden-rail'd,
    Burnt like a fringe of fire.

Likewise the deep-set windows, stain'd and
    traced,
  Would seem slow-flaming crimson
      fires
From shadow'd grots of arches interlaced,
    And tipt with frost-like spires.

★

Full of long-sounding corridors it was,
  That over-vaulted grateful gloom,
Thro' which the livelong day my soul did
    pass,
    Well-pleased, from room to room.

Full of great rooms and small the palace stood,
All various, each a perfect whole
From living Nature, fit for every mood
And change of my still soul.

For some were hung with arras green and blue,
Showing a gaudy summer-morn,
Where with puff'd cheek the belted hunter blew
His wreathed bugle-horn.

One seem'd all dark and red — a tract of sand,
And some one pacing there alone,
Who paced for ever in a glimmering land,
Lit with a low large moon.

One show'd an iron coast and angry waves.
You seem'd to hear them climb and fall
And roar rock-thwarted under bellowing caves
Beneath the windy wall.

And one, a full-fed river winding slow
By herds upon an endless plain,
The ragged rims of thunder brooding low
With shadow-streaks of rain.

And one, the reapers at their sultry toil.
  In front they bound the sheaves. Behind
Were realms of upland, prodigal in oil,
    And hoary to the wind.

And one, a foreground black with stones
    and slags,
  Beyond, a line of heights, and higher
All barr'd with long white cloud the scornful
      crags,
    And highest, snow and fire.

And one, an English home — grey twilight
    pour'd
  On dewy pastures, dewy trees,
Softer than sleep — all things in order
      stored,
    A haunt of ancient Peace.

Nor these alone, but every landscape fair,
  As fit for every mood of mind,
Or gay, or grave, or sweet, or stern,
    was there,
Not less than truth design'd.

★

Or the maid-mother by a crucifix,
  In tracts of pasture sunny-warm,
Beneath branch-work of costly sardonyx

Sat smiling, babe in arm.

Or in a clear-wall'd city on the sea,
Near gilded organ-pipes, her hair
Wound with white roses, slept St. Cecily;
An angel look'd at her.

Or thronging all one porch of Paradise,
A group of Houris bow'd to see
The dying Islamite, with hands and eyes
That said, We wait for thee.

Or mythic Uther's deeply-wounded son
In some fair space of sloping greens
Lay, dozing in the vale of Avalon,
And watch'd by weeping queens.

Or hollowing one hand against his ear,
To list a foot-fall, ere he saw
The wood-nymph, stay'd the Ausonian king to hear
Of wisdom and of law.

Or over hills with peaky tops engrail'd,
And many a tract of palm and rice,
The throne of Indian Cama slowly sail'd
A summer fann'd with spice.

Or sweet Europa's mantle blew unclasp'd,
From off her shoulder backward bourne:

From one hand droop'd a crocus:
one hand grasp'd
The mild bull's golden horn.

Or else flush'd Ganymede, his rosy thigh
Half-buried in the Eagle's down
Sole as a flying star shot thro' the sky
Above the pillar'd town.
Nor these alone: but every legend fair
Which the supreme Caucasian mind
Carved out of Nature for itself, was there,
Not less than life, design'd.

*

Then in the towers I placed great bells that
swung,
Moved of themselves, with silver sound;
And with choice paintings of wise men I
hung
The royal dais round.

For there was Milton like a seraph strong,
Beside him Shakespeare bland and mild;
And there the world-worn Dante grasp'd his
song,
And somewhat grimly smiled.

And there the Ionian father of the rest;
A million wrinkles carved his skin;

A hundred winters snow'd upon his breast,
From cheek and throat and chin.

Above, the fair hall-ceiling stately-set
Many an arch high up did lift,
And angels rising and descending met
With interchange of gift.

Below was all mosaic choicely plann'd
With cycles of the human tale
Of this wide world, the times of every land
So wrought, they will not fail.

The people here, a beast of burden slow,
Toil'd onward, prick'd with goads and
stings;
Here play'd, a tiger, rolling to and fro
The heads and crowns of kings;

Here rose, an athlete, strong to break or
bind
All force in bonds that might endure,
And here once more like some sick man
declined
And trusted any cure.

But over these she trod: and those great
bells
Began to chime. She took her throne:
She sat betwixt the shining Oriels,

To sing her songs alone.

And thro' the topmost Oriels' colour'd flame
Two godlike faces gazed below;
Plato the wise, and large-brow'd Verulam,
The first of those who know.

And all those names, that in their motion were
Full-welling fountain-heads of change,
Betwixt the slender shafts were blazon'd fair
In diverse raiment strange:

Thro' which the lights, rose, amber,
emerald, blue,
Flush'd in her temples and her eyes,
And from her lips, as morn from
Memnon, drew
Rivers of melodies.

No nightingale delighteth to prolong
Her low preamble all alone
More than my soul to hear her echo'd song
Throb thro' the ribbed stone;

Singing and murmuring in her feastful
mirth,
Joying to feel herself alive,
Lord over Nature, Lord of the visible earth,
Lord of the senses five;

Communing with herself: 'All these are mine,
And let the world have peace or wars,
'Tis one to me.' She — when young night divine
Crown'd dying day with stars,

Making sweet close of his delicious toils —
Lit light in wreaths and anadems,
And pure quintessences of precious oils
In hollow'd moons of gems,

To mimic heaven; and clapt her hands and cried,
'I marvel if my still delight
In this great house so royal-rich, and wide,
Be flatter'd to the height.

'O all things fair to sate my various eyes!
O shapes and hues that please me well!
O silent faces of the Great and Wise,
My Gods, with whom I dwell!

'O God-like isolation which art mine,
I can but count thee perfect gain,
What time I watch the darkening droves of swine
That range on yonder plain.

'In filthy sloughs they roll a prurient skin,

They graze and wallow, breed and sleep;
And oft some brainless devil enters in,
And drives them to the deep.'

Then of the moral instinct would she prate,
And of the rising from the dead,
As hers by right of full-accomplish'd Fate;
And at the last she said:
'I take possession of man's mind and deed.
I care not what the sects may brawl.
I sit as God holding no form of creed,
But contemplating all.'

★

Full oft the riddle of the painful earth
Flash'd thro' her as she sat alone,
Yet not the less held she her solemn mirth,
And intellectual throne.

And so she throve and prosper'd: so three years
She prosper'd: on the fourth she fell
Like Herod, when the shout was in his ears,
Struck thro' with pangs of hell.

Lest she should fail and perish utterly,
God, before whom ever lie bare
The abysmal deeps of Personality,
Plagued her with sore despair.

When she would think, where'er she turn'd
her sight,
The airy hand confusion wrought,
Wrote 'Mene, mene,' and divided quite
The kingdom of her thought.

Deep dread and loathing of her solitude
Fell on her, from which mood was born
Scorn of herself; again, from out that mood
Laughter at her self-scorn.

'What! is not this my place of strength,'
she said,
'My spacious mansion built for me
Whereof the strong foundation-stones were
laid
Since my first memory?'

But in dark corners of her palace stood
Uncertain shapes; and unawares
On white-eyed phantasms weeping tears of
blood,
And horrible nightmares,

And hollow shades enclosing hearts of
flame,
And, with dim fretted foreheads all,
On corpses three-months-old at noon she
came,
That stood against the wall.

A spot of dull stagnation, without light
Or power of movement, seem'd my soul,
'Mid onward-sloping motions infinite
Making for one sure goal.

A still salt pool, lock'd in with bars of sand;
Left on the shore; that hears all night
The plunging seas draw backward from the land
Their moon-led waters white.

A star that with the choral starry dance
Join'd not, but stood, and standing saw
The hollow orb of moving Circumstance
Roll'd round by one fix'd law.

Back on herself her serpent pride had curl'd.
'No voice,' she shriek'd in that lone hall,
'No voice breaks thro' the stillness of this world:
One deep, deep silence all!'

She, mouldering with the dull earth's mouldering sod,
Inwrapt tenfold in slothful shame,
Lay there exiled from eternal God,
Lost to her place and name;

And death and life she hated equally,
And nothing saw, for her despair,

But dreadful time, dreadful eternity,
No comfort anywhere;

Remaining utterly confused with fears,
And ever worse with growing time,
And ever unrelieved by dismal tears,
And all alone in crime:

Shut up as in a crumbling tomb, girt round
With blackness as a solid wall,
Far off she seem'd to hear the dully sound
Of human footsteps fall.

As in strange lands a traveller walking slow,
In doubt and great perplexity,
A little before moon-rise hears the low
Moan of an unknown sea;

And knows not if it be thunder, or a sound
Of rocks thrown down, or one deep cry
Of great wild beasts; then thinketh,
'I have found
A new land, but I die.'

She howl'd aloud, 'I am on fire within.
There comes no murmur of reply.
What is it that will take away my sin,
And save me lest I die?'

So when four years were wholly finished,

She threw her royal robes away.
'Make me a cottage in the vale,' she said,
Where I may mourn and pray.

'Yet pull not down my palace towers, that are
So lightly, beautifully built:
Perchance I may return with others there
When I have purged my guilt.'

The May Queen

You must wake and call me early, call me early, mother dear;
To-morrow 'ill be the happiest time of all the glad New-year;
Of all the glad New-year, mother, the maddest merriest day;
For I'm to be Queen o' the May, mother, I'm to be Queen o' the May.

There's many a black black eye, they say, but none so bright as mine;
There's Margaret and Mary, there's Kate and Caroline:
But none so fair as little Alice in all the land they say,
So I'm to be Queen o' the May, mother, I'm to be Queen o' the May.

I sleep so sound all night, mother,
    that I shall never wake,
If you do not call me loud when the day
    begins to break:
But I must gather knots of flowers,
    and buds and garlands gay,
For I'm to be Queen o' the May, mother,
    I'm to be Queen o' the May.

As I came up the valley whom think ye
    should I see,
But Robin leaning on the bridge beneath
    the hazel-tree?
He thought of that sharp look, mother,
    I gave him yesterday, —
But I'm to be Queen o' the May, mother,
    I'm to be Queen o' the May.

He thought I was a ghost, mother,
    for I was all in white,
And I ran by him without speaking,
    like a flash of light.
They call me cruel-hearted,
    but I care not what they say,
For I'm to be Queen o' the May, mother,
    I'm to be Queen o' the May.

They say he's dying all for love,
    but that can never be:
They say his heart is breaking,

mother — what is that to me?
There's many a bolder lad 'ill woo me any
summer day,
And I'm to be Queen o' the May, mother,
I'm to be Queen o' the May.
Little Effie shall go with me to-morrow to
the green,
And you'll be there, too, mother,
to see me made the Queen;
For the shepherd lads on every side 'ill come
from far away,
And I'm to be Queen o' the May, mother,
I'm to be Queen o' the May.

The honeysuckle round the porch has
wov'n its wavy bowers,
And by the meadow-trenches blow the faint
sweet cuckoo-flowers;
And the wild marsh-marigold shines like
fire in swamps and hollows grey,
And I'm to be Queen o' the May, mother,
I'm to be Queen o' the May.

The night-winds come and go, mother,
upon the meadowgrass,
And the happy stars above them seem to
brighten as they pass;
There will not be a drop of rain the whole of
the livelong day,
And I'm to be Queen o' the May, mother,

I'm to be Queen o' the May.

All the valley, mother, 'ill be fresh and green
and still,
And the cowslip and the crowfoot are over
all the hill,
And the rivulet in the flowery dale 'ill
merrily glance and play,
For I'm to be Queen o' the May, mother,
I'm to be Queen o' the May.

So you must wake and call me early,
call me early, mother dear,
To-morrow 'ill be the happiest time of all
the glad New-year:
To-morrow 'ill be of all the year the maddest
merriest day,
For I'm to be Queen o' the May, mother,
I'm to be Queen o' the May.

New Year's Eve

If you're waking call me early, call me early,
mother dear,
For I would see the sun rise upon the glad
New-year.
It is the last New-year that I shall ever see,
Then you may lay me low i' the mould and
think no more of me.

To-night I saw the sun set: he set and left behind
The good old year, the dear old time, and all my peace of mind;
And the New-year's coming up, mother, but I shall never see
The blossom on the blackthorn, the leaf upon the tree.

Last May we made a crown of flowers: we had a merry day;
Beneath the hawthorn on the green they made me Queen of May;
And we danced about the may-pole and in the hazel copse,
Till Charles's Wain came out above the tall white chimney-tops.

There's not a flower on all the hills: the frost is on the pane:
I only wish to live till the snowdrops come again:
I wish the snow would melt and the sun come out on high:
I long to see a flower so before the day I die.

The building rook 'ill caw from the windy tall elm-tree
And the tufted plover pipe along the fallow lea,

And the swallow 'ill come back again with
summer o'er the wave,
But I shall lie alone, mother, within the
mouldering grave.
Upon the chancel-casement, and upon that
grave of mine,
In the early early morning the summer sun
'ill shine,
Before the red cock crows from the farm
upon the hill,
When you are warm-asleep, mother, and all
the world is still.

When the flowers come again, mother,
beneath the waning light
You'll never see me more in the long grey
fields at night;
When from the dry dark wold the summer
airs blow cool
On the oat-grass and the sword-grass,
and the bulrush in the pool.

You'll bury me, my mother, just beneath the
hawthorn shade,
And you'll come sometimes and see me
where I am lowly laid.
I shall not forget you, mother, I shall hear
you when you pass,
With your feet above my head in the long
and pleasant grass.

I have been wild and wayward,
but you'll forgive me now;
You'll kiss me, my own mother,
and forgive me ere I go;
Nay, nay, you must not weep,
nor let your grief be wild,
You should not fret for me, mother,
you have another child.

If I can I'll come again, mother,
from out my resting-place;
Tho' you'll not see me, mother,
I shall look upon your face;
Tho' I cannot speak a word,
I shall hearken what you say,
And be often, often with you when you
think I'm far away.

Goodnight, goodnight, when I have said
goodnight for evermore,
And you see me carried out from the
threshold of the door;
Don't let Effie come to see me till my grave
be growing green:
She'll be a better child to you than ever I
have been.
She'll find my garden-tools upon the
granary floor:
Let her take 'em: they are hers:
I shall never garden more:

But tell her, when I'm gone,
to train the rose-bush that I set
About the parlour-window and the
box of mignonette.

Goodnight, sweet mother: call me before
the day is born.
All night I lie awake, but I fall asleep at morn;
But I would see the sun rise upon the glad
New-year,
So, if you're waking, call me, call me early,
mother dear.

Conclusion

I thought to pass away before, and yet alive
I am;
And in the fields all round I hear the
bleating of the lamb.
How sadly, I remember, rose the morning of
the year!
To die before the snowdrop came, and now
the violet's here.

O sweet is the new violet, that comes
beneath the skies,
And sweeter is the young lamb's voice to me
that cannot rise,
And sweet is all the land about, and all the

flowers that blow,
And sweeter far is death than life to me that
long to go.

It seem'd so hard at first, mother,
to leave the blessed sun,
And now it seems as hard to stay,
and yet His will be done!
But still I think it can't be long before I
find release;
And that good man, the clergyman,
has told me words of peace.

O blessings on his kindly voice and on his
silver hair!
And blessings on his whole life long,
until he meet me there!
O blessings on his kindly heart and on
his silver head!
A thousand times I blest him,
as he knelt beside my bed.

He taught me all the mercy,
for he show'd me all the sin.
Now, tho' my lamp was lighted late,
there's One will let me in:
Nor would I now be well, mother,
again if that could be,
For my desire is but to pass to Him that died
for me.

I did not hear the dog howl, mother,
or the deathwatch beat,
There came a sweeter token when the night
and morning meet:
But sit beside my bed, mother,
and put your hand in mine,
And Effie on the other side,
and I will tell the sign.

All in the wild March-morning I heard the
angels call;
It was when the moon was setting,
and the dark was over all;
The trees began to whisper
and the wind began to roll,
And in the wild March-morning I heard
them call my soul.

For lying broad awake I thought of you and
Effie dear;
I saw you sitting in the house,
and I no longer here;
With all my strength I pray'd for both,
and so I felt resign'd,
And up the valley came a swell of music on
the wind.

I thought that it was fancy, and I listen'd in
my bed,
And then did something speak to me —

I know not what was said;
For great delight and shuddering took hold
of all my mind,
And up the valley came again the music on
the wind.

But you were sleeping; and I said,
'It's not for them: it's mine.'
And if it comes three times, I thought,
I take it for a sign.
And once again it came, and close beside
the window-bars,
Then seem'd to go right up to Heaven and
die among the stars.

So now I think my time is near. I trust it is,
I know
The blessed music went that way my soul
will have to go.
And for myself, indeed, I care not if I go
to-day.
But, Effie, you must comfort *her* when I am
past away.

And say to Robin a kind word,
and tell him not to fret;
There's many worthier than I,
would make him happy yet.
If I had lived — I cannot tell —
I might have been his wife;

But all these things have ceased to be,
with my desire of life.

O look! the sun begins to rise,
the heavens are in a glow;
He shines upon a hundred fields,
and all of them I know.
And there I move no longer now,
and there his light may shine —
Wild flowers in the valley for other hands
than mine.

O sweet and strange it seems to me,
that ere this day is done
The voice, that now is speaking,
may be beyond the sun —
For ever and for ever with those just souls
and true —
And what is life, that we should moan?
why make we such ado?

For ever and for ever, all in a blessed
home —
And there to wait a little while till you and
Effie come —
To lie within the light of God, as I lie upon
your breast —
And the wicked cease from troubling,
and the weary are at rest.

The Lotos-Eaters

'Courage!' he said, and pointed toward the
    land,
'This mounting wave will roll us shoreward
    soon.'
In the afternoon they came unto a land
In which it seemed always afternoon.
All round the coast the languid air did
    swoon,
Breathing like one that hath a weary dream.
Full-faced above the valley stood the moon;
And like a downward smoke, the slender
    stream
Along the cliff to fall and pause and fall did
    seem.

A land of streams! some, like a downward
    smoke,
Slow-dropping veils of thinnest lawn,
    did go;
And some thro' wavering lights and
    shadows broke,
Rolling a slumbrous sheet of foam below.
They saw the gleaming river seaward flow
From the inner land: far off, three
    mountain-tops,
Three silent pinnacles of aged snow,
Stood sunset-flush'd: and, dew'd with
    showery drops,

Up-clomb the shadowy pine above the
woven copse.

The charmed sunset linger'd low adown
In the red West: thro' mountain clefts the
dale
Was seen far inland, and the yellow down
Border'd with palm, and many a winding
vale
And meadow, set with slender galingale;
A land where all things always seem'd the
same!
And round about the keel with faces pale,
Dark faces pale against that rosy flame,
The mild-eyed melancholy Lotos-eaters
came.

Branches they bore of that enchanted stem,
Laden with flower and fruit, whereof they
gave
To each, but whoso did receive of them,
And taste, to him the gushing of the wave
Far far away did seem to mourn and rave
On alien shores; and if his fellow spake,
His voice was thin, as voices from the grave;
And deep-asleep he seem'd, yet all awake,
And music in his ears his beating heart did
make.
They sat them down upon the yellow sand,
Between the sun and moon upon the shore;

And sweet it was to dream of Fatherland,
Of child, and wife, and slave; but evermore
Most weary seem'd the sea, weary the oar,
Weary the wandering fields of barren foam.
Then some one said, 'We will return no more;
And all at once they sang, 'Our island home
Is far beyond the wave; we will no longer
roam.'

Choric Song

I

There is sweet music here that softer falls
Than petals from blown roses on the grass,
Or night-dews on still waters between walls
Of shadowy granite, in a gleaming pass;
Music that gentlier on the spirit lies,
Than tir'd eyelids upon tir'd eyes;
Music that brings sweet sleep down from
the blissful skies.
Here are cool mosses deep,
And thro' the moss the ivies creep,
And in the stream the long-leaved flowers
weep,
And from the craggy ledge the poppy hangs
in sleep.

II

Why are we weigh'd upon with heaviness,
And utterly consumed with sharp distress,
While all things else have rest from
  weariness?
All things have rest: why should we toil
  alone,
We only toil, who are the first of things,
And make perpetual moan,
Still from one sorrow to another thrown:
Nor ever fold our wings,
And cease from wanderings,
Nor steep our brows in slumber's holy balm;
Nor hearken what the inner spirit sings,
'There is no joy but calm!'
Why should we only toil, the roof and crown
  of things?

III

Lo! in the middle of the wood,
The folded leaf is woo'd from out the bud
With winds upon the branch, and there
Grows green and broad, and takes no care
Sun-steep'd at noon, and in the moon
Nightly dew-fed; and turning yellow
Falls, and floats adown the air.
Lo! sweeten'd with the summer light,

The full-juiced apple, waxing over-mellow,
Drops in a silent autumn night.
All its allotted length of days,
The flower ripens in its place,
Ripens and fades, and falls, and hath no toil,
Fast-rooted in the fruitful soil.

IV

Hateful is the dark-blue sky,
Vaulted o'er the dark-blue sea.
Death is the end of life; ah, why
Should life all labour be?
Let us alone. Time driveth onward fast,
And in a little while our lips are dumb.
Let us alone, What is it that will last?
All things are taken from us, and become
Portions and parcels of the dreadful Past.
Let us alone. What pleasure can we have
To war with evil? Is there any peace
In ever climbing up the climbing wave?
All things have rest, and ripen toward the
grave
In silence; ripen, fall and cease:
Give us long rest or death, dark death, or
dreamful ease.

V

How sweet it were, hearing the downward
stream,
With half-shut eyes ever to seem
Falling asleep in a half-dream!
To dream and dream, like yonder amber light,
Which will not leave the myrrh-bush on the
height;
To hear each other's whisper'd speech;
Eating the Lotos day by day,
To watch the crisping ripples on the beach,
And tender curving lines of creamy spray;
To lend our hearts and spirits wholly
To the influence of mild-minded
melancholy;
To muse and brood and live again in
memory,
With those old faces of our infancy
Heap'd over with a mound of grass,
Two handfuls of white dust, shut in an urn
of brass!

VI

Dear is the memory of our wedded lives,
And dear the last embraces of our wives
And their warm tears: but all hath suffer'd
change;

For surely now our household hearths are
cold:
Our sons inherit us: our looks are strange:
And we should come like ghosts to trouble
joy.
Or else the island princes over-bold
Have eat our substance, and the minstrel
sings
Before them of the ten-years' war in Troy,
And our great deeds, as half-forgotten
things.
Is there confusion in the little isle?
Let what is broken so remain.
The Gods are hard to reconcile:
'Tis hard to settle order once again.
There is confusion worse than death,
Trouble on trouble, pain on pain,
Long labour unto aged breath,
Sore task to hearts worn out with many
wars
And eyes grown dim with gazing on the
pilot-stars.

VII

But, propt on beds of amaranth and moly,
How sweet (while warm airs lull us, blowing
lowly)
With half-dropt eyelids still,

Beneath a heaven dark and holy,
To watch the long bright river drawing slowly
His waters from the purple hill —
To hear the dewy echoes calling
From cave to cave thro' the thick-twined
vine —
To watch the emerald-colour'd water falling
Thro' many a wov'n acanthus-wreath
divine!
Only to hear and see the far-off sparkling
brine,
Only to hear were sweet, stretch'd out
beneath the pine.

VIII

The Lotos blooms below the barren peak:
The Lotos blows by every winding creek:
All day the wind breathes low with mellower
tone:
Thro' every hollow cave and alley lone
Round and round the spicy downs the
yellow Lotos-dust is blown.
We have had enough of action, and of
motion we.
Roll'd to starboard, roll'd to larboard, when
the surge was seething free,
Where the wallowing monster spouted his
foam-fountains in the sea.

Let us swear an oath, and keep it with an equal mind,
In the hollow Lotos-land to live and lie reclined
On the hills like Gods together, careless of mankind.
For they lie beside their nectar, and the bolts are hurl'd
Far below them in the valleys, and the clouds are lightly curl'd
Round their golden houses, girdled with the gleaming world:
Where they smile in secret, looking over wasted lands,
Blight and famine, plague and earthquake, roaring deeps and fiery sands,
Clanging fights, and flaming towns, and sinking ships, and praying hands.
But they smile, they find a music centred in a doleful song
Steaming up, a lamentation and an ancient tale of wrong,
Like a tale of little meaning tho' the words are strong;
Chanted from an ill-used race of men that cleave the soil,
Sow the seed, and reap the harvest with enduring toil,
Storing yearly little dues of wheat, and wine and oil;

Till they perish and they suffer — some, 'tis whisper'd — down in hell
Suffer endless anguish, others in Elysian valleys dwell
Resting weary limbs at last on beds of asphodel.
Surely, surely, slumber is more sweet than toil, the shore
Than labour in the deep mid-ocean, wind and wave and oar;
Oh rest ye, brother mariners, we will not wander more.

Rosalind

I

My Rosalind, my Rosalind,
My frolic falcon, with bright eyes,
Whose free delight, from any height of rapid flight,
Stoops at all game that wing the skies,
My Rosalind, my Rosalind,
My bright-eyed, wild-eyed falcon, whither.
Careless both of wind and weather,
Whither fly ye, what game spy ye,
Up or down the streaming wind?

II

The quick lark's closest-caroll'd strains,
The shadow rushing up the sea,
The lightning-flash atween the rains,
The sunlight driving down the lea,
The leaping stream, the very wind,
That will not stay, upon his way,
To stoop the cowslip to the plains,
Is not so clear and bold and free
As you, my falcon Rosalind.
You care not for another's pains,
Because you are the soul of joy,
Bright metal all without alloy.
Life shoots and glances thro' your veins,
And flashes off a thousand ways,
Through lips and eyes in subtle rays.
Your hawk-eyes are keen and bright,
Keen with triumph, watching still
To pierce me through with pointed light;
But oftentimes they flash and glitter
Like sunshine on a dancing rill,
And your words are seeming-bitter,
Sharp and few, but seeming-bitter
From excess of swift delight.

III

Come down, come home, my Rosalind,

My gay young hawk, my Rosalind:
Too long you keep the upper skies;
Too long you roam and wheel at will;
But we must hood your random eyes,
That care not whom they kill,
And your cheek, whose brilliant hue
Is so sparkling-fresh to view,
Some red heath-flower in the dew,
Touched with sunrise. We must bind
And keep you fast, my Rosalind,
Fast, fast, my wild-eyed Rosalind,
And clip your wings, and make you love:
When we have lured you from above,
And that delight of frolic flight,
    by day or night,
From North to South;
We'll bind you fast in silken cords,
And kiss away the bitter words
From off your rosy mouth.

A Dream of Fair Women

I read, before my eyelids dropt their shade,
  '*The Legend of Good Women*,' long ago
Sung by the morning star of song, who made
  His music heard below;

Dan Chaucer, the first warbler, whose sweet
    breath

Preluded those melodious bursts that fill
The spacious times of great Elizabeth
With sounds that echo still.

And, for a while, the knowledge of his art
Held me above the subject, as strong gales
Hold swollen clouds from raining, tho' my heart,
Brimful of those wild tales,

Charged both mine eyes with tears. In every land
I saw, wherever light illumineth,
Beauty and anguish walking hand in hand
The downward slope to death

Those far-renowned brides of ancient song
Peopled the hollow dark, like burning stars,
And I heard sounds of insult, shame, and wrong,
And trumpets blown for wars;

And clattering flints batter'd with clanging hoofs:
And I saw crowds in column'd sanctuaries;
And forms that pass'd at windows and on roofs
Of marble palaces;

Corpses across the threshold; heroes tall
Dislodging pinnacle and parapet
Upon the tortoise creeping to the wall;
Lances in ambush set;

And high shrine-doors burst thro' with heated blasts
That run before the fluttering tongues of fire;
White surf wind-scatter'd over sails and masts,
And ever climbing higher;

Squadrons and squares of men in brazen plates,
Scaffolds, still sheets of water, divers woes,
Ranges of glimmering vaults with iron grates,
And hush'd seraglios.

So shape chased shape as swift as, when to land
Bluster the winds and tides the self-same way,
Crisp foam-flakes scud along the level sand,
Torn from the fringe of spray.

I started once, or seem'd to start in pain,
Resolved on noble things, and strove to speak,

As when a great thought strikes along the brain,
And flushes all the cheek.

And once my arm was lifted to hew down
A cavalier from off his saddle-bow,
That bore a lady from a leaguer'd town;
And then, I know not how,

All those sharp fancies, by down-lapsing thought
Stream'd onward, lost their edges, and did creep
Roll'd on each other, rounded, smooth'd, and brought
Into the gulfs of sleep.

At last methought that I had wander'd far
In an old wood: fresh-wash'd in coolest dew,
The maiden splendours of the morning star
Shook in the steadfast blue.

Enormous elm-tree-boles did stoop and lean
Upon the dusky brushwood underneath
Their broad curved branches, fledged with clearest green,
New from its silken sheath.

The dim red morn had died, her journey
done,
And with dead lips smiled at the twilight
plain,
Half-fall'n across the threshold of the sun,
Never to rise again.

There was no motion in the dumb dead air,
Not any song of bird or sound of rill;
Gross darkness of the inner sepulchre
Is not so deadly still

As that wide forest. Growths of jasmine
turn'd
Their humid arms festooning tree to tree,
And at the root thro' lush green grasses
burn'd
The red anemone.

I knew the flowers, I knew the leaves, I knew
The tearful glimmer of the languid dawn
On those long, rank, dark wood-walks
drench'd in dew,
Leading from lawn to lawn.

The smell of violets, hidden in the green,
Pour'd back into my empty soul and
frame
The times when I remember to have been
Joyful and free from blame.

And from within me a clear under-tone
  Thrill'd thro' mine ears in that unblissful
    clime,
'Pass freely thro': the wood is all thine own,
  Until the end of time.'

At length I saw a lady with call,
  Stiller than chisell'd marble, standing
    there;
A daughter of the gods, divinely tall,
  And most divinely fair.

Her loveliness with shame and with surprise
  Froze my swift speech: she turning on my
    face
The star-like sorrows of immortal eyes,
  Spoke slowly in her place.

'I had great beauty: ask thou not my name:
  No one can be more wise than destiny.
Many drew swords and died.
    Where'er I came
  I brought calamity.'

'No marvel, sovereign lady: in fair field
  Myself for such a face had boldly died,'
I answer'd free; and turning I appeal'd
  To one that stood beside.

But she, with sick and scornful looks averse,

To her full height her stately stature draws;
'My youth,' she said, 'was blasted with a
curse:
This woman was the cause.

'I was cut off from hope in that sad place,
Which yet to name my spirit loathes and
fears:
My father held his hand upon his face;
I, blinded with my tears,

'Still strove to speak: my voice was thick
with sighs
As in a dream. Dimly I could descry
The stern black-bearded kings with wolfish
eyes,
Waiting to see me die.

'The high masts flicker'd as they lay afloat;
The crowds, the temples, waver'd, and the
shore;
The bright death quiver'd at the victim's
throat;
Touch'd; and I knew no more.'

Whereto the other with a downward brow:
'I would the white cold heavy-plunging
foam,
Whirl'd by the wind, had roll'd me deep
below,

Then when I left my home.'

Her slow full words sank thro' the silence drear,
As thunder-drops fall on a sleeping sea:
Sudden I heard a voice that cried, 'Come here,
That I may look on thee.'

I turning saw, throned on a flowery rise,
One sitting on a crimson scarf unroll'd;
A queen, with swarthy cheeks and bold black eyes,
Brow-bound with burning gold.

She, flashing forth a haughty smile, began:
'I govern'd men by change, and so I sway'd
All moods. 'Tis long since I have seen a man.
Once, like the moon, I made

'The ever-shifting currents of the blood
According to my humour ebb and flow.
I have no men to govern in this wood:
That makes my only woe.

'Nay — yet it chafes me that I could not bend
One will; nor tame and tutor with mine eye

That dull cold-blooded Caesar. Prythee, friend,
Where is Mark Antony?

'The man, my lover, with whom I rode sublime
On Fortune's neck: we sat as God by God:
The Nilus would have risen before his time
And flooded at our nod.

'We drank the Libyan Sun to sleep, and lit
Lamps which outburn'd Canopus. O my life
In Egypt! O the dalliance and the wit,
The flattery and the strife,

'And the wild kiss, when fresh from war's alarms.
My Hercules, my Roman Antony,
My mailed Bacchus leapt into my arms,
Contented there to die!

'And there he died: and when I heard my name
Sigh'd forth with life I would not brook my fear
Of the other: with a worm I balk'd his fame,
What else was left? look here!'

(With that she tore her robe apart, and half
The polish'd argent of her breast to sight
Laid bare. Thereto she pointed with a laugh,
Showing the aspick's bite.)

'I died a Queen. The Roman soldier found
Me lying dead, my crown about my brows,
A name for ever! — lying robed and crown'd,
Worthy a Roman spouse.'

Her warbling voice, a lyre of widest range
Struck by all passion, did fall down and glance
From tone to tone, and glided thro' all change
Of liveliest utterance.

When she made pause I knew not for delight;
Because with sudden motion from the ground
She raised her piercing orbs, and fill'd with light
The interval of sound.

Still with their fires Love tipt his keenest darts;

As once they drew into two burning rings
All beams of Love, melting the mighty
hearts
Of captains and of kings.

Slowly my sense undazzled, Then I heard
A noise of some one coming thro' the
lawn,
And singing clearer than the crested bird,
That claps his wings at dawn.

'The torrent brooks of hallow'd Israel
From craggy hollows pouring, late and
soon,
Sound all night long, in falling thro' the
dell,
Far-heard beneath the moon.

'The balmy moon of blessed Israel
Floods all the deep-blue gloom with
beams divine:
All night the splinter'd crags that wall the
dell
With spires of silver shine.'

As one that museth where broad sunshine
laves
The lawn by some cathedral, thro' the
door
Hearing the holy organ rolling waves

Of sound on roof and floor
Within, and anthem sung, is charm'd and tied
To where he stands, — so stood I, when that flow
Of music left the lips of her that died
To save her father's vow;

The daughter of the warrior Gileadite,
A maiden pure; as when she went along
From Mizpeh's tower'd gate with welcome light,
With timbrel and with song.

My words leapt forth: 'Heaven heads the count of crimes
With that wild oath.' She render'd answer high:
'Not so, nor once alone; a thousand times
I would be born and die.

'Single I grew, like some green plant, whose root
Creeps to the garden water-pipes beneath,
Feeding the flower; but ere my flower to fruit
Changed, I was ripe for death.

'My God, my land, my father — these did move

Me from my bliss of life, that Nature gave,
Lower'd softly with a threefold cord of love
Down to a silent grave.

'And I went mourning, "No fair Hebrew boy
Shall smile away my maiden blame among
The Hebrew mothers" — emptied of all joy,
Leaving the dance and song,

'Leaving the olive-gardens far below,
Leaving the promise of my bridal bower,
The valleys of grape-loaded vines that glow
Beneath the battled tower.

'The light white cloud swam over us. Anon
We heard the lion roaring from his den;
We saw the large white stars rise one by one,
Or, from the darken'd glen,

'Saw God divide the night with flying flame,
And thunder on the everlasting hills.
I heard Him, for He spake, and grief became
A solemn scorn of ills.

'When the next moon was roll'd into the sky.
Strength came to me that equall'd my desire.
How beautiful a thing it was to die

For God and for my sire!

'It comforts me in this one thought to dwell,
That I subdued me to my father's will;
Because the kiss he gave me, ere I fell,
Sweetens the spirit still.

'Moreover it is written that my race
Hew'd Ammon, hip and thigh, from
Aroer
On Arnon unto Minneth,' Here her face
Glow'd, as I look'd at her.

She lock'd her lips: she left me where I
stood:
'Glory to God,' she sang, and past afar,
Thridding the sombre boskage of the wood,
Toward the morning-star.

Losing her carol I stood pensively,
As one that from a casement leans his
head,
When midnight bells cease ringing
suddenly,
And the old year is dead.

'Alas! alas!' a low voice, full of care
Murmur'd beside me: 'Turn and look on
me:
I am that Rosamond, whom men call fair,

If what I was I be.

'Would I had been some maiden coarse and poor!
O me, that I should ever see the light!
Those dragon eyes of anger'd Elëanor
Do hunt me, day and night.'

She ceased in tears, fallen from hope and trust:
To whom the Egyptian: 'O, you tamely died!
You should have clung to Fulvia's waist, and thrust
The dagger thro' her side.'

With that sharp sound the white dawn's creeping beams,
Stol'n to my brain, dissolved the mystery
Of folded sleep. The captain of my dreams
Ruled in the eastern sky.

Morn broaden'd on the borders of the dark,
Ere I saw her, who clasp'd in her last trance
Her murder'd father's head, orJoan of Arc,
A light of ancient France;

Or her, who knew that Love can vanquish Death,

Who kneeling, with one arm about her king,
Drew forth the poison with her balmy breath,
Sweet as new buds in Spring.

No memory labours longer from the deep
Gold-mines of thought to lift the hidden ore
That glimpses, moving up, than I from sleep
To gather and tell o'er

Each little sound and sight. With what dull pain
Compass'd, how eagerly I sought to strike
Into that wondrous track of dreams again!
But no two dreams are like.

As when a soul laments, which hath been blest,
Desiring what is mingled with past years,
In yearnings that can never be exprest
By signs or groans or tears;

Because all words, tho' cull'd with choicest art,
Failing to give the bitter of the sweet
Wither beneath the palate, and the heart
Faints, faded by its heat.

Margaret

I

O sweet pale Margaret,
O rare pale Margaret,
What lit your eyes with tearful power,
Like moonlight on a falling shower?
Who lent you, love, your mortal dower
Of pensive thought and aspect pale,
Your melancholy sweet and frail
As perfume of the cuckoo-flower?
From the westward-winding flood,
From the evening-lighted wood,
From all things outward you have won
A tearful grace, as tho' you stood
Between the rainbow and the sun.
The very smile before you speak,
That dimples your transparent cheek,
Encircles all the heart, and feedeth
The senses with a still delight
Of dainty sorrow without sound,
Like the tender amber round,
Which the moon about her spreadeth,
Moving thro' a fleecy night.

II

You love, remaining peacefully,

To hear the murmur of the strife,
But enter not the toil of life.
Your spirit is the calmed sea,
Laid by the tumult of the fight.
You are the evening star, alway
Remaining betwixt dark and bright:
Lull'd echoes of laborious day
Come to you, gleams of mellow light
Float by you on the verge of night.

III

What can it matter, Margaret
What songs below the waning stars
The lion-heart, Plantagenet,
Sang looking thro' his prison bars?
Exquisite Margaret, who can tell
The last wild thought of Chatelet,
Just ere the falling axe did part
The burning brain from the true heart,
Even in her sight he loved so well?

IV

A fairy shield your Genius made
And gave you on your natal day.
Your sorrow, only sorrow's shade,
Keeps real sorrow far away.

You move not in such solitudes,
    You are not less divine,
But more human in your moods,
    Than your twin-sister, Adeline.
Your hair is darker, and your eyes
    Touch'd with a somewhat darker hue,
    And less aërially blue
    But ever trembling thro' the dew
Of dainty-woeful sympathies.

V

    O sweet pale Margaret,
    O rare pale Margaret,
Come down, come down, and hear me
    speak:
Tie up the ringlets on your cheek:
    The sun is just about to set,
The arching limes are tall and shady,
    And faint, rainy lights are seen,
      Moving in the leavy beech.
Rise from the feast of sorrow, lady,
    Where all day long you sit between
      Joy and woe, and whisper each.
Or only look across the lawn,
  Look out below your bower-eaves,
Look down, and let your blue eyes dawn
  Upon me thro' the jasmine-leaves.

Kate

I know her by her angry air,
Her bright black eyes, her bright black hair,
    Her rapid laughters wild and shrill,
As laughter of the woodpecker
    From the bosom of a hill.
    'Tis Kate — she sayeth what she will:
For Kate hath an unbridled tongue,
    Clear as the twanging of a harp.
        Her heart is like a throbbing star.
Kate hath a spirit ever strung
    Like a new bow, and bright and sharp
        As edges of the scymetar.
Whence shall she take a fitting mate?
    For Kate no common love will feel;
My woman-soldier, gallant Kate,
    As pure and true as blades of steel.

Kate saith 'the world is void of might.'
    Kate saith 'the men are gilded flies.'
        Kate snaps her fingers at my vows;
    Kate will not hear of lover's sighs.
I would I were an armèd knight,
    Far-famed for well-won enterprise,
        And wearing on my swarthy brows
    The garland of new-wreathed emprise
        For in a moment I would pierce
The blackest files of clanging fight,
And strongly strike to left and right,

In dreaming of my lady's eyes.
Oh! Kate loves well the bold and fierce;
But none are bold enough for Kate,
She cannot find a fitting mate.

Sonnet

on the result of the late Russian invasion of Poland

How long, O God, shall men be ridden down,
And trampled under by the last and least
Of men? The heart of Poland hath not ceased
To quiver, though her sacred blood doth drown
The fields; and out of every smouldering town
Cries to Thee, lest brute Power be increased,
Till that o'ergrown Barbarian in the East
Transgress his ample bound to some new crown: —
Cries to Thee, 'Lord, how long shall these things be?
How long shall the icy-hearted Muscovite
Oppress the region?' Us, O Just and Good,

Forgive, who smiled when she was torn in
three;
Us, who stand *now,* when we should aid the
right —
A matter to be wept with tears of blood!

Sonnet

As when with downcast eyes we muse and
brood,
And ebb into a former life, or seem
To lapse far back in a confused dream
To states of mystical similitude;
If one but speaks or hems or stirs his chair,
Ever the wonder waxeth more and more,
So that we say, 'All this hath been before,
All this *hath* been, I know not when or
where.'
So, friend, when first I look'd upon your
face,
Our thought gave answer, each to each, so
true,
Opposed mirrors each reflecting each —
Altho' I knew not in what time or place,
Methought that I had often met with you,
And each had lived in the other's mind and
speech.

The Death of the Old Year

Full knee-deep lies the winter snow,
And the winter winds are wearily sighing:
Toll ye the church-bell sad and slow,
And tread softly and speak low,
For the old year lies a-dying.
        Old year, you must not die;
        You came to us so readily,
        You lived with us so steadily,
        Old year, you shall not die.
He lieth still: he doth not move:
He will not see the dawn of day.
He hath no other life above.
He gave me a friend, and a true true-love,
And the New-year will take 'em away.
        Old year, you must not go;
        O long as you have been with us,
        Such joy as you have seen with us,
        Old year, you shall not go.

He froth'd his bumpers to the brim;
A jollier year we shall not see.
But tho' his eyes are waxing dim,
And tho' his foes speak ill of him,
He was a friend to me.
        Old year, you shall not die;
        We did so laugh and cry with you,
        I've half a mind to die with you,
        Old year, if you must die.

He was full of joke and jest,
But all his merry quips are o'er.
To see him die, across the waste
His son and heir doth ride post-haste,
But he'll be dead before.
Every one for his own.
The night is starry and cold, my friend,
And the New-year blithe and bold, my friend,
Comes up to take his own.

How hard he breathes! over the snow
I heard just now the crowing cock.
The shadows flicker to and fro:
The cricket chirps: the light burns low:
'Tis nearly twelve o'clock.
Shake hands, before you die.
Old year, we'll dearly rue for you:
What is it we can do for you?
Speak out before you die.

His face is growing sharp and thin.
Alack! our friend is gone.
Close up his eyes: tie up his chin:
Step from the corpse, and let him in
That standeth there alone,
And waiteth at the door.
There's a new foot on the floor, my friend,

And a new face at the door, my
friend,
A new face at the door.

To J. S.

The wind, that beats the mountain, blows
More softly round the open wold,
And gently comes the world to those
That are cast in gentle mould.

And me this knowledge bolder made,
Or else I had not dared to flow
In these words toward you, and invade
Even with a verse your holy woe.

'Tis strange that those we lean on most,
Those in whose laps our limbs are
nursed,
Fall into shadow, soonest lost:
Those we love first are taken first.

God gives us love, Something to love
He lends us; but, when love is grown
To ripeness, that on which it throve
Falls off, and love is left alone.

This is the curse of time. Alas!
In grief I am not all unlearn'd:

Once thro' mine own doors Death did pass;
    One went, who never hath return'd.

He will not smile — not speak to me
    Once more. Two years his chair is seen
Empty before us. That was he
    Without whose life I had not been.

Your loss is rarer; for this star
    Rose with you thro' a little arc
Of heaven, nor having wander'd far
    Shot on the sudden into dark.

I knew your brother: his mute dust
    I honour and his living worth:
A man more pure and bold and just
    Was never born into the earth.

I have not look'd upon you nigh,
    Since that dear soul hath fall'n asleep.
Great Nature is more wise than I:
    I will not tell you not to weep.

And tho' mine own eyes fill with dew,
    Drawn from the spirit thro' the brain,
I will not even preach to you,
    'Weep, weeping dulls the inward pain.'

Let Grief be her own mistress still.
    She loveth her own anguish deep

More than much pleasure. Let her will
Be done — to weep or not to weep.

I will not say 'God's ordinance
Of Death is blown in every wind;'
For that is not a common chance
That takes away a noble mind.

His memory long, will live alone
In all our hearts, as mournful light
That broods above the fallen sun,
And dwells in heaven half the night.

Vain solace! Memory standing near
Cast down her eyes, and in her throat
Her voice seem'd distant, and a tear
Dropt on the letters as I wrote.

I wrote I know not what. In truth,
How *should* I soothe you anyway,
Who miss the brother of your youth?
Yet something I did wish to say:

For he too was a friend to me:
Both are my friends, and my true breast
Bleedeth for both; yet it may be
That only silence suiteth best.

Words weaker than your grief would make
Grief more. 'Twere better I should cease;

Although myself could almost take
The place of him that sleeps in peace.

Sleep sweetly, tender heart, in peace:
Sleep, holy spirit, blessed soul,
While the stars burn, the moons increase,
And the great ages onward roll.

Sleep till the end, true soul and sweet.
Nothing comes to thee new or strange.
Sleep full of rest from head to feet;
Lie still, dry dust, secure of change.

St Agnes' Eve

Deep on the convent-roof the snows
Are sparkling to the moon:
My breath to heaven like vapour goes:
May my soul follow soon!
The shadows of the convent-towers
Slant down the snowy sward,
Still creeping with the creeping hours
That lead me to my Lord:
Make Thou my spirit pure and clear
As are the frosty skies,
Or this first snowdrop of the year
That in my bosom lies.

As these white robes are soil'd and dark,

To yonder shining ground;
As this pale taper's earthly spark,
To yonder argent round;
So shows my soul before the Lamb,
My spirit before Thee;
So in mine earthly house I am,
To that I hope to be.
Break up the heavens, O Lord! and far,
Thro' all yon starlight keen,
Draw me, thy bride, a glittering star,
In raiment white and clean.

He lifts me to the golden doors;
The flashes come and go;
All heaven bursts her starry floors,
And strows her lights below,
And deepens on and up! the gates
Roll back, and far within
For me the Heavenly Bridegroom waits,
To make me pure of sin.
The sabbaths of Eternity,
One sabbath deep and wide —
A light upon the shining sea —
The Bridegroom with his bride!

Lady Clara Vere de Vere

Lady Clara Vere de Vere,
    Of me you shall not win renown:
You thought to break a country heart
    For pastime, ere you went to town.
At me you smiled, but unbeguiled
    I saw the snare, and I retired:
The daughter of a hundred Earls,
    You are not one to be desired.

Lady Clara Vere de Vere,
    I know you proud to bear your name,
Your pride is yet no mate for mine,
    Too proud to care from whence I came.
Nor would I break for your sweet sake
    A heart that doats on truer charms.
A simple maiden in her flower
    Is worth a hundred coats-of-arms.

Lady Clara Vere de Vere,
    Some meeker pupil you must find,
For were you queen of all that is,
    I could not stoop to such a mind.
You sought to prove how I could love,
    And my disdain is my reply.
The lion on your old stone gates
    Is not more cold to you than I.

Lady Clara Vere de Vere,
    You put strange memories in my head.
Not thrice your branching limes have blown
    Since I beheld young Laurence dead.
Oh your sweet eyes, your low replies:
    A great enchantress you may be;
But there was that across his throat
    Which you had hardly cared to see.

Lady Clara Vere de Vere,
    When thus he met his mother's view,
She had the passions of her kind,
    She spake some certain truths of you.
Indeed I heard one bitter word
    That scarce is fit for you to hear;
Her manners had not that repose
    Which stamps the caste of Vere de Vere.
Lady Clara Vere de Vere,
    There stands a spectre in your hall:
The guilt of blood is at your door:
    You changed a wholesome heart to gall.
You held your course without remorse,
    To make him trust his modest worth,
And, last, you fix'd a vacant stare,
    And slew him with your noble birth.

Trust me, Clara Vere de Vere,
    From yon blue heavens above us bent
The grand old gardener and his wife
    Smile at the claims of long descent.

Howe'er it be, it seems to me,
  'Tis only noble to be good.
Kind hearts are more than coronets,
  And simple faith than Norman blood.

I know you, Clara Vere de Vere:
  You pine among your halls and towers:
The languid light of your proud eyes
  Is wearied of the rolling hours.
In glowing health, with boundless wealth,
  But sickening of a vague disease,
You know so ill to deal with time,
  You needs must play such pranks as
    these.

Clara, Clara Vere de Vere,
  If time be heavy on your hands,
Are there no beggars at your gate,
  Nor any poor about your lands?
Oh! teach the orphan-boy to read,
  Or teach the orphan-girl to sew,
Pray Heaven for a human heart,
  And let the foolish yeoman go.

The Blackbird

O Blackbird! sing me something well:
 While all the neighbours shoot thee
   round,

I keep smooth plats of fruitful ground,
Where thou may'st warble, eat and dwell.

The espaliers and the standards all
Are thine; the range of lawn and park:
The unnetted black-hearts ripen dark,
All thine, against the garden wall.

Yet, tho' I spared thee all the spring,
Thy sole delight is, sitting still,
With that gold dagger of thy bill
To fret the summer jenneting.

A golden bill! the silver tongue,
Cold February loved, is dry:
Plenty corrupts the melody
That made thee famous once, when young:

And in the sultry garden-squares,
Now thy flute-notes are changed to coarse,
I hear thee not at all, or hoarse
As when a hawker hawks his wares.

Take warning! he that will not sing
While yon sun prospers in the blue,
Shall sing for want, ere leaves are new,
Caught in the frozen palms of Spring.

You ask Me, Why, tho' Ill at Ease

You ask me, why, tho' ill at ease,
   Within this region I subsist,
   Whose spirits falter in the mist,
And languish for the purple seas.

It is the land that freemen till,
   That sober-suited Freedom chose,
   The land, where girt with friends or foes
A man may speak the thing he will;

A land of settled government,
   A land of just and old renown,
   Where Freedom broadens slowly down
From precedent to precedent:

Where faction seldom gathers head,
   But by degrees to fullness wrought,
   The strength of some diffusive thought
Hath time and space to work and spread.

Should banded unions persecute
   Opinion, and induce a time
   When single thought is civil crime,
And individual freedom mute;

Tho' Power should make from land to land
   The name of Britain trebly great —
   Tho' every channel of the State

Should fill and choke with golden sand —

Yet waft me from the harbour-mouth,
  Wild wind! I seek a warmer sky,
  And I will see before I die
The palms and temples of the South.

Of Old sat Freedom on the Heights

Of old sat Freedom on the heights,
  The thunders breaking at her feet:
Above her shook the starry lights:
  She heard the torrents meet.

There in her place she did rejoice,
  Self-gather'd in her prophet-mind,
But fragments of her mighty voice
  Came rolling on the wind.

Then stept she down thro' town and field
  To mingle with the human race,
And part by part to men reveal'd
  The fullness of her face —

Grave mother of majestic works,
  From her isle-altar gazing down,
Who, God-like, grasps the triple forks,
  And, King-like, wears the crown:

Her open eyes desire the truth.
  The wisdom of a thousand years
Is in them. May perpetual youth
  Keep dry their light from tears;

That her fair form may stand and shine,
  Make bright our days and light our
    dreams,
Turning to scorn with lips divine
  The falsehood of extremes!

Love Thou thy Land, with Love far Brought

Love thou thy land, with love far-brought
  From out the storied Past, and used
  Within the Present, but transfused
Thro' future time by power of thought.

True love turn'd round on fixed poles,
  Love, that endures not sordid ends,
  For English natures, freemen, friends,
Thy brothers and immortal souls.

But pamper not a hasty time,
  Nor feed with crude imaginings
  The herd, wild hearts and feeble wings,
That every sophister can lime.

Deliver not the tasks of might
  To weakness, neither hide the ray
  From those, not blind, who wait for day,
Tho' sitting girt with doubtful light.

Make knowledge circle with the winds;
  But let her herald, Reverence, fly
  Before her to whatever sky
Bear seed of men and growth of minds.

Watch what main-currents draw the years:
  Cut Prejudice against the grain:
  But gentle words are always gain:
Regard the weakness of thy peers:

Nor toil for title, place, or touch
  Of pension, neither count on praise:
  It grows to guerdon after-days:
Nor deal in watch-words overmuch;

Not clinging to some ancient saw;
  Not master'd by some modern term;
  Not swift nor slow to change, but firm
And in its season bring the law;

That from Discussion's lip may fall
  With Life, that, working strongly, binds —
  Set in all lights by many minds,
To close the interests of all.

For Nature also, cold and warm,
  And moist and dry, devising long,
  Thro' many agents making strong,
Matures the individual form.

Meet is it changes should control
  Our being, lest we rust in ease.
  We all are changed by still degrees
All but the basis of the soul.

So let the change which comes be free
  To ingroove itself with that which flies,
  And work, a joint of state, that plies
Its office, moved with sympathy.

A saying, hard to shape in act;
  For all the past of Time reveals
  A bridal dawn of thunder-peals,
Wherever Thought hath wedded Fact.

Ev'n now we hear with inward strife
  A motion toiling in the gloom —
  The Spirit of the years to come
Yearning to mix himself with Life.

A slow-develop'd strength awaits
  Completion in a painful school;
  Phantoms of other forms of rule,
New Majesties of mighty States —

The warders of the growing hour,
  But vague in vapour, hard to mark;
  And round them sea and air are dark
With great contrivances of Power.

Of many changes, aptly join'd,
  Is bodied forth the second whole.
  Regard gradation, lest the soul
Of Discord race the rising wind;

A wind to puff your idol-fires,
  And heap their ashes on the head;
  To shame the boast so often made,
That we are wiser than our sires.

Oh yet, if Nature's evil star
  Drive men in manhood, as in youth,
  To follow flying steps of Truth
Across the brazen bridge of war —

If New and Old, disastrous feud,
  Must ever shock, like armed foes,
  And this be true, till Time shall close
That Principles are rain'd in blood;

Not yet the wise of heart would cease
  To hold his hope thro' shame and guilt,
  But with his hand against the hilt,
Would pace the troubled land, like Peace;

Not less, tho' dogs of Faction bay,
  Would serve his kind in deed and word,
  Certain, if knowledge bring the sword,
That knowledge takes the sword away —

Would love the gleams of good that broke
  From either side, nor veil his eyes
  And if some dreadful need should rise
Would strike, and firmly, and one stroke:

To-morrow yet would reap to-day,
  As we bear blossom of the dead;
  Earn well the thrifty months, nor wed
Raw Haste, half-sister to Delay.

The Goose

I knew an old wife lean and poor,
  Her rags scarce held together;
There strode a stranger to the door,
  And it was windy weather.

He held a goose upon his arm,
  He utter'd rhyme and reason,
'Here, take the goose, and keep you warm,
  It is a stormy season.'

She caught the white goose by the leg,
  A goose — 'twas no great matter.

The goose let fall a golden egg
  With cackle and with clatter.

She dropt the goose, and caught the pelf,
  And ran to tell her neighbours;
And bless'd herself, and cursed herself
  And rested from her labours.

And feeding high, and living soft,
  Grew plump and able-bodied;
Until the grave churchwarden doff'd.
  The parson smirk'd and nodded.

So sitting, served by man and maid,
  She felt her heart grow prouder:
But ah! the more the white goose laid
  It clack'd and cackled louder.

It clutter'd here, it chuckled there;
  It stirr'd the old wife's mettle:
She shifted in her elbow-chair,
  And hurl'd the pan and kettle.

'A quinsy choke thy cursed note!'
  Then wax'd her anger stronger.
'Go, take the goose and wring her throat,
  I will not bear it longer.'

Then yelp'd the cur, and yawl'd the cat;
  Ran Gaffer, stumbled Gammer.

The goose flew this way and flew that,
  And fill'd the house with clamour.

As head and heels upon the floor
  They flounder'd all together,
There strode a stranger to the door
  And it was windy weather:

He took the goose upon his arm,
  He utter'd words of scorning;
'So keep you cold, or keep you warm,
  It is a stormy morning.'

The wild wind rang from park and plain,
  And round the attics rumbled,
Till all the tables danced again,
  And half the chimneys tumbled.

The glass blew in, the fire blew out,
  The blast was hard and harder.
Her cap blew off, her gown blew up,
  And a whirlwind clear'd the larder;

And while on all sides breaking loose
  Her household fled the danger,
Quoth she, 'The Devil take the goose,
  And God forget the stranger!'

The Epic

At Francis Allen's on the Christmas-eve —
The game of forfeits done — the girls all
kiss'd
Beneath the sacred bush and past away —
The parson Holmes, the poet Everard Hall,
The host, and I sat round the wassail-bowl,
Then half-way ebb'd: and there we held a
talk,
How all the old honour had from Christmas
gone,
Or gone, or dwindled down to some odd
games
In some odd nooks like this; till I, tired out
With cutting eights that day upon the pond,
Where, three times slipping from the outer
edge,
I bump'd the ice into three several stars,
Fell in a doze; and half-awake I heard
The parson taking wide and wider sweeps,
Now harping on the church-commissioners,
Now hawking at Geology and schism;
Until I woke, and found him settled down
Upon the general decay of faith
Right thro' the world, 'at home was little
left,
And none abroad: there was no anchor, none,
To hold by.' Francis, laughing, clapt his
hand

On Everard's shoulder, with 'I hold by him.'
'And I,' quoth Everard, 'by the wassail bowl.'
'Why yes,' I said, 'we knew your gift that way
At college: but another which you had,
I mean of verse (for so we held it then),
What came of that?' 'You know,' said Frank, 'he burnt
His epic, his King Arthur, some twelve books' —
And then to me demanding why? 'Oh, sir,
He thought that nothing new was said, or else
Something so said 'twas nothing — that a truth
Looks freshest in the fashion of the day:
God knows: he has a mint of reasons: ask.
It pleased me well enough.' 'Nay, nay,' said Hall,
'Why take the style of those heroic times?
For nature brings not back the Mastodon,
Nor we those times; and why should any man
Remodel models? these twelve books of mine
Were faint Homeric echoes, nothing-worth,
Mere chaff and draff, much better burnt.' 'But I,'
Said Francis, 'pick'd the eleventh from this hearth,

And have it: keep a thing, its use will come.
I hoard it as a sugar-plum for Holmes.'
He laugh'd, and I, though sleepy, like a
    horse
That hears the corn-bin open, prick'd my
    ears;
For I remember'd Everard's college fame
When we were Freshmen: then at my
    request
He brought it; and the poet little urged,
But with some prelude of disparagement,
Read, mouthing out his hollow oes and aes,
Deep-chested music, and to this result.

Morte d'Arthur

So all day long the noise of battle roll'd
Among the mountains by the winter sea;
Until King Arthur's table, man by man,
Had fall'n in Lyonnesse about their Lord,
King Arthur: then, because his wound was
    deep,
The bold Sir Bedivere uplifted him,
Sir Bedivere, the last of all his knights,
And bore him to a chapel nigh the field,
A broken chancel with a broken cross,
That stood on a dark strait of barren land.
On one side lay the Ocean, and on one
Lay a great water, and the moon was full.

Then spake King Arthur to Sir Bedivere:
'The sequel of to-day unsolders all
The goodliest fellowship of famous knights
Whereof this world holds record. Such a sleep
They sleep — the men I loved, I think that we
Shall never more, at any future time,
Delight our souls with talk of knightly deeds,
Walking about the gardens and the halls
Of Camelot, as in the days that were.
I perish by this people which I made, —
Tho' Merlin sware that I should come again
To rule once more — but let what will be, be,
I am so deeply smitten thro' the helm
That without help I cannot last till morn.
Thou therefore take my brand Excalibur,
Which was my pride: for thou rememberest how
In those old days, one summer noon, an arm
Rose up from out the bosom of the lake,
Clothed in white samite, mystic, wonderful,
Holding the sword — and how I row'd across
And took it, and have worn it, like a king:
And, wheresoever I am sung or told
In aftertime this also shall be known:
But now delay not: take Excalibur,

And fling him far into the middle mere:
Watch what thou seëst, and lightly bring me word.'
To him replied the bold Sir Bedivere:
'It is not meet, Sir King, to leave thee thus,
Aidless, alone, and smitten thro' the helm.
A little thing may harm a wounded man.
Yet I thy hest will all perform at full,
Watch what I see, and lightly bring thee wold.'
So saying, from the ruin'd shrine he stept
And in the moon athwart the place of tombs,
Where lay the mighty bones of ancient men,
Old knights, and over them the sea-wind sang
Shrill, chill, with flakes of foam. He, stepping down
By zig-zag paths, and juts of pointed rock,
Came on the shining levels of the lake.
There drew he forth the brand Excalibur,
And o'er him, drawing it, the winter moon,
Brightening the skirts of a long cloud, ran forth
And sparkled keen with frost against the hilt:
For all the haft twinkled with diamond sparks,
Myriads of topaz-lights, and jacinth-work
Of subtlest jewellery. He gazed so long

That both his eyes were dazzled, as he stood,
This way and that dividing the swift mind,
In act to throw: but at the last it seem'd
Better to leave Excalibur conceal'd
There in the many-knotted waterfiags,
That whistled stiff and dry about the marge.
So strode he back slow to the wounded King.
Then spake King Arthur to Sir Bedivere:
'Hast thou perform'd my mission which I gave?
What is it thou hast seen? or what hast heard?'
And answer made the bold Sir Bedivere:
'I heard the ripple washing in the reeds,
And the wild water lapping on the crag.'
To whom replied King Arthur, faint and pale:
'Thou hast betray'd thy nature and thy name,
Not rendering true answer, as beseem'd
Thy fëalty, nor like a noble knight:
For surer sign had follow'd, either hand,
Or voice, or else a motion of the mere.
This is a shameful thing for men to lie.
Yet now, I charge thee, quickly go again
As thou art lief and dear, and do the thing
I bad thee, watch, and lightly bring me word.'

Then went Sir Bedivere the second time
Across the ridge, and paced beside the
mere,
Counting the dewy pebbles, fix'd in
thought;
But when he saw the wonder of the hilt,
How curiously and strangely chased, he
smote
His palms together, and he cried aloud,
'And if indeed I cast the brand away,
Surely a precious thing, one worthy note,
Should thus be lost for ever from the earth,
Which might have pleased the eyes of many
men.
What good should follow this, if this were
done?
What harm, undone? deep harm to disobey,
Seeing obedience is the bond of rule.
Were it well to obey then, if a king demand
An act unprofitable, against himself?
The King is sick, and knows not what he
does.
What record, or what relic of my lord
Should be to aftertime, but empty breath
And rumours of a doubt? but were this kept,
Stored in some treasure-house of mighty
kings,
Some one might show it at a joust of arms,
Saying, "King Arthur's sword, Excalibur
Wrought by the lonely maiden of the Lake,

Nine years she wrought it, sitting in the deeps
Upon the hidden bases of the hills."
So might some old man speak in the aftertime
To all the people, winning reverence.
But now much honour and much fame were lost.'

So spake he, clouded with his own conceit,
And hid Excalibur the second time,
And so strode back slow to the wounded King.

Then spoke King Arthur, breathing heavily:
'What is it thou hast seen? or what hast heard?'

And answer made the bold Sir Bedivere:
'I heard the water lapping on the crag,
And the long ripple washing in the reeds.'

To whom replied King Arthur, much in wrath:
'Ah, miserable and unkind, untrue,
Unknightly, traitor-hearted! Woe is me!
Authority forgets a dying king,
Laid widow'd of the power in his eye
That bow'd the will. I see thee what thou art,
For thou, the latest-left of all my knights,
In whom should meet the offices of all,

Thou wouldst betray me for the precious hilt;
Either from lust of gold, or like a girl
Valuing the giddy pleasure of the eyes.
Yet, for a man may fail in duty twice,
And the third time may prosper, get thee hence:
But, if thou spare to fling Excalibur,
I will arise and slay thee with my hands.'

Then quickly rose Sir Bedivere, and ran,
And, leaping down the ridges lightly, plunged
Among the bulrush-beds, and clutch'd the sword,
And strongly wheel'd and threw it. The great brand
Made lightnings in the splendour of the moon
And flashing round and round, and whirl'd in an arch,
Shot like a streamer of the northern morn,
Seen where the moving isles of winter shock
By night, with noises of the northern sea.
So flash'd and fell the brand Excalibur:
But ere he dipt the surface, rose an arm
Clothed in white samite, mystic, wonderful
And caught him by the hilt, and brandish'd him
Three times, and drew him under in the mere.

And lightly went the other to the King.
Then spoke King Arthur, drawing thicker breath:
'Now see I by thine eyes that this is done.
Speak out: what is it thou hast heard, or seen?'
And answer made the bold Sir Bedivere:
'Sir King, I closed mine eyelids, lest the gems
Should blind my purpose, for I never saw,
Nor shall see, here or elsewhere, till I die,
Not tho' I live three lives of mortal men,
So great a miracle as yonder hilt.
Then with both hands I flung him, wheeling him;
But when I look'd again, behold an arm,
Clothed in white samite, mystic, wonderful,
That caught him by the hilt, and brandish'd him
Three times, and drew him under in the mere.'
And answer made King Arthur, breathing hard:
'My end draws nigh; 'tis time that I were gone.
Make broad thy shoulders to receive my weight,
And bear me to the margin; yet I fear
My wound hath taken cold, and I shall die.'
So saying, from the pavement he half rose,

Slowly, with pain, reclining on his arm,
And looking wistfully with wide blue eyes
As in a picture. Him Sir Bedivere
Remorsefully regarded thro' his tears,
And would have spoken, but he found not
words,
Then took with care, and kneeling on one
knee,
O'er both his shoulders drew the languid
hands,
And rising bore him thro' the place of
tombs.
But, as he walk'd, King Arthur panted
hard,
Like one that feels a nightmare on his bed
When all the house is mute. So sigh'd the
King,
Muttering and murmuring at his ear,
'Quick, quick!
I fear it is too late, and I shall die.'
But the other swiftly strode from ridge to
ridge,
Clothed with his breath, and looking, as he
walk'd,
Larger than human on the frozen hills.
He heard the deep behind him, and a cry
Before. His own thought drove him like a
goad.
Dry clash'd his harness in the icy caves
And barren chasms, and all to left and right

The bare black cliff clang'd round him, as he based
His feet on juts of slippery crag that rang
Sharp-smitten with the dint of armed heels —
And on a sudden, lo! the level lake,
And the long glories of the winter moon.
Then saw they how there hove a dusky barge,
Dark as a funeral scarf from stem to stern,
Beneath them; and descending they were ware
That all the decks were dense with stately forms
Black-stoled, black-hooded, like a dream — by these
Three Queens with crowns of gold — and from them rose
A cry that shiver'd to the tingling stars,
And, as it were one voice, an agony
Of lamentation, like a wind, that shrills
All night in a waste land, where no one comes,
Or hath come, since the making of the world.
Then murmur'd Arthur, 'Place me in the barge,
And to the barge they came. There those three Queens
Put forth their hands, and took the King, and wept.

But she, that rose the tallest of them all
And fairest, laid his head upon her lap,
And loosed the shatter'd casque, and chafed his hands,
And call'd him by his name, complaining loud,
And dropping bitter tears against his brow
Striped with dark blood: for all his face was white
And colourless, and like the wither'd moon
Smote by the fresh beam of the springing east;
And all his greaves and cuisses dash'd with drops
Of onset; and the light and lustrous curls —
That made his forehead like a rising sun
High from the dais-throne — were parch'd with dust;
Or, clotted into points and hanging loose,
Mix'd with the knightly growth that fringed his lips.
So like a shatter'd column lay the King;
Not like that Arthur who, with lance in rest,
From spur to plume a star of tournament,
Shot thro' the lists at Camelot, and charged
Before the eyes of ladies and of kings.
Then loudly cried the bold Sir Bedivere,
'Ah! my Lord Arthur, whither shall I go?
Where shall I hide my forehead and my eyes?

For now I see the true old times are dead,
When every morning brought a noble chance,
And every chance brought out a noble
knight.
Such times have been not since the light that
led
The holy Elders with the gift of myrrh.
But now the whole ROUND TABLE is
dissolved
Which was an image of the mighty world;
And I, the last, go forth companionless,
And the days darken round me, and the
years,
Among new men, strange faces, other
minds.'

And slowly answered Arthur from the
barge:
'The old order changeth, yielding place to
new,
And God fulfils Himself in many ways,
Lest one good custom should cormpt the
world.
Comfort thyself: what comfort is in me?
I have lived my life, and that which I have
done
May He within Himself make pure! but
thou,
If thou shouldst never see my face again,
Pray for my soul. More things are wrought
by prayer

Than this world dreams of. Wherefore, let thy voice
Rise like a fountain for me night and day.
For what are men better than sheep or goats
That nourish a blind life within the brain,
If, knowing God, they lift not hands of prayer
Both for themselves and those who call them friend?
For so the whole round earth is every way
Bound by gold chains about the feet of God.
But now farewell. I am going a long way
With these thou seëist — if indeed I go —
(For all my mind is clouded with a doubt)
To the island-valley of Avilion;
Where falls not hail, or rain, or any snow,
Nor ever wind blows loudly, but it lies
Deep-meadow'd, happy, fair with orchard-lawns
And bowery hollows crown'd with summer sea,
Where I will heal me of my grievous wound.'
So said he, and the barge with oar and sail
Moved from the brink, like some full-breasted swan
That, fluting a wild carol ere her death,
Ruffles her pure cold plume, and takes the flood
With swarthy webs. Long stood Sir Bedivere

Revolving many memories, till the hull
Look'd one black dot against the verge of
dawn,
And on the mere the wailing died away.

★

Here ended Hall, and our last light, that
long
Had wink'd and threaten'd darkness, flared
and fell:
At which the Parson, sent to sleep with
sound,
And waked with silence, grunted 'Good!'
but we
Sat rapt: it was the tone with which he
read —
Perhaps some modern touches here and
there
Redeem'd it from the charge of
nothingness —
Or else we loved the man and prized his
work;
I know not: but we sitting, as I said,
The cock crew loud; as at that time of year
The lusty bird takes every hour for dawn:
Then Francis, muttering, like a man ill
used,
'There now — that's nothing!' drew a little
back,

And drove his heel into the smoulder'd log
That sent a blast of sparkles up the flue
And so to bed; where yet in sleep I seem'd
To sail with Arthur under looming shores,
Point after point; till on to dawn, when dreams
Begin to feel the truth and stir of day,
To me, methought, who waited with a crowd,
There came a bark that, blowing forward, bore
King Arthur, like a modern gentleman
Of stateliest port; and all the people cried
'Arthur is come again: he cannot die.'
Then those that stood upon the hills behind
Repeated — 'Come again and thrice as fair;'
And, further inland, voices echoed — 'Come
With all good things, and war shall be no more.'
At this a hundred bells began to peal,
That with the sound I woke, and heard indeed
The clear church-bells ring in the Christmas morn.

The Gardener's Daughter; or the Pictures

This morning is the morning of the day,
When I and Eustace from the city went
To see the Gardener's Daughter; I and he,
Brothers in Art; a friendship so complete
Portion'd in halves between us, that we
grew
The fable of the city where we dwelt.
My Eustace might have sat for Hercules;
So muscular he spread, so broad of breast.
He, by some law that holds in love, and
draws
The greater to the lesser, long desired
A certain miracle of symmetry,
A miniature of loveliness, all grace
Summ'd up and closed in little, — Juliet she
So light of foot, so light of spirit — oh, she
To me myself, for some three careless
moons,
The summer pilot of an empty heart
Unto the shores of nothing! Know you not
Such touches are but embassies of love,
To tamper with the feelings, ere he found
Empire for life? but Eustace painted her,
And said to me, she sitting with us then,
'When will *you* paint like this?' and I
replied,

(My words were half in earnest, half in jest,)
' 'Tis not your work, but Love's. Love,
unperceived,
A more ideal Artist he than all,
Came, drew your pencil from you, made
those eyes
Darker than darkest pansies, and that hair
More black than ashbuds in the front of
March.'
And Juliet answer'd laughing, 'Go and see
The Gardener's daughter: trust me, after
that
You scarce can fail to match his
masterpiece.'
And up we rose, and on the spur we went.
Not wholly in the busy world, nor quite
Beyond it, blooms the garden that I love.
News from the humming city comes to it
In sound of funeral or of marriage bells;
And, sitting muffled in dark leaves,
you hear
The windy clanging of the minster clock;
Although between it and the garden lies
A league of grass, wash'd by a slow broad
stream,
That, stirr'd with languid pulses of the oar,
Waves all its lazy lilies, and creeps on,
Barge-laden, to three arches of a bridge
Crown'd with the minster-towers.
The fields between

Are dewy-fresh, browsed by deep-udder'd kine,
And all about the large lime feathers low,
The lime a summer home of murmurous wings.
In that still place she, hoarded in herself,
Grew, seldom seen: not less among us lived
Her fame from lip to lip, Who had not heard
Of Rose, the Gardener's daughter?
Where was he,
So blunt in memory, so old at heart,
At such a distance from his youth in grief,
That, having seen, forgot? The common mouth,
So gross to express delight, in praise of her
Grew oratory. Such a lord is Love,
And Beauty such a mistress of the world.
And if I said that Fancy, led by Love,
Would play with flying forms and images,
Yet this is also true, that, long before
I look'd upon her, when I heard her name
My heart was like a prophet to my heart,
And told me I should love. A crowd of hopes,
That sought to sow themselves like winged seeds,
Born out of everything I heard and saw,
Flutter'd about my senses and my soul;
And vague desires, like fitful blasts of balm
To one that travels quickly, made the air

Of Life delicious, and all kinds of thought,
That verged upon them, sweeter than the
dream
Dream'd by a happy man, when the dark
East,
Unseen, is brightening to his bridal morn.
And sure this orbit of the memory folds
For ever in itself the day we went
To see her. All the land in flowery squares,
Beneath a broad and equal-blowing wind,
Smelt of the coming summer, as one large
cloud
Drew downward: but all else of Heaven was
pure
Up to the Sun, and May from verge to verge,
And May with me from head to heel.
And now,
As tho' 'twere yesterday, as tho' it were
The hour just flown, that morn with all its
sound,
(For those old Mays had thrice the life of
these,)
Rings in mine ears. The steer forgot to graze,
And, where the hedge-row cuts the pathway,
stood,
Leaning his horns into the neighbour field,
And lowing to his fellows. From the woods
Came voices of the well-contented doves.
The lark could scarce get out his notes for
joy,

But shook his song together as he near'd
His happy home, the ground. To left and right,
The cuckoo told his name to all the hills;
The mellow ouzel fluted in the elm;
The redcap whistled; and the nightingale
Sang loud, as tho' he were the bird of day.

And Eustace turn'd, and smiling said to me,
'Hear how the bushes echo! by my life,
These birds have joyful thoughts. Think you they sing
Like poets, from the vanity of song?
Or have they any sense of why they sing?
And would they praise the heavens for what they have?'
And I made answer, 'Were there nothing else
For which to praise the heavens but only love,
That only love were cause enough for praise.'

Lightly he laugh'd, as one that read my thought,
And on we went; but ere an hour had pass'd
We reach'd a meadow slanting to the North;
Down which a well-worn pathway courted us

To one green wicket in a privet hedge;
This, yielding, gave into a grassy walk
Thro' crowded lilac-ambush trimly pruned;
And one warm gust, full-fed with perfume, blew
Beyond us, as we enter'd in the cool.
The garden stretches southward. In the midst
A cedar spread his dark-green layers of shade.
The garden-glasses shone, and momently
The twinkling laurel scatter'd silver lights.
'Eustace,' I said, 'this wonder keeps the house.'
He nodded, but a moment afterwards
He cried, 'Look! look!' Before he ceased I turn'd,
And, ere a star can wink, beheld her there.
For up the porch there grew an Eastern rose,
That, flowering high, the last night's gale had caught,
And blown across the walk. One arm aloft —
Gown'd in pure white, that fitted to the shape —
Holding the bush, to fix it back, she stood.
A single stream of all her soft brown hair
Pour'd on one side: the shadow of the flowers

Stole all the golden gloss, and, wavering
Lovingly lower, trembled on her waist —
Ah, happy shade — and still went wavering down,
But, ere it touch'd a foot, that might have danced
The greensward into greener circles, dipt,
And mix'd with shadows of the common ground!
But the full day dwelt on her brows, and sunn'd
Her violet eyes, and all her Hebe bloom,
And doubled his own warmth against her lips,
And on the bounteous wave of such a breast
As never pencil drew. Half light, half shade,
She stood, a sight to make an old man young.
  So rapt, we near'd the house, but she, a Rose
In roses, mingled with her fragrant toil,
Nor heard us come, nor from her tendance turn'd
Into the world without; till close at hand,
And almost ere I knew mine own intent,
This murmur broke the stillness of that air
Which brooded round about her:
                                        'Ah, one rose,
One rose, but one, by those fair fingers cull'd,

Were worth a hundred kisses press'd on lips
Less exquisite than thine.'
She look'd: but all
Suffused with blushes — neither self possess'd
Nor startled, but betwixt this mood and that,
Divided in a graceful quiet — paused,
And dropt the branch she held, and turning, wound
Her looser hair in braid, and stirr'd her lips
For some sweet answer, tho' no answer came,
Nor yet refused the rose, but granted it,
And moved away, and left me, statue-like,
In act to render thanks.
I, that whole day
Saw her no more, altho' I linger'd there
Till every daisy slept, and Love's white star
Beam'd thro' the thicken'd cedar in the dusk.
So home we went, and all the livelong way
With solemn gibe did Eustace banter me.
'Now,' said he, 'will you climb the top of Art.
You cannot fail but work in hues to dim
The Titianic Flora, Will you match
My Juliet? you, not you, — the Master, Love,
A more ideal Artist he than all.'
So home I went, but could not sleep for joy,

Reading her perfect features in the gloom,
Kissing the rose she gave me o'er and o'er,
And shaping faithful record of the glance
That graced the giving — such a noise of life
Swarm'd in the golden present, such a voice
Call'd to me from the years to come, and such
A length of bright horizon rimm'd the dark.
And all that night I heard the watchman peal
The sliding season: all that night I heard
The heavy clocks knolling the drowsy hours.
The drowsy hours, dispensers of all good,
O'er the mute city stole with folded wings,
Distilling odours on me as they went
To greet their fairer sisters of the East.

Love at first sight, first-born, and heir to all,
Made this night thus. Henceforward squall nor storm
Could keep me from that Eden where she dwelt.
Light pretexts drew me: sometimes a Dutch love
For tulips; then for roses, moss or musk
To grace my city-rooms; or fruits and cream
Served in the weeping elm; and more and more

A word could bring the colour to my cheek;
A thought would fill my eyes with happy
  dew;
Love trebled life within me, and with each
The year increased.
                 The daughters of the year,
One after one, thro' that still garden pass'd:
Each garlanded with her peculiar flower
Danced into light, and died into the shade;
And each in passing touch'd with some new
  grace
Or seem'd to touch her, so that day by day,
Like one that never can be wholly known,
Her beauty grew; till Autumn brought an
  hour
For Eustace, when I heard his deep 'I will',
Breathed, like the covenant of a God, to
  hold
From thence thro' all the worlds: but I
  rose up
Full of his bliss, and following her dark eyes
Felt earth as air beneath me, till I reach'd
The wicket-gate, and found her standing
  there.
  There sat we down upon a garden mound,
Two mutually enfolded; Love, the third,
Between us, in the circle of his arms
Enwound us both; and over many a range
Of waning lime the grey cathedral towers,
Across a hazy glimmer of the west,

Reveal'd their shining windows: from them clash'd
The bells; we listen'd; with the time we play'd;
We spoke of other things; we coursed about
The subject most at heart, more near and near,
Like doves about a dovecote, wheeling round
The central wish, until we settled there.
Then, in that time and place, I spoke to her,
Requiring, tho' I knew it was mine own
Yet for the pleasure that I took to hear,
Requiring at her hand the greatest gift,
A woman's heart, the heart of her I loved;
And in that time and place she answer'd me,
And in the compass of three little words,
More musical than ever came in one,
The silver fragments of a broken voice,
Made me most happy, faltering 'I am thine.'
Shall I cease here? Is this enough to say
That my desire, like all strongest hopes
By its own energy fulfill'd itself,
Merged in completion? Would you learn at full
How passion rose thro' circumstantial grades
Beyond all grades develop'd? and indeed
I had not staid so long to tell you all,

But while I mused came Memory with sad eyes,
Holding the folded annals of my youth;
And while I mused, Love with knit brows went by,
And with a flying finger swept my lips,
And spake, 'Be wise: not easily forgiven
Are those, who setting wide the doors, that bar
The secret bridal chambers of the heart,
Let in the day.' Here, then, my words have end.

Yet might I tell of meetings, of farewells —
Of that which came between, more sweet than each,
In whispers like the whispers of the leaves
That tremble round a nightingale — in sighs
Which perfect Joy, perplex'd for utterance,
Stole from her sister Sorrow. Might I not tell
Of difference, reconcilement, pledges given,
And vows, where there was never need of vows,
And kisses, where the heart on one wild leap
Hung tranced from all pulsation, as above
The heavens between their fairy fleeces pale
Sow'd all their mystic gulfs with fleeting stars;
Or while the balmy glooming, crescent-lit,
Spread the light haze along the river-shores,

And in the hollows; or as once we met
Unheedful, tho' beneath a whispering rain
Night slid down one long stream of sighing wind,
And in her bosom bore the baby, Sleep.
But this whole hour your eyes have been intent
On that veil'd picture — veil'd, for what it holds
May not be dwelt on by the common day.
This prelude has prepared thee. Raise thy soul;
Make thine heart ready with thine eyes: the time
Is come to raise the veil.
Behold her there,
As I beheld her ere she knew my heart,
My first, last love; the idol of my youth,
The darling of my manhood, and, alas!
Now the most blessed memory of mine age.

Dora

With farmer Allan at the farm abode
William and Dora. William was his son,
And she his niece. He often look'd at them,
And often thought 'I'll make them man and wife.'
Now Dora felt her uncle's will in all,

And yearn'd towards William; but the youth, because
He had been always with her in the house,
Thought not of Dora.
Then there came a day
When Allan call'd his son, and said,
'My son: I married late, but I would wish to see
My grandchild on my knees before I die:
And I have set my heart upon a match.
Now therefore look to Dora; she is well
To look to; thrifty too beyond her age.
She is my brother's daughter: he and I
Had once hard words, and parted, and he died
In foreign lands; but for his sake I bred
His daughter Dora: take her for your wife;
For I have wish'd this marriage, night and day,
For many years.' But William answer'd short;
'I cannot marry Dora; by my life,
I will not marry Dora.' Then the old man
Was wroth, and doubled up his hands, and said:
'You will not, boy! you dare to answer thus!
But in my time a father's word was law,
And so it shall be now for me. Look to it;
Consider, William: take a month to think,
And let me have an answer to my wish;

Or, by the Lord that made me, you shall pack,
And never more darken my doors again.'
But William answer'd madly; bit his lips,
And broke away. The more he look'd at her
The less he liked her; and his ways were harsh;
But Dora bore them meekly. Then before
The month was out he left his father's house,
And hired himself to work within the fields;
And half in love, half spite, he woo'd and wed
A labourer's daughter, Mary Morrison.

Then, when the bells were ringing, Allan call'd
His niece and said: 'My girl, I love you well;
But if you speak with him that was my son,
Or change a word with her he calls his wife,
My home is none of yours. My will is law.'
And Dora promised, being meek. She thought,
'It cannot be: my uncle's mind will change!'

And days went on, and there was born a boy
To William; then distresses came on him;
And day by day he pass'd his father's gate,
Heart-broken, and his father help'd him not.

But Dora stored what little she could save,
And sent it them by stealth, nor did they know
Who sent it; till at last a fever seized
On William, and in harvest time he died.
Then Dora went to Mary. Mary sat
And look'd with tears upon her boy, and thought
Hard things of Dora. Dora came and said:
'I have obey'd my uncle until now,
And I have sinn'd, for it was all thro' me
This evil came on William at the first.
But, Mary, for the sake of him that's gone,
And for your sake, the woman that he chose,
And for this orphan, I am come to you:
You know there has not been for these five years
So full a harvest: let me take the boy,
And I will set him in my uncle's eye
Among the wheat; that when his heart is glad
Of the full harvest, he may see the boy,
And bless him for the sake of him that's gone.
And Dora took the child, and went her way
Across the wheat, and sat upon a mound
That was unsown, where many poppies grew.
Far off the farmer came into the field

And spied her not; for none of all his men
Dare tell him Dora waited with the child;
And Dora would have risen and gone to him
But her heart fail'd her; and the reapers
reap'd,
And the sun fell, and all the land was dark.
But when the morrow came, she rose and
took
The child once more, and sat upon the
mound;
And made a little wreath of all the flowers
That grew about, and tied it round his hat
To make him pleasing in her uncle's eye.
Then when the farmer pass'd into the field
He spied her, and he left his men at work,
And came and said; 'Where were you
yesterday?
Whose child is that? What are you doing
here?'
So Dora cast her eyes upon the ground,
And answer'd softly, 'This is William's
child!'
'And did I not,' said Allan, 'did I not
Forbid you, Dora?' Dora said again;
'Do with me as you will, but take the child
And bless him for the sake of him that's
gone!'
And Allan said, 'I see it is a trick
Got up betwixt you and the woman there.
I must be taught my duty, and by you!

You knew my word was law, and yet you dared
To slight it. Well — for I will take the boy;
But go you hence, and never see me more.'
  So saying, he took the boy, that cried aloud
And struggled hard. The wreath of flowers fell
At Dora's feet. She bow'd upon her hands,
And the boy's cry came to her from the field,
More and more distant. She bow'd down her head,
Remembering the day when first she came
And all the things that had been. She bow'd down
And wept in secret; and the reapers reap'd,
And the sun fell, and all the land was dark.
  Then Dora went to Mary's house, and stood
Upon the threshold. Mary saw the boy
Was not with Dora. She broke out in praise
To God, that help'd her in her widowhood
And Dora said, 'My uncle took the boy;
But, Mary, let me live and work with you:
He says that he will never see me more.'
Then answer'd Mary, 'This shall never be,
That thou shouldst take my trouble on thyself
And, now I think, he shall not have the boy,
For he will teach him hardness, and to slight

His mother; therefore thou and I will go,
And I will have my boy, and bring him home;
And I will beg of him to take thee back:
But if he will not take thee back again,
Then thou and I will live within one house,
And work for William's child, until he grows
Of age to help us.'
So the women kiss'd
Each other, and set out, and reach'd the farm
The door was off the latch they peep'd, and saw
The boy set up betwixt his grandsire's knees,
Who thrust him in the hollows of his arm,
And clapt him on the hands and on the cheeks,
Like one that loved him: and the lad stretch'd out
And babbled for the golden seal, that hung
From Allan's watch, and sparkled by the fire.
Then they came in: but when the boy beheld
His mother, he cried out to come to her:
And Allan set him down, and Mary said:
'O Father! — if you let me call you so —
I never came a-begging for myself,
Or William, or this child; but now I come
For Dora: take her back; she loves you well.

O Sir, when William died, he died at peace
With all men; for I ask'd him, and he said,
He could not ever rue his marrying me —
I had been a patient wife but, Sir, he said
That he was wrong to cross his father thus:
"God bless him!" he said, "and may he never know
The troubles I have gone thro'!" Then he turn'd
His face and pass'd — unhappy that I am!
But now, Sir, let me have my boy, for you
Will make him hard, and he will learn to slight
His father's memory, and take Dora back,
And let all this be as it was before.'
So Mary said, and Dora hid her face
By Mary. There was silence in the room;
And all at once the old man burst in sobs: —
'I have been to blame — to blame. I have kill'd my son.
I have kill'd him — but I loved him — my dear son.
May God forgive me! — I have been to blame.
Kiss me, my children.'
Then they clung about
The old man's neck, and kiss'd him many times.
And all the man was broken with remorse;
And all his love came back a hundredfold;

And for three hours he sobb'd o'er William's child,
Thinking of William.
So those four abode
Within one house together; and as years
Went forward, Mary took another mate;
But Dora lived unmarried till her death.

Audley Court

'The Bull, the Fleece are cramm'd, and not a room
For love or money. Let us picnic there
At Audley Court.'
I spoke, while Audley feast
Humm'd like a hive all round the narrow quay,
To Francis, with a basket on his arm,
To Francis just alighted from the boat,
And breathing of the sea. 'With all my heart,'
Said Francis. Then we shoulder'd thro' the swarm,
And rounded by the stillness of the beach
To where the bay runs up its latest horn.
We left the dying ebb that faintly lipp'd
The flat red granite; so by many a sweep
Of meadow smooth from aftermath we reach'd

The griffin-guarded gates, and pass'd thro' all
The pillar'd dusk of sounding sycamores,
And cross'd the garden to the gardener's lodge,
With all its casements bedded, and its walls
And chimneys muffled in the leafy vine.
   There, on a slope of orchard, Francis laid
A damask napkin wrought with horse and hound,
Brought out a dusky loaf that smelt of home,
And, half-cut-down, a pasty costly-made,
Where quail and pigeon, lark and leveret lay,
Like fossils of the rock, with golden yolks
Imbedded and injellied; last, with these,
A flask of cider from his father's vats,
Prime, which I knew; and so we sat and eat
And talk'd old matters over; who was dead,
Who married, who was like to be, and how
The races went, and who would rent the hall:
Then touch'd upon the game, how scarce it was
This season; glancing thence, discuss'd the farm,
The four-field system, and the price of grain;

And struck upon the corn-laws, where we
split,
And came again together on the king
With heated faces; till he laugh'd aloud;
And, while the blackbird on the pippin hung
To hear him, clapt his hand in mine and
sang —
'Oh! who would fight and march and
countermarch,
Be shot for sixpence in a battle-field,
And shovell'd up into a bloody trench
Where no one knows? but let me live my life.
'Oh! who would cast and balance at a
desk,
Perch'd like a crow upon a three-legg'd
stool,
Till all his juice is dried, and all his joints
Are full of chalk? but let me live my life.
'Who'd serve the state? for if I carved my
name
Upon the cliffs that guard my native land,
I might as well have traced it in the sands
The sea wastes all: but let me live my life.
'Oh! who would love? I woo'd a woman
once,
But she was sharper than an eastern wind,
And all my heart turn'd from her, as a thorn
Turns from the sea: but let me live my life.'
He sang his song, and I replied with mine:
I found it in a volume, all of songs

Knock'd down to me, when old Sir Robert's
pride,
His books — the more the pity, so I said —
Came to the hammer here in March — and
this —
I set the words, and added names I knew.
'Sleep, Ellen Aubrey, sleep, and dream of
me:
Sleep, Ellen, folded in thy sister's arm,
And sleeping, haply dream her arm is mine.
'Sleep, Ellen, folded in Emilia's arm;
Emilia, fairer than all else but thou,
For thou art fairer than all else that is.
'Sleep, breathing health and peace upon
her breast:
Sleep breathing love and trust against her
lip:
I go to-night: I come to-morrow morn.
'I go, but I return: I would I were
The pilot of the darkness and the dream.
Sleep, Ellen Aubrey, love and dream of me.'
So sang we each to either, Francis Hale,
The farmer's son, who lived across the bay
My friend; and I, that having wherewithal,
And in the fallow leisure of my life
A rolling stone of here and everywhere,
Did what I would; but ere the night we rose
And saunter'd home beneath a moon, that,
just
In crescent, dimly rain'd about the leaf

Twilights of airy silver, till we reach'd
The limit of the hills, and as we sank
From rock to rock upon the glooming quay,
The town was hush'd beneath us: lower down
The bay was oily-calm; the harbour-buoy
With one green sparkle ever and anon
Dipt by itself, and we were glad at heart.

Walking to the Mail

John. I'm glad I walk'd, How fresh the meadows look
Above the river, and, but a month ago,
The whole hill-side was redder than a fox.
Is yon plantation where this byway joins
The turnpike?
James. Yes.
John. And when does this come by?
James. The mail? At one o'clock.
John. What is it now?
James. A quarter to.
John. Whose house is that I see?
No, not the County Member's with the vane:
Up higher with the yew-tree by it, and half
A score of gables.
James. That? Sir Edward Head's:
But he's abroad: the place is to be sold.
John. Oh, his. He was not broken.

James. No, sir, he,
Vex'd with a morbid devil in his blood
That veil'd the world with jaundice, hid his face
From all men, and commercing with himself,
He lost the sense that handles daily life —
That keeps us all in order more or less —
And sick of home went overseas for change.
John. And whither?
James. Nay, who knows? he's here and there.
But let him go; his devil goes with him,
As well as with his tenant, Jocky Dawes.
John. What's that?
James. You saw the man — on Monday, was it? —
There by the humpback'd willow; half stands up
And bristles; half has fall'n and made a bridge;
And there he caught the younker tickling trout —
Caught *in flagrante* — what's the Latin word? —
Delicto: but his house, for so they say,
Was haunted with a jolly ghost, that shook
The curtains, whined in lobbies, tapt at doors
And rummaged like a rat: no servant stay'd:

The farmer vext packs up his beds and chairs,
And all his household stuff; and with his boy
Betwixt his knees, his wife upon the tilt,
Sets out, and meets a friend who hails him, 'What!
You're flitting!' 'Yes, we're flitting,' says the ghost
(For they had pack'd the thing among the beds,)
'Oh well,' says he, 'you flitting with us too —
Jack, turn the horses' heads and home again.'

John. He left *his* wife behind; for so I heard.

James. He left her, yes. I met my lady once:
A woman like a butt, and harsh as crabs.

John. Oh yet but I remember, ten years back —
'Tis now at least ten years — and then she was —
You could not light upon a sweeter thing:
A body slight and round, and like a pear
In growing, modest eyes, a hand, a foot,
Lessening in perfect cadence, and a skin
As clean and white as privet when it flowers.

James. Aye, aye, the blossom fades, and they that loved
At first like dove and dove were cat and dog.

She was the daughter of a cottager
Out of her sphere. What betwixt shame and pride,
New things and old, himself and her, she sour'd
To what she is: a nature never kind!
Like men, like manners: like breeds like, they say.
Kind nature is the best: those manners next
That fit us like a nature second-hand;
Which are indeed the manners of the great.
John. But I had heard it was this bill that past,
And fear of change at home, that drove him hence.
James. That was the last drop in the cup of gall.
I once was near him, when his bailiff brought
A Chartist pike. You should have seen him wince
As from a venomous thing: he thought himself
A mark for all, and shudder'd, lest a cry
Should break his sleep by night, and his nice eyes
Should see the raw mechanic's bloody thumbs
Sweat on his blazon'd chairs; but, sir, you know

That these two parties still divide the
world —
Of those that want, and those that have: and
still
The same old sore breaks out from age to age
With much the same result. Now I myself,
A Tory to the quick, was as a boy
Destructive, when I had not what I would.
I was at school — a college in the South:
There lived a flayflint near; we stole his
fruit,
His hens, his eggs; but there was law for us;
We paid in person. He had a sow, sir. She,
With meditative grunts of much content,
Lay great with pig, wallowing in sun and
mud.
By night we dragg'd her to the college tower
From her warm bed, and up the corkscrew
stair
With hand and rope we haled the groaning
sow,
And on the leads we kept her till she pigg'd.
Large range of prospect had the mother
sow,
And but for daily loss of one she loved,
As one by one we took them —
but for this —
As never sow was higher in this world —
Might have been happy: but what lot is
pure?

We took them all, till she was left alone
Upon her tower, the Niobe of swine,
And so return'd unfarrow'd to her sty.
John. They found you out?
James. Not they.
John. Well — after all —
What know we of the secret of a man?
His nerves were wrong. What ails us, who are sound,
That we should mimic this raw fool the world,
Which charts us all in its coarse blacks or whites,
As ruthless as a baby with a worm
As cruel as a schoolboy ere he grows
To Pity — more from ignorance than will.
But put your best foot forward, or I fear
That we shall miss the mail: and here it comes
With five at top: as quaint a four-in-hand
As you shall see — three piebalds and a roan.

St Simeon Stylites

Altho' I be the basest of mankind,
From scalp to sole one slough and crust of sin,
Unfit for earth, unfit for heaven, scarce meet

For troops of devils, mad with blasphemy,
I will not cease to grasp the hope I hold
Of saintdom, and to clamour, mourn and sob,
Battering the gates of heaven with storms of prayer,
Have mercy, Lord, and take away my sin.
Let this avail, just, dreadful, mighty God,
This not be all in vain, that thrice ten years,
Thrice multiplied by superhuman pangs,
In hungers and in thirsts, fevers and cold,
In coughs, aches, stitches, ulcerous throes and cramps,
A sign betwixt the meadow and the cloud,
Patient on this tall pillar I have borne
Rain, wind, frost, heat, hail, damp, and sleet, and snow;
And I had hoped that ere this period closed
Thou wouldst have caught me up into thy rest,
Denying not these weather-beaten limbs
The meed of saints, the white robe and the palm.
O take the meaning, Lord: I do not breathe,
Not whisper, any murmur of complaint.
Pain heap'd ten-hundred-fold to this, were still
Less burthen, by ten-hundred-fold, to bear,

Than were those lead-like tons of sin, that crush'd
My spirit flat before thee.
O Lord, Lord,
Thou knowest I bore this better at the first,
For I was strong and hale of body then;
And tho' my teeth, which now are dropt away,
Would chatter with the cold, and all my beard
Was tagg'd with icy fringes in the moon,
I drown'd the whoopings of the owl with sound
Of pious hymns and psalms, and sometimes saw
An angel stand and watch me, as I sang.
Now am I feeble grown; my end draws nigh;
I hope my end draws nigh: half deaf I am,
So that I scarce can hear the people hum
About the column's base, and almost blind
And scarce can recognize the fields I know,
And both my thighs are rotted with the dew;
Yet cease I not to clamour and to cry,
While my stiff spine can hold my weary head,
Till all my limbs drop piecemeal from the stone,
Have mercy, mercy: take away my sin.
O Jesus, if thou wilt not save my soul,
Who may be saved? who is it may be saved?

Who may be made a saint, if I fail here?
Show me the man hath suffer'd more than I.
For did not all thy martyrs die one death?
For either they were stoned or crucified
Or burn'd in fire, or boil'd in oil, or sawn
In twain beneath the ribs; but I die here
To-day, and whole years long, a life of death.
Bear witness, if I could have found a way
(And heedfully I sifted all my thought)
More slowly-painful to subdue this home
Of sin, my flesh, which I despise and hate,
I had not stinted practice, O my God.
  For not alone this pillar-punishment,
Not this alone I bore: but while I lived
In the white convent down the valley there,
For many weeks about my loins I wore
The rope that haled the buckets from the well,
Twisted as tight as I could knot the noose;
And spake not of it to a single soul,
Until the ulcer, eating thro' my skin,
Betray'd my secret penance, so that all
My brethren marvell'd greatly. More than this
I bore, whereof, O God, thou knowest all.
  Three winters, that my soul might grow to thee,
I lived up there on yonder mountain side.
My right leg chain'd into the crag, I lay
Pent in a roofless close of ragged stones;

Inswathed sometimes in wandering mist, and twice
Black'd with thy branding thunder, and sometimes
Sucking the damps for drink, and eating not,
Except the spare chance-gift of those that came
To touch my body and be heal'd, and live:
And they say then that I work'd miracles,
Whereof my fame is loud amongst man kind,
Cured lameness, palsies, cancers. Thou, O God,
Knowest alone whether this was or no.
Have mercy, mercy; cover all my sin.

Then, that I might be more alone with thee,
Three years I lived upon a pillar, high
Six cubits, and three years on one of twelve;
And twice three years I crouch'd on one that rose
Twenty by measure; last of all, I grew
Twice ten long weary weary years to this,
That numbers forty cubits from the soil.

I think that I have borne as much as this —
Or else I dream — and for so long a time,
If I may measure time by yon slow light,
And this high dial, which my sorrow crowns —
So much — even so.

And yet I know not well,
For that the evil ones come here, and say,
'Fall down, O Simeon: thou hast suffer'd long
For ages and for ages!' then they prate
Of penances I cannot have gone thro',
Perplexing me with lies; and oft I fall,
Maybe for months, in such blind lethargies
That Heaven, and Earth, and Time are choked.

But yet
Bethink thee, Lord, while thou and all the saints
Enjoy themselves in heaven, and men on earth
House in the shade of comfortable roofs
Sit with their wives by fires, eat wholesome food
And wear warm clothes, and even beasts have stalls,
I, 'tween the spring and downfall of the light
Bow down one thousand and two hundred times,
To Christ, the Virgin Mother, and the, Saints;
Or in the night, after a little sleep,
I wake: the chill stars sparkle; I am wet
With drenching dews, or stiff with crackling frost.

I wear an undress'd goatskin on my back;
A grazing iron collar grinds my neck;
And in my weak, lean arms I lift the cross,
And strive and wrestle with thee till I die:
O mercy, mercy! wash away my sin.
O Lord, thou knowest what a man I am;
A sinful man, conceived and born in sin:
'Tis their own doing; this is none of mine;
Lay it not to me. Am I to blame for this,
That here come those that worship me?
Ha! ha!
They think that I am somewhat. What am I?
The silly people take me for a saint,
And bring me offerings of fruit and flowers:
And I, in truth (thou wilt bear witness here)
Have all in all endured as much, and more
Than many just and holy men, whose names
Are register'd and calendar'd for saints.
Good people, you do ill to kneel to me.
What is it I can have done to merit this?
I am a sinner viler than you all.
It may be I have wrought some miracles
And cured some halt and maim'd, but what of that?
It may be, no one, even among the saints,
May match his pains with mine; but what of that?
Yet do not rise: for you may look on me,
And in your looking you may kneel to God.
Speak! is there any of you halt or maim'd?

I think you know I have some power with Heaven
From my long penance: let him speak his wish.
 Yes, I can heal him. Power goes forth from me.
They say that they are heal'd. Ah, hark! they shout
'St. Simeon Stylites.' Why, if so,
God reaps a harvest in me. O my soul,
God reaps a harvest in thee. If this be,
Can I work miracles and not be saved?
This is not told of any. They were saints.
It cannot be but that I shall be saved;
Yea, crown'd a saint. They shout, 'Behold a saint!',
And lower voices saint me from above.
Courage, St. Simeon! This dull chrysalis
Cracks into shining wings, and hope ere death
Spreads more and more and more, that God hath now
Sponged and made blank of crimeful record all
My mortal archives.
 O my sons, my sons,
I, Simeon of the pillar, by surname
Stylites, among men; I, Simeon,
The watcher on the column till the end;
I, Simeon, whose brain the sunshine bakes;

I, whose bald brows in silent hours become
Unnaturally hoar with rime, do now
From my high nest of penance here proclaim
That Pontius and Iscariot by my side
Show'd like fair seraphs. On the coals I lay,
A vessel full of sin: all hell beneath
Made me boil over. Devils pluck'd my sleeve;
Abaddon and Asmodeus caught at me.
I smote them with the cross; they swarm'd again.
In bed like monstrous apes they crush'd my chest:
They flapp'd my light out as I read: I saw
Their faces grow between me and my book:
With colt-like whinny and with hoggish whine
They burst my prayer. Yet this way was left,
And by this way I 'scaped them. Mortify
Your flesh, like me, with scourges and with thorns;
Smite, shrink not, spare not. If it may be, fast
Whole Lents, and pray. I hardly, with slow steps,
With slow, faint steps, and much exceeding pain,
Have scrambled past those pits of fire, that still

Sing in mine ears. But yield not me the
praise:
God only thro' his bounty hath thought fit,
Among the powers and princes of this
world,
To make me an example to mankind,
Which few can reach to. Yet I do not say
But that a time may come — yea, even now,
Now, now, his footsteps smite the threshold
stairs
Of life — I say, that time is at the doors
When you may worship me without
reproach;
For I will leave my relics in your land,
And you may carve a shrine about my dust,
And burn a fragrant lamp before my bones,
When I am gather'd to the glorious saints.
While I spake then, a sting of shrewdest
pain
Ran shrivelling thro' me, and a cloudlike
change,
In passing, with a grosser film made thick
These heavy, horny eyes. The end! the end!
Surely the end! What's here? a shape, a
shade,
A flash of light, Is that the angel there
That holds a crown? Come, blessed brother,
come.
I know thy glittering face. I waited long;
My brows are ready. What! deny it now?

Nay, draw, draw, draw nigh. So I clutch it.
    Christ!
'Tis gone: 'tis here again; the crown! the
    crown!
So now 'tis fitted on and grows to me,
And from it melt the dews of Paradise,
Sweet! sweet! spikenard, and balm, and
    frankincense.
Ah! let me not be fool'd, sweet saints: I trust
That I am whole, and clean, and meet for
    Heaven.
  Speak, if there be a priest, a man of God
Among you there, and let him presently
Approach, and lean a ladder on the shaft,
And climbing up into my airy home,
Deliver me the blessed sacrament.
For by the warning of the Holy Ghost,
I prophesy that I shall die to-night,
A quarter before twelve.
                          Put thou, O Lord,
Aid all this foolish people; let them take
Example, pattern: lead them to thy light.

The Talking Oak

Once more the gate behind me falls;
  Once more before my face
I see the moulder'd Abbey-walls,
  That stand within the chace.

Beyond the lodge the city lies,
  Beneath its drift of smoke;
And ah! with what delighted eyes
  I turn to yonder oak.

For when my passion first began,
  Ere that, which in me burn'd,
The love, that makes me thrice a man,
  Could hope itself return'd;

To yonder oak within the field
  I spoke without restraint,
And with a larger faith appeal'd
  Than Papist unto Saint.

For oft I talk'd with him apart,
  And told him of my choice,
Until he plagiarized a heart,
  And answer'd with a voice.

Tho' what he whisper'd, under Heaven
  None else could understand;
I found him garmiously given,
  A babbler in the land.

But since I heard him make reply
  Is many a weary hour;
'Twere well to question him, and try
  If yet he keeps the power.

Hail, hidden to the knees in fern,
  Broad Oak of Sumner-chace,
Whose topmost branches can discern
  The roofs of Sumner-place!

Say thou, whereon I carved her name,
  If ever maid or spouse,
As fair as my Olivia, came
  To rest beneath thy boughs. —

'O Walter, I have shelter'd here
  Whatever maiden grace
The good old Summers, year by year,
  Made ripe in Sumner-chace:

'Old Summers, when the monk was fat,
  And, issuing shorn and sleek,
Would twist his girdle tight, and pat
  The girls upon the cheek,

'Ere yet, in scorn of Peter's-pence,
  And number'd bead, and shrift,
Bluff Harry broke into the spence,
  And turn'd the cowls adrift:

'And I have seen some score of those
  Fresh faces, that would thrive
When his man-minded offset rose
  To chase the deer at five;

‘And all that from the town would stroll
  Till that wild wind made work
In which the gloomy brewer’s soul
  Went by me, like a stork:

‘The slight she-slips of loyal blood,
  And others, passing praise,
Strait-laced, but all-too-full in bud
  For puritanic stays:

‘And I have shadow’d many a group
  Of beauties, that were born
In teacup-times of hood and hoop,
  Or while the patch was worn;

‘And, leg and arm with love-knots gay,
  About me leap’d and laugh’d
The modish Cupid of the day,
  And shrill’d his tinsel shaft.

‘I swear (and else may insects prick
  Each leaf into a gall)
This girl, for whom your heart is sick,
  Is three times worth them all;

‘For those and theirs, by Nature’s law,
  Have faded long ago;
But in these latter springs I saw
  Your own Olivia blow,

'From when she gamboll'd on the greens,
  A baby-germ, to when
The maiden blossoms of her teens
  Could number five from ten.

'I swear, by leaf, and wind, and rain,
  (And hear me with thine ears,)
That, tho' I circle in the grain
  Five hundred rings of years —

'Yet, since I first could cast a shade,
  Did never creature pass
So slightly, musically made,
  So light upon the grass:

'For as to fairies, that will flit
  To make the greensward fresh,
I hold them exquisitely knit,
  But far too spare of flesh.'

Oh, hide thy knotted knees in fern,
  And overlook the chace;
And from thy topmost branch discern
  The roofs of Sumner-place.

But thou, whereon I carved her name,
  That oft hast heard my vows,
Declare when last Olivia came
  To sport beneath thy boughs.

'O yesterday, you know, the fair
  Was holden at the town;
Her father left his good arm-chair,
  And rode his hunter down.

'And with him Albert came on his.
  I look'd at him with joy:
As cowslip unto oxlip is,
  So seems she to the boy.

'An hour had past — and, sitting straight
  Within the low-wheel'd chaise,
Her mother trundled to the gate
  Behind the dappled greys.

'But, as for her, she stay'd at home,
  And on the roof she went,
And down the way you use to come,
  She look'd with discontent.

'She left the novel half-uncut
  Upon the rosewood shelf;
She left the new piano shut:
  She could not please herself.

'Then ran she, gamesome as the colt,
  And livelier than a lark
She sent her voice thro' all the holt
  Before her, and the park.

‘A light wind chased her on the wing,
  And in the chase grew wild,
As close as might be would he cling
  About the darling child:

‘But light as any wind that blows
  So fleetly did she stir,
The flower, she touch’d on, dipt and rose,
  And turn’d to look at her.

‘And here she came, and round me play’d,
  And sang to me the whole
Of those three stanzas that you made
  About my “giant bole”;

‘And in a fit of frolic mirth
  She strove to span my waist:
Alas, I was so broad of girth,
  I could not be embraced.

‘I wish’d myself the fair young beech
  That here beside me stands,
That round me, clasping each in each,
  She might have lock’d her hands.

‘Yet seem’d the pressure thrice as sweet
  As woodbine’s fragile hold
Or when I feel about my feet
  The berried briony fold.’

O muffle round thy knees with fern,
  And shadow Sumner-chace!
Long may thy topmost branch discern
  The roofs of Sumner-place!

But tell me, did she read the name
  I carved with many vows
When last with throbbing heart I came
  To rest beneath thy boughs?

'O yes, she wander'd round and round
  These knotted knees of mine,
And found, and kiss'd the name she found,
  And sweetly murmur'd thine.

'A teardrop trembled from its source,
  And down my surface crept.
My sense of touch is something coarse,
  But I believe she wept.

'Then flush'd her cheek with rosy light,
  She glanced across the plain;
But not a creature was in sight:
  She kiss'd me once again.

'Her kisses were so close and kind,
  That, trust me on my word,
Hard wood I am, and wrinkled rind,
  But yet my sap was stirr'd:

'And even into my inmost ring
  A pleasure I discern'd,
Like those blind motions of the Spring,
  That show the year is turn'd.

'Thrice-happy he that may caress
  The ringlet's waving balm —
The cushions of whose touch may press
  The maiden's tender palm.

'I, rooted here among the groves,
  But languidly adjust
My vapid vegetable loves
  With anthers and with dust:

'For ah! my friend, the days were brief
  Whereof the poets talk,
When that, which breathes within the leaf,
  Could slip its bark and walk.

'But could I, as in times foregone,
  From spray, and branch, and stem,
Have suck'd and gather'd into one
  The life that spreads in them,

'She had not found me so remiss;
  But lightly issuing thro',
I would have paid her kiss for kiss
  With usury thereto.'

O flourish high, with leafy towers,
  And overlook the lea,
Pursue thy loves among the bowers,
  But leave thou mine to me.

O flourish, hidden deep in fern,
  Old oak, I love thee well
A thousand thanks for what I learn
  And what remains to tell.

' 'Tis little more: the day was warm;
  At last, tired out with play,
She sank her head upon her arm,
  And at my feet she lay.

'Her eyelids dropp'd their silken eaves.
  I breathed upon her eyes
Thro' all the summer of my leaves
  A welcome mix'd with sighs.

'I took the swarming sound of life —
  The music from the town —
The murmurs of the drum and fife
  And lull'd them in my own.

'Sometimes I let a sunbeam slip,
  To light her shaded eye;
A second flutter'd round her lip
  Like a golden butterfly;

‘A third would glimmer on her neck
  To make the necklace shine;
Another slid, a sunny fleck,
  From head to ankle fine,

‘Then close and dark my arms I spread,
  And shadow’d all her rest —
Dropt dews upon her golden head,
  An acorn in her breast.

‘But in a pet she started up,
  And pluck’d it out, and drew
My little oakling from the cup,
  And flung him in the dew.

‘And yet it was a graceful gift —
  I felt a pang within
As when I see the woodman lift
  His axe to slay my kin.

‘I shook him down because he was
  The finest on the tree.
He lies beside thee on the grass.
  O kiss him once for me.

‘O kiss him twice and thrice for me.
  That have no lips to kiss,
For never yet was oak on lea
  Shall grow so fair as this.’

Step deeper yet in herb and fern,
   Look further thro' the chace
Spread upward till thy boughs discern
   The front of Sumner-place.

This fruit of thine by Love is blest,
   That but a moment lay
Where fairer fruit of Love may rest
   Some happy future day.

I kiss it twice, I kiss it thrice,
   The warmth it thence shall win
To riper life may magnetize
   The baby-oak within.

But thou, while kingdoms overset,
   Or lapse from hand to hand,
Thy leaf shall never fail, nor yet
   Thine acorn in the land.

May never saw dismember thee,
   Nor wielded axe disjoint,
That art the fairest-spoken tree
   From here to Lizard-point.

O rock upon thy towery top
   All throats that gurgle sweet!
All starry culmination drop
   Balm-dews to bathe thy feet!

All grass of silky feather grow —
   And while he sinks or swells
The full south-breeze around thee blow
   The sound of minster bells.

The fat earth feed thy branchy root,
   That under deeply strikes!
The northern morning o'er thee shoot,
   High up, in silver spikes!

Nor ever lightning char thy grain,
   But, rolling as in sleep
Low thunders bring the mellow rain,
   That makes thee broad and deep!

And hear me swear a solemn oath,
   That only by thy side
Will I to Olive plight my troth,
   And gain her for my bride.

And when my marriage morn may fall,
   She, Dryad-like, shall wear
Alternate leaf and acorn-ball
   In wreath about her hair.

And I will work in prose and rhyme,
   And praise thee more in both
Than bard has honour'd beech or lime,
   Or that Thessalian growth,

In which the swarthy ringdove sat,
  And mystic sentence spoke;
And more than England honours that,
  Thy famous brother-oak,

Wherein the younger Charles abode
  Till all the paths were dim,
And far below the Roundhead rode,
  And humm'd a surly hymn.

Love and Duty

Of love that never found his earthly close,
What sequel? Streaming eyes and breaking
    hearts?
Or all the same as if he had not been?
  Not so. Shall Error in the round of time
Still father Truth? O shall the braggart
    shout
For some blind glimpse of freedom work
    itself
Thro' madness, hated by the wise, to law
System and empire? Sin itself be found
The cloudy porch oft opening on the Sun?
And only he, this wonder, dead, become
Mere highway dust? or year by year alone
Sit brooding in the ruins of a life,
Nightmare of youth, the spectre of himself?
  If this were thus, if this, indeed, were all,

Better the narrow brain, the stony heart,
The staring eye glazed o'er with sapless days,
The long mechanic pacings to and fro,
The set grey life, and apathetic end.
But am I not the nobler thro' thy love?
O three times less unworthy! likewise thou
Art more thro' Love, and greater than thy years.
The Sun will run his orbit, and the Moon
Her circle. Wait, and Love himself will bring
The drooping flower of knowledge changed to fruit
Of wisdom. Wait: my faith is large in Time,
And that which shapes it to some perfect end.
Will some one say, then why not ill for good?
Why took ye not your pastime? To that man
My work shall answer, since I knew the right
And did it; for a man is not as God,
But then most Godlike being most a man.
— So let me think 'tis well for thee and me —
— Ill-fated that I am, what lot is mine
Whose foresight preaches peace, my heart so slow
To feel it! For how hard it seem'd to me,
When eyes, love-languid thro' half-tears, would dwell

One earnest, earnest moment upon mine,
Then not to dare to see! when thy low voice,
Faltering, would break its syllables, to keep
My own full-tuned, — hold passion in a leash,
And not leap forth and fall about thy neck,
And on thy bosom (deep-desired relief!)
Rain out the heavy mist of tears, that
weigh'd
Upon my brain, my senses and my soul!
For Love himself took part against himself
To warn us off, and Duty loved of Love —
O this world's curse, — beloved but
hated — came
Like Death betwixt thy dear embrace and
mine,
And crying, 'Who is this? behold thy bride,'
She push'd me from thee.
If the sense is hard
To alien ears, I did not speak to these —
No, not to thee, but to thyself in me:
Hard is my doom and thine: thou knowest it
all.

Could Love part thus? was it not well to
speak,
To have spoken once? It could not but be
well.
The slow sweet hours that bring us all things
good,
The slow sad hours that bring us all things
ill,

And all good things from evil, brought the
night
In which we sat together and alone,
And to the want, that hollow'd all the heart
Gave utterance by the yearning of an eye,
That burn'd upon its object thro' such tears
As flow but once a life.
The trance gave way
To those caresses, when a hundred times
In that last kiss, which never was the last,
Farewell, like endless welcome,
lived and died.
Then follow'd counsel, comfort,
and the words
That make a man feel strong in speaking
truth;
Till now the dark was worn, and overhead
The lights of sunset and of sunrise mix'd
In that brief night; the summer night,
that paused
Among her stars to hear us; stars that hung
Love-charmed to listen: all the wheels
of Time
Spun round in station, but the end had
come.
O then like those, who clench their nerves
to rush
Upon their dissolution, we two rose,
There — closing like an individual life —
In one blind cry of passion and of pain,

Like bitter accusation ev'n to death,
Caught up the whole of love and utter'd it,
And bade adieu for ever.
Live — yet live —
Shall sharpest pathos blight us, knowing all
Life needs for life is possible to will —
Live happy; tend thy flowers; be tended by
My blessing! Should my Shadow cross thy thoughts
Too sadly for their peace, remand it thou
For calmer hours to Memory's darkest hold,
If not to be forgotten — not at once —
Not all forgotten. Should it cross thy dreams,
O might it come like one that looks content,
With quiet eyes unfaithful to the truth,
And point thee forward to a distant light
Or seem to lift a burthen from thy heart
And leave thee freër, till thou wake refresh'd,
Then when the first low matin-chirp hath grown
Full quire, and morning driv'n her plow of pearl
Far furrowing into light the mounded rack,
Beyond the fair green field and eastern sea.

Ulysses

It little profits that an idle king,
By this still hearth, among these barren crags,
Match'd with an aged wife, I mete and dole
Unequal laws unto a savage race,
That hoard, and sleep, and feed, and know not me.
I cannot rest from travel: I will drink
Life to the lees: all times I have enjoy'd
Greatly, have suffer'd greatly, both with those
That loved me, and alone; on shore, and when
Thro' scudding drifts the rainy Hyades
Vext the dim sea: I am become a name;
For always roaming with a hungry heart
Much have I seen and known; cities of men
And manners, climates, councils, governments,
Myself not least, but honour'd of them all;
And drunk delight of battle with my peers,
Far on the ringing plains of windy Troy.
I am a part of all that I have met;
Yet all experience is an arch wherethro'
Gleams that untravell'd world, whose margin fades
For ever and for ever when I move.
How dull it is to pause, to make an end,

To rust unburnish'd, not to shine in use!
As tho' to breathe were life. Life piled on life
Were all too little, and of one to me
Little remains: but every hour is saved
From that eternal silence, something more,
A bringer of new things; and vile it were
For some three suns to store and hoard
myself,
And this grey spirit yearning in desire
To follow knowledge, like a sinking star,
Beyond the utmost bound of human
thought.

This is my son, mine own Telemachus,
To whom I leave the sceptre and the isle —
Well-loved of me, discerning to fulfil
This labour, by slow prudence to make mild
A rugged people, and thro' soft degrees
Subdue them to the useful and the good.
Most blameless is he, centred in the sphere
Of common duties, decent not to fail
In offices of tenderness, and pay
Meet adoration to my household gods,
When I am gone. He works his work, I mine.

There lies the port: the vessel puffs her
sail:
There gloom the dark broad seas.
My mariners,
Souls that have toil'd, and wrought, and
thought with me —
That ever with a frolic welcome took

The thunder and the sunshine, and opposed
Free hearts, free foreheads — you and I are old;
Old age hath yet his honour and his toil;
Death closes all: but something ere the end,
Some work of noble note, may yet be done,
Not unbecoming men that strove with Gods.
The lights begin to twinkle from the rocks:
The long day wanes: the slow moon climbs: the deep
Moans round with many voices. Come, my friends,
'Tis not too late to seek a newer world.
Push off, and sitting well in order smite
The sounding furrows; for my purpose holds
To sail beyond the sunset, and the baths
Of all the western stars, until I die.
It may be that the gulfs will wash us down:
It may be we shall touch the Happy Isles,
And see the great Achilles, whom we knew.
Tho' much is taken, much abides; and tho'
We are not now that strength which in old days
Moved earth and heaven; that which we are, we are;
One equal temper of heroic hearts,
Made weak by time and fate, but strong in will
To strive, to seek, to find, and not to yield.

Locksley Hall

Comradeses, leave me here a little,
    while as yet 'tis early morn:
Leave me here, and when you want me,
    sound upon the bugle horn.

'Tis the place, and all around it, as of old,
    the curlews call,
Dreary gleams about the moorland flying
    over Locksley Hall;

Locksley Hall, that in the distance overlooks
    the sandy tracts,
And the hollow ocean-ridges roaring into
    cataracts.

Many a night from yonder ivied casement,
    ere I went to rest,
Did I look on great Orion sloping slowly to
    the West.

Many a night I saw the Pleiads, rising thro'
    the mellow shade,
Glitter like a swarm of fire-flies tangled in a
    silver braid.

Here about the beach I wander'd,
    nourishing a youth sublime
With the fairy tales of science,

and the long result of Time;

When the centuries behind me like a fruitful
land reposed;
When I clung to all the present for the
promise that it closed:

When I dipt into the future far as human eye
could see;
Saw the Vision of the world, and all the
wonder that would be. —

In the Spring a fuller crimson comes upon
the robin's breast;
In the Spring the wanton lapwing gets
himself another crest;

In the Spring a livelier iris changes on the
burnish'd dove;
In the Spring a young man's fancy lightly
turns to thoughts of love.

Then her cheek was pale and thinner than
should be for one so young,
And her eyes on all my motions with a mute
observance hung.

And I said, 'My cousin Amy, speak,
and speak the truth to me,
Trust me, cousin, all the current of

my being sets to thee.'

On her pallid cheek and forehead came a colour and a light,
As I have seen the rosy red flushing in the northern night.

And she turn'd — her bosom shaken with a sudden storm of sighs —
All the spirit deeply dawning in the dark of hazel eyes —

Saying, 'I have hid my feelings, fearing they should do me wrong;'
Saying, 'Dost thou love me, cousin?' weeping, 'I have loved thee long.'

Love took up the glass of Time, and turn'd it in his glowing hands;
Every moment, lightly shaken, ran itself in golden sands.

Love took up the harp of Life, and smote on all the chords with might;
Smote the chord of Self, that, trembling, pass'd in music out of sight.

Many a morning on the moorland did we hear the copses ring,
And her whisper throng'd my pulses

with the fullness of the Spring.

Many an evening by the waters did we watch
the stately ships,
And our spirits rush'd together at the
touching of the lips.

O my cousin, shallow-hearted! O my Amy,
mine no more!
O the dreary, dreary moorland!
O the barren, barren shore!

Falser than all fancy fathoms, falser than all
songs have sung
Puppet to a father's threat, and servile to a
shrewish tongue!

Is it well to wish thee happy? —
having known me — to decline
On a range of lower feelings and a narrower
heart than mine!

Yet it shall be: thou shalt lower to his level
day by day,
What is fine within thee growing coarse to
sympathize with clay.

As the husband is, the wife is:
thou art mated with a clown,
And the grossness of his nature will have

weight to drag thee down.

He will hold thee, when his passion shall
have spent its novel force,
Something better than his dog,
a little dearer than his horse.

What is this? his eyes are heavy:
think not they are glazed with wine.
Go to him: it is thy duty: kiss him:
take his hand in thine.

It may be my lord is weary, that his
brain is overwrought:
Soothe him with thy finer fancies,
touch him with thy lighter thought.

He will answer to the purpose, easy things
to understand —
Better thou wert dead before me,
tho' I slew thee with my hand!

Better thou and I were lying,
hidden from the heart's disgrace,
Roll'd in one anothers arms,
and silent in a last embrace.

Cursed be the social wants that sin against
the strength of youth!
Cursed be the social lies that warp us from

the living truth!

Cursed be the sickly forms that err from
honest Nature's rule!
Cursed be the gold that gilds the straiten'd
forehead of the fool!

Well — 'tis well that I should bluster! —
Hadst thou less unworthy proved —
Would to God — for I had loved thee more
than ever wife was loved.

Am I mad, that I should cherish that which
bears but bitter fruit?
I will pluck it from my bosom, tho' my heart
be at the root.

Never, tho' my mortal summers to such
length of years should come
As the many-winter'd crow that leads the
clanging rookery home.

Where is comfort? in division of the records
of the mind?
Can I part her from herself, and love her,
as I knew her, kind?

I remember one that perish'd: sweetly did
she speak and move:
Such a one do I remember,

whom to look at was to love.

Can I think of her as dead, and love her for
the love she bore?
No — she never loved me truly: love is love
for evermore.

Comfort? comfort scorn'd of devils!
this is truth the poet sings,
That a sorrow's crown of sorrow is
remembering happier things.

Drug thy memories, lest thou learn it,
lest thy heart be put to proof,
In the dead unhappy night, and when
the rain is on the roof.

Like a dog, he hunts in dreams, and thou art
staring at the wall,
Where the dying night-lamp flickers,
and the shadows rise and fall.

Then a hand shall pass before thee,
pointing to his drunken sleep,
To thy widow'd marriage-pillows,
to the tears that thou wilt weep.

Thou shalt hear the 'Never, never,'
whisper'd by the phantom years,
And a song from out the distance in the

ringing of thine ears;

And an eye shall vex thee, looking ancient
kindness on thy pain.
Turn thee, turn thee on thy pillow:
get thee to thy rest again.

Nay, but Nature brings thee solace;
for a tender voice will cry.
'Tis a purer life than thine; a lip to drain
thy trouble dry.

Baby lips will laugh me down: my latest rival
brings thee rest.
Baby fingers, waxen touches, press me from
the mother's breast.

O, the child too clothes the father with a
dearness not his due.
Half is thine and half is his: it will be worthy
of the two.

O, I see thee old and formal, fitted to thy
petty part,
With a little hoard of maxims preaching
down a daughter's heart.

'They were dangerous guides the feelings —
she herself was not exempt —
Truly, she herself had suffer'd' —

Perish in thy self contempt!

Overlive it — lower yet — be happy!
wherefore should I care?
I myself must mix with action,
lest I wither by despair.

What is that which I should turn to,
lighting upon days like these?
Every door is barr'd with gold,
and opens but to golden keys.

Every gate is throng'd with suitors,
all the markets overflow.
I have but an angry fancy: what is that
which I should do?

I had been content to perish, falling
on the foeman's ground
When the ranks are roll'd in vapour,
and the winds are laid with sound.

But the jingling of the guinea helps
the hurt that Honour feels,
And the nations do but murmur,
snarling at each other's heels.

Can I but relive in sadness? I will turn
that earlier page.
Hide me from my deep emotion,

O thou wondrous Mother-Age!

Make me feel the wild pulsation that I felt
before the strife,
When I heard my days before me,
and the tumult of my life;

Yearning for the large excitement
that the coming years would yield,
Eager-hearted as a boy when first he
leaves his father's field,

And at night along the dusky highway near
and nearer drawn,
Sees in heaven the light of London flaring
like a dreary dawn;

And his spirit leaps within him to be gone
before him then,
Underneath the light he looks at,
in among the throngs of men;

Men, my brothers, men the workers,
ever reaping something new:
That which they have done but earnest of
the things that they shall do:

For I dipt into the future, far as human eye
could see,
Saw the Vision of the world,

and all the wonder that would be;

Saw the heavens fill with commerce,
argosies of magic sails,
Pilots of the purple twilight, dropping
down with costly bales;

Heard the heavens fill with shouting,
and there rain'd a ghostly dew
From the nations' airy navies grappling in
the central blue;

Far along the world-wide whisper of
the south-wind rushing warm,
With the standards of the peoples
plunging thro' the thunder-storm;

Till the war-drum throbb'd no longer,
and the battleflags were furl'd
In the Parliament of man, the Federation
of the world.

There the common sense of most shall hold
a fretful realm in awe,
And the kindly earth shall slumber,
lapt in universal law.

So I triumph'd ere my passion sweeping
thro' me left me dry,
Left me with the palsied heart, and left me

with the jaundiced eye;

Eye, to which all order festers,
all things here are out of joint:
Science moves, but slowly slowly,
creeping on from point to point:

Slowly comes a hungry people, as a lion,
creeping nigher,
Glares at one that nods and winks behind a
slowly-dying fire.

Yet I doubt not thro' the ages one increasing
purpose runs,
And the thoughts of men are widen'd with
the process of the suns.

What is that to him that reaps not harvest of
his youthful joys,
Tho' the deep heart of existence beat for
ever like a boy's?

Knowledge comes, but wisdom lingers,
and I linger on the shore,
And the individual withers, and the world is
more and more.

Knowledge comes, but wisdom lingers,
and he bears a laden breast,
Full of sad experience, moving toward the

stillness of his rest.

Hark, my merry comrades call me,
sounding on the bugle-horn,
They to whom my foolish passion were a
target for their scorn:

Shall it not be scorn to me to harp on such a
moulder'd string?
I am shamed thro' all my nature to have
loved so slight a thing.

Weakness to be wroth with weakness!
woman's pleasure, woman's pain —
Nature made them blinder motions
bounded in a shallower brain:

Woman is the lesser man, and all thy
passions, match'd with mine,
Are as moonlight unto sunlight,
and as water unto wine —

Here at least, where nature sickens, nothing.
Ah, for some retreat
Deep in yonder shining Orient, where my
life began to beat;

Where in wild Mahratta-battle fell my
father evil-starr'd; —
I was left a trampled orphan,

and a selfish uncle's ward.

Or to burst all links of habit —
there to wander far away,
On from island unto island at the
gateways of the day.

Larger constellations burning,
mellow moons and happy skies,
Breadths of tropic shade and palms
in cluster, knots of Paradise.

Never comes the trader, never floats an
European flag,
Slides the bird o'er lustrous woodland,
swings the trailer from the crag;

Droops the heavy-blossom'd bower, hangs
the heavy-fruited tree —
Summer isles of Eden lying in dark-purple
spheres of sea.

There methinks would be enjoyment more
than in this march of mind,
In the steamship, in the railway,
in the thoughts that shake mankind.

There the passions cramp'd no longer
shall have scope and breathing-space;
I will take some savage woman, she shall

rear my dusky race.

Iron-jointed, supple-sinew'd,
they shall dive, and they shall run,
Catch the wild goat by the hair,
and hurl their lances in the sun;

Whistle back the parrot's call, and leap the
rainbows of the brooks,
Not with blinded eyesight poring over
miserable books —

Fool, again the dream, the fancy!
but I *know* my words are wild,
But I count the grey barbarian lower than
the Christian child.

I, to herd with narrow foreheads,
vacant of our glorious gains,
Like a beast with lower pleasures,
like a beast with lower pains!

Mated with a squalid savage —
what to me were sun or clime?
I the heir of all the ages, in the foremost files
of time —

I that rather held it better men should
perish one by one,
Than that earth should stand at gaze like

Joshua's moon in Ajalon!

Not in vain the distance beacons Forward,
forward let us range
Let the great world spin for ever down the
ringing grooves of change

Thro' the shadow of the globe we sweep into
the younger day:
Better fifty years of Europe than a cycle of
Cathay.

Mother-Age (for mine I knew not)
help me as when life begun:
Rift the hills, and roll the waters,
flash the lightnings, weigh the Sun —

O, I see the crescent promise of my spirit
hath not set.
Ancient founts of inspiration well thro' all
my fancy yet.

Howsoever these things be, a long farewell
to Locksley Hall!
Now for me the woods may wither,
now for me the roof-tree fall.

Comes a vapour from the margin,
blackening over heath and holt,
Cramming all the blast before it,

in its breast a thunderbolt.

Let it fall on Locksley Hall, with rain or hail, or fire or snow;
For the mighty wind arises, roaring seaward, and I go.

Godiva

I waited for the train at Coventry;
I hung with grooms and porters on the bridge,
To watch the three tall spires; and there I shaped
The city's ancient legend into this: —
Not only we, the latest seed of Time,
New men, that in the flying of a wheel
Cry down the past, not only we, that prate
Of rights and wrongs, have loved the people well,
And loathed to see them overtax'd;
but she
Did more, and underwent, and overcame,
The woman of a thousand summers back,
Godiva, wife to that grim Earl, who ruled
In Coventry: for when he laid a tax
Upon his town, and all the mothers brought
Their children, clamouring, 'If we pay, we starve!'

She sought her lord, and found him, where he strode
About the hall, among his dogs, alone,
His beard a foot before him, and his hair
A yard behind. She told him of their tears,
And pray'd him, 'If they pay this tax, they starve.'
Whereat he stared, replying, half-amazed,
'You would not let your little finger ache
For such as *these?*' — 'But I would die,' said she.
He laugh'd, and swore by Peter and by Paul:
Then fillip'd at the diamond in her ear;
'O aye, aye, aye, you talk!' — 'Alas!' she said,
'But prove me what it is I would not do.'
And from a heart as rough as Esau's hand,
He answer'd, 'Ride you naked thro' the town,
And I repeal it;' and nodding, as in scorn,
He parted, with great strides among his dogs.
So left alone, the passions of her mind,
As winds from all the compass shift and blow,
Made war upon each other for an hour,
Till pity won. She sent a herald forth,
And bade him cry, with sound of trumpet, all
The hard condition; but that she would loose

The people: therefore, as they loved her well,
From then till noon no foot should pace the street,
No eye look down, she passing; but that all
Should keep within, door shut, and window barr'd.

Then fled she to her inmost bower, and there
Unclasp'd the wedded eagles of her belt,
The grim Earl's gift; but ever at a breath
She linger'd, looking like a summer moon
Half-dipt in cloud: anon she shook her head
And shower'd the rippled ringlets to her knee,
Unclad herself in haste; adown the stair
Stole on; and, like a creeping sunbeam, slid
From pillar unto pillar, until she reach'd
The gateway; there she found her palfrey trapt
In purple blazon'd with armorial gold.
Then she rode forth, clothed on with chastity:
The deep air listen'd round her as she rode,
And all the low wind hardly breathed for fear.
The little wide-mouth'd heads upon the spout
Had cunning eyes to see: the barking cur

Made her cheek flame: her palfrey's footfall shot
Light horrors thro' her pulses: the blind walls
Were full of chinks and holes; and overhead
Fantastic gables, crowding, stared: but she
Not less thro' all bore up, till, last, she saw
The white-flower'd elder-thicket from the field
Gleam thro' the Gothic archways in the wall.
Then she rode back, clothed on with chastity:
And one low churl, compact of thankless earth,
The fatal byword of all years to come,
Boring a little auger-hole in fear
Peep'd — but his eyes, before they had their will,
Were shrivell'd into darkness in his head,
And dropt before him. So the Powers, who wait
On noble deeds, cancell'd a sense misused;
And she, that knew not, pass'd: and all at once,
With twelve great shocks of sound, the shameless noon
Was clash'd and hammer'd from a hundred towers,
One after one: but even then she gain'd

Her bower; whence reissuing,
robed and crown'd,
To meet her lord, she took the tax away,
And built herself an everlasting name.

The Two Voices

A still small voice spake unto me,
'Thou art so full of misery,
Were it not better not to be?'

Then to the still small voice I said
'Let me not cast in endless shade
What is so wonderfully made.'

To which the voice did urge reply;
'To-day I saw the dragon-fly
Come from the wells where he did lie.

'An inner impulse rent the veil
Of his old husk: from head to tail
Came out clear plates of sapphire mail.

'He dried his wings: like gauze they grew:
Thro' crofts and pastures wet with dew
A living flash of light he flew.'

I said, 'When first the world began,
Young Nature thro' five cycles ran,

And in the sixth she moulded man.

'She gave him mind, the lordliest
Proportion, and, above the rest,
Dominion in the head and breast.'

Thereto the silent voice replied;
'Self-blinded are you by your pride:
Look up thro' night: the world is wide.

'This truth within thy mind rehearse,
That in a boundless universe
Is boundless better, boundless worse.

'Think you this mould of hopes and fears
Could find no statelier than his peers
In yonder hundred million spheres?'

It spake, moreover, in my mind:
'Tho' thou wert scatter'd to the wind,
Yet is there plenty of the kind.'

Then did my response clearer fall:
'No compound of this earthly ball
Is like another, all in all.'

To which he answer'd scoffingly;
'Good soul! suppose I grant it thee,
Who'll weep for thy deficiency?

‘Or will one beam be less intense,
When thy peculiar difference
Is cancell’d in the world of sense?’

I would have said, ’Thou canst not know,’
But my full heart, that work’d below,
Rain’d thro’ my sight its overflow.

Again the voice spake unto me:
‘Thou art so steep’d in misery,
Surely ’twere better not to be.

‘Thine anguish will not let thee sleep,
Nor any train of reason keep:
Thou canst not think, but thou wilt weep.’

I said, ‘The years with change advance:
If I make dark my countenance,
I shut my life from happier chance.

‘Some turn this sickness yet might take,
Ev’n yet.’ But he: ‘What drug can make
A wither’d palsy cease to shake?’

I wept: ‘Tho’ I should die, I know
That ail about the thorn will blow
In tufts of rosy-tinted snow;

‘And men, thro’ novel spheres of thought
Still moving after truth long sought,

Will learn new things when I am not.'

'Yet,' said the secret voice, 'some time,
Sooner or later, will grey prime
Make thy grass hoar with early rime.

'Not less swift souls that yearn for light,
Rapt after heaven's starry flight,
Would sweep the tracts of day and night.

'Not less the bee would range her cells,
The furzy prickle fire the dells,
The foxglove cluster dappled bells.'

I said that 'all the years invent;
Each month is various to present
The world with some development.

'Were this not well, to bide mine hour,
Tho' watching from a ruin'd tower
How grows the day of human power?'

'The highest-mounted mind,' he said,
'Still sees the sacred morning spread
The silent summit overhead.

'Will thirty seasons render plain
Those lonely lights that still remain,
Just breaking over land and main?

‘Or make that morn, from his cold crown
And crystal silence creeping down,
Flood with full daylight glebe and town?

‘Forerun thy peers, thy time, and let
Thy feet, millenniums hence, be set
In midst of knowledge, dream’d not yet.

‘Thou hast not gain’d a real height,
Nor art thou nearer to the light,
Because the scale is infinite.

‘ ’Twere better not to breathe or speak,
Than cry for strength, remaining weak,
And seem to find, but still to seek.

‘Moreover, but to seem to find
Asks what thou lackest, thought resign’d,
A healthy frame, a quiet mind.’

I said, ‘When I am gone away,
“He dared not tarry,” men will say,
Doing dishonour to my clay.’

‘This is more vile,’ he made reply
‘To breathe and loathe, to live and sigh,
Than once from dread of pain to die.

‘Sick art thou — a divided will
Still heaping on the fear of ill

The fear of men, a coward still.

'Do men love thee? Art thou so bound
To men, that how thy name may sound
Will vex thee lying underground?

'The memory of the wither'd leaf
In endless time is scarce more brief
Than of the garner'd Autumn-sheaf.

'Go, vexed Spirit, sleep in trust;
The right ear, that is fill'd with dust,
Hears little of the false or just.'

'Hard task, to pluck resolve,' I cried,
'From emptiness and the waste wide
Of that abyss, or scornful pride!

'Nay — rather yet that I could raise
One hope that warm'd me in the days
While still I yearn'd for human praise.

'When, wide in soul and bold of tongue,
Among the tents I paused and sung,
The distant battle flash'd and rung.

'I sung the joyful Paean clear,
And, sitting, burnish'd without fear
The brand, the buckler, and the spear —

‘Waiting to strive a happy strife,
To war with falsehood to the knife,
And not to lose the good of life —

‘Some hidden principle to move,
To put together, part and prove,
And mete the bounds of hate and love —

‘As far as might be, to carve out
Free space for every human doubt,
That the whole mind might orb about —

‘To search thro’ all I felt or saw,
The springs of life, the depths of awe,
And reach the law within the law:

‘At least, not rotting like a weed,
But, having sown some generous seed,
Fruitful of further thought and deed,

‘To pass, when Life her light withdraws,
Not void of righteous self-applause,
Nor in a merely selfish cause —

‘In some good cause, not in mine own,
To perish, wept for, honour’d, known,
And like a warrior overthrown;

‘Whose eyes are dim with glorious tears,
When, soil’d with noble dust, he hears

His country's war-song thrill his ears:

'Then dying of a mortal stroke,
That time the foeman's line is broke,
And all the war is roll'd in smoke.'

'Yea!' said the voice, 'thy dream was good,
While thou abodest in the bud.
It was the stirring of the blood.

'If Nature put not forth her power
About the opening of the flower,
Who is it that could live an hour?

'Then comes the check, the change, the fall
Pain rises up, old pleasures pall.
There is one remedy for all.

'Yet hadst thou, thro' enduring pain,
Link'd month to month with such a chain
Of knitted purport, all were vain.

'Thou hadst not between death and birth
Dissolved the riddle of the earth.
So were thy labour little-worth.

'That men with knowledge merely play'd,
I told thee — hardly nigher made,
Tho' scaling slow from grade to grade;

'Much less this dreamer, deaf and blind
Named man, may hope some truth to find
That bears relation to the mind.

'For every worm beneath the moon
Draws different threads, and late and soon
Spins, toiling out his own cocoon.

'Cry, faint not: either Truth is born
Beyond the polar gleam forlorn,
Or in the gateways of the morn.

'Cry, faint not, climb: the summits slope
Beyond the furthest flights of hope,
Wrapt in dense cloud from base to cope.

'Sometimes a little corner shines,
As over rainy mist inclines
A gleaming crag with belts of pines.

'I will go forward, sayest thou,
I shall not fail to find her now.
Look up, the fold is on her brow.

'If straight thy track, or if oblique,
Thou know'st not. Shadows thou dost strike,
Embracing cloud, Ixion-like;

'And owning but a little more
Than beasts, abidest lame and poor,

Calling thyself a little lower

'Than angels. Cease to wail and brawl!
Why inch by inch to darkness crawl?
There is one remedy for all.'

'O dull, one-sided voice,' said I,
Wilt thou make everything a lie,
To flatter me that I may die?

'I know that age to age succeeds,
Blowing a noise of tongues and deeds,
A dust of systems and of creeds.

'I cannot hide that some have striven,
Achieving calm, to whom was given
The joy that mixes man with Heaven:

'Who, rowing hard against the stream,
Saw distant gates of Eden gleam,
And did not dream it was a dream;

'But heard, by secret transport led,
Ev'n in the charnels of the dead,
The murmur of the fountain-head —

'Which did accomplish their desire,
Bore and forbore, and did not tire,
Like Stephen, an unquenched fire.

'He heeded not reviling tones,
Nor sold his heart to idle moans,
Tho' cursed and scorn'd, and bruised with
stones:

'But looking upward, full of grace,
He pray'd, and from a happy place
God's glory smote him on the face.'

The sullen answer slid betwixt:
Not that the grounds of hope were fix'd,
The elements were kindlier mix'd.'

I said, 'I toil beneath the curse,
But, knowing not the universe,
I fear to slide from bad to worse.

'And that, in seeking to undo
One riddle, and to find the true,
I knit a hundred others new:

'Or that this anguish fleeting hence,
Unmanacled from bonds of sense,
Be fix'd and froz'n to permanence:

'For I go, weak from suffering here;
Naked I go, and void of cheer:
What is it that I may not fear?'

'Consider well,' the voice replied,

'His face, that two hours since hath died
Wilt thou find passion, pain or pride?

'Will he obey when one commands?
Or answer should one press his hands?
He answers not, nor understands.

'His palms are folded on his breast:
There is no other thing express'd
But long disquiet merged in rest.

'His lips are very mild and meek:
Tho' one should smite him on the cheek,
And on the mouth, he will not speak.

'His little daughter, whose sweet face
He kiss'd, taking his last embrace,
Becomes dishonour to her race —

'His sons grow up that bear his name,
Some grow to honour some to shame, —
But he is chill to praise or blame.

'He will not hear the north-wind rave,
Nor, moaning, household shelter crave
From winter rains that beat his grave.

'High up the vapours fold and swim:
About him broods the twilight dim:
The place he knew forgetteth him.'

'If all be dark, vague voice,' I said,
'These things are wrapt in doubt and dread,
Nor canst thou show the dead are dead.

'The sap dries up: the plant declines.
A deeper tale my heart divines.
Know I not Death? the outward signs?

'I found him when my years were few;
A shadow on the graves I knew,
And darkness in the village yew.

'From grave to grave the shadow crept:
In her still place the morning wept:
Touch'd by his feet the daisy slept.

'The simple senses crown'd his head:
"Omega! thou art Lord," they said,
"We find no motion in the dead."

'Why, if man rot in dreamless ease,
Should that plain fact, as taught by these,
Not make him sure that he shall cease?

'Who forged that other influence,
That heat of inward evidence,
By which he doubts against the sense?

'He owns the fatal gift of eyes,
That read his spirit blindly wise,

Not simple as a thing that dies.

'Here sits he shaping wings to fly:
His heart forebodes a mystery:
He names the name Eternity.

'That type of Perfect in his mind
In Nature can he nowhere find.
He sows himself on every wind.

'He seems to hear a Heavenly Friend,
And thro' thick veils to apprehend
A labour working to an end.

'The end and the beginning vex
His reason: many things perplex,
With motions, checks, and counterchecks.

'He knows a baseness in his blood
At such strange war with something good,
He may not do the thing he would.

'Heaven opens inward, chasms yawn,
Vast images in glimmering dawn,
Half shown, are broken and withdrawn.

'Ah! sure within him and without,
Could his dark wisdom find it out,
There must be answer to his doubt.

'But thou canst answer not again.
With thine own weapon art thou slain,
Or thou wilt answer but in vain.

'The doubt would rest, I dare not solve.
In the same circle we revolve.
Assurance only breeds resolve.'

As when a billow, blown against,
Falls back, the voice with which I fenced
A little ceased, but recommenced.

'Where wert thou when thy father play'd
In his free field, and pastime made,
A merry boy in sun and shade?

'A merry boy they called him then.
He sat upon the knees of men
In days that never come again.

'Before the little ducts began.
To feed thy bones with lime, and ran
Their course, till thou wert also man:

'Who took a wife, who rear'd his race,
Whose wrinkles gather'd on his face,
Whose troubles number with his days:

'A life of nothings, nothing-worth,
From that first nothing ere his birth

To that last nothing under earth!'

'These words,' I said, 'are like the rest,
No certain clearness, but at best
A vague suspicion of the breast:

'But if I grant, thou might'st defend
The thesis which thy words intend —
That to begin implies to end;

'Yet how should I for certain hold,
Because my memory is so cold,
That I first was in human mould?

'I cannot make this matter plain,
But I would shoot, howe'er in vain,
A random arrow from the brain.

'It may be that no life is found,
Which only to one engine bound
Falls off, but cycles always round.

'As old mythologies relate,
Some draught of Lethe might await
The slipping thro' from state to state.

'As here we find in trances, men
Forget the dream that happens then,
Until they fall in trance again.

‘So might we, if our state were such
As one before, remember much,
For those two likes might meet and touch

‘But, if I lapsed from nobler place,
Some legend of a fallen race
Alone might hint of my disgrace;

‘Some vague emotion of delight
In gazing up an Alpine height,
Some yearning toward the lamps of night.

‘Or if thro’ lower lives I came —
Tho’ all experience past became
Consolidate in mind and frame —

‘I might forget my weaker lot;
For is not our first year forgot?
The haunts of memory echo not.

‘And men, whose reason long was blind,
From cells of madness unconfined,
Oft lose whole years of darker mind.

‘Much more, if first I floated free,
As naked essence, must I be
Incompetent of memory:

‘For memory dealing but with time,
And he with matter, could she climb

Beyond her own material prime?

'Moreover, something is or seems,
That touches me with mystic gleams,
Like glimpses of forgotten dreams —

'Of something felt, like something here;
Of something done, I know not where;
Such as no language may declare.'

The still voice laugh'd. 'I talk,' said he,
'Not with thy dreams. Suffice it thee
Thy pain is a reality.'

'But thou,' said I, 'hast miss'd thy mark,
Who sought'st to wreck my mortal ark,
By making all the horizon dark.

'Why not set forth, if I should do
This rashness, that which might ensue
With this old soul in organs new?

'Whatever crazy sorrow saith,
No life that breathes with human breath
Has ever truly long'd for death.

' 'Tis life, whereof our nerves are scant,
Oh life, not death, for which we pant;
More life, and fuller, that I want.'

I ceased, and sat as one forlorn,
Then said the voice, in quiet scorn,
'Behold, it is the Sabbath morn.'

And I arose, and I released
The casement, and the light increased
With freshness in the dawning east.

Like soften'd airs that blowing steal,
When meres begin to uncongeal,
The sweet church bells began to peal.

On to God's house the people prest:
Passing the place where each must rest,
Each enter'd like a welcome guest.

One walk'd between his wife and child,
With measur'd footfall firm and mild
And now and then he gravely smiled.

The prudent partner of his blood
Lean'd on him, faithful, gentle, good,
Wearing the rose of womanhood.

And in their double love secure
The little maiden walk'd demure
Pacing with downward eyelids pure.

These three made unity so sweet,
My frozen heart began to beat,

Remembering its ancient heat.

I blest them, and they wander'd on:
I spoke, but answer came there none:
The dull and bitter voice was gone.

A second voice was at mine ear,
A little whisper silver-clear,
A murmur, 'Be of better cheer.'

As from some blissful neighbourhood
A notice faintly understood,
'I see the end, and know the good.'

A little hint to solace woe,
A hint, a whisper breathing low
'I may not speak of what I know.'

Like an Aeolian harp that wakes
No certain air, but overtakes
Far thought with music that it makes

Such seem'd the whisper at my side:
'What is it thou knowest, sweet voice?' I
cried.
'A hidden hope,' the voice replied:

So heavenly-toned, that in that hour
From out my sullen heart a power
Broke, like the rainbow from the shower,

To feel, altho' no tongue can prove,
That every cloud, that spreads above
And veileth love, itself is love.

And forth into the fields I went,
And Nature's living motion lent
The pulse of hope to discontent.

I wonder'd at the bounteous hours,
The slow result of winter showers:
You scarce could see the grass for flowers.

I wonder'd, while I paced along:
The woods were fill'd so full with song,
There seem'd no room for sense of wrong.

So variously seem'd all things wrought,
I marvell'd how the mind was brought
To anchor by one gloomy thought;

And wherefore rather I made choice
To commune with that barren voice,
Than him that said, 'Rejoice! rejoice!'

The Day-Dream

Prologue

O Lady Flora, let me speak:
  A pleasant hour has past away
While, dreaming on your damask cheek,
  The dewy sister-eyelids lay.
As by the lattice you reclined,
  I went thro' many wayward moods
To see you dreaming — and, behind,
  A summer crisp with shining woods.
And I too dream'd, until at last
  Across my fancy, brooding warm,
The reflex of a legend past,
  And loosely settled into form.
And would you have the thought I had,
  And see the vision that I saw,
Then take the broidery-frame, and add
  A crimson to the quaint Macaw,
And I will tell it. Turn your face,
  Nor look with that too-earnest eye —
The rhymes are dazzled from their place,
  And order'd words asunder fly.

The Sleeping Palace

I

The varying year with blade and sheaf
  Clothes and reclothes the happy plains;
Here rests the sap within the leaf,
  Here stays the blood along the veins.
Faint shadows, vapours lightly curl'd,
  Faint murmurs from the meadows come,
Like hints and echoes of the world
  To spirits folded in the womb.

II

Soft lustre bathes the range of urns
  On every slanting terrace-lawn.
The fountain to his place returns
  Deep in the garden lake withdrawn.
Here droops the banner on the tower,
  On the hall-hearths the festal fires,
The peacock in his laurel bower,
  The parrot in his gilded wires.

III

Roof-haunting martins warm their eggs:
  In these, in those the life is stay'd.

The mantles from the golden pegs
  Droop sleepily: no sound is made,
Not even of a gnat that sings.
  More like a picture seemeth all
Than those old portraits of old kings,
  That watch the sleepers from the wall.

IV

Here sits the Butler with a flask
  Between his knees, half-drain'd; and there
The wrinkled steward at his task,
  The maid-of-honour blooming fair:
The page has caught her hand in his:
  Her lips are sever'd as to speak:
His own are pouted to a kiss:
  The blush is fix'd upon her cheek.

V

Till all the hundred summers pass,
  The beams, that thro' the Oriel shine,
Make prisms in every carven glass,
  And beaker brimm'd with noble wine.
Each baron at the banquet sleeps,
  Grave faces gather'd in a ring.
His state the king reposing keeps.
  He must have been a jovial king.

VI

All round a hedge upshoots, and shows
  At distance like a little wood;
Thorns, ivies, woodbine, mistletoes,
  And grapes with bunches red as blood;
All creeping plants, a wall of green
  Close-matted, bur and brake and brier,
And glimpsing over these, just seen,
  Highup, the topmost palace-spire.

VII

When will the hundred summers die,
  And thought and time be born again,
And newer knowledge, drawing nigh,
  Bring truth that sways the soul of men?
Here all things in their place remain,
  As all were order'd, ages since.
Come, Care and Pleasure, Hope and Pain,
  And bring the fated fairy Prince.

I

Year after year unto her feet,
  She lying on her couch alone,
Across the purpled coverlet,
  The maiden's jet-black hair has grown,
On either side her tranced form
  Forth streaming from a braid of pearl:
The slumbrous light is rich and warm,
  And moves not on the rounded curl.

II

The silk star-broider'd coverlid
  Unto her limbs itself doth mould
Languidly ever; and, amid
  Her full black ringlets downward roll'd,
Glows forth each softly-shadow'd arm
  With bracelets of the diamond bright:
Her constant beauty doth inform
  Stillness with love, and day with light.

III

She sleeps: her breathings are not heard
  In palace chambers far apart.

The fragrant tresses are not stirr'd
  That lie upon her charmed heart
She sleeps: on either hand upswells
  The gold-fringed pillow lightly prest:
She sleeps, nor dreams, but ever dwells
  A perfect form in perfect rest.

The Arrival

I

All precious things, discover'd late,
  To those that seek them issue forth;
For love in sequel works with fate,
  And draws the veil from hidden worth.
He travels far from other skies —
  His mantle glitters on the rocks —
A fairy Prince, with joyful eyes
  And lighter-footed than the foe.

II

The bodies and the bones of those
  That strove in other days to pass,
Are wither'd in the thorny close,
  Or scatter'd blanching on the grass.
He gazes on the silent dead:
  'They perish'd in their daring deeds.'

This proverb flashes thro' his head
  'The many fail: the one succeeds.'

III

He comes, scarce knowing what he seeks:
  He breaks the hedge: he enters there:
The colour flies into his cheeks:
  He trusts to light on something fair;
For all his life the charm did talk
  About his path, and hover near
With words of promise in his walk,
  And whisper'd voices at his ear.

IV

More close and close his footsteps wind;
  The Magic Music in his heart
Beats quick and quicker, till he find
  The quiet chamber far apart.
His spirit flutters like a lark,
  He stoops — to kiss her — on his knee.
'Love, if thy tresses be so dark,
  How dark those hidden eyes must be!'

I

A touch, a kiss! the charm was snapt.
  There rose a noise of striking clocks,
And feet that ran, and doors that clapt,
  And barking dogs, and crowing cocks;
A fuller light illumined all,
  A breeze thro' all the garden swept,
A sudden hubbub shook the hall
  And sixty feet the fountain leapt.

II

The hedge broke in, the banner blew,
  The butler drank, the steward scrawl'd,
The fire shot up, the martin flew,
  The parrot scream'd, the peacock
    squall'd,
The maid and page renew'd their strife,
  The palace bang'd, and buzz'd and clackt,
And all the long-pent stream of life
  Dash'd downward in a cataract.

III

And last with these the king awoke,

And in his chair himself uprear'd,
And yawn'd, and rubb'd his face, and spoke,
'By holy rood, a royal beard!
How say you? we have slept, my lords.
My beard has grown into my lap.'
The barons swore, with many words,
'Twas but an after-dinner's nap.

IV

'Pardy,' return'd the king, 'but still
My joints are something stiff or so.
My lord, and shall we pass the bill
I mention'd half an hour ago?'
The chancellor, sedate and vain,
In courteous words return'd reply:
But dallied with his golden chain,
And, smiling, put the question by.

The Departure

I

And on her lover's arm she leant,
And round her waist she felt it fold,
And far across the hills they went
In that new world which is the old:
Across the hills, and far away

Beyond their utmost purple rim,
And deep into the dying day
The happy princess follow'd him.

II

'I'd sleep another hundred years,
O love, for such another kiss;'
'O wake for ever, love,' she hears,
'O love, 'twas such as this and this.'
And o'er them many a sliding star,
And many a merry wind was borne,
And, stream'd thro' many a golden bar,
The twilight melted into morn.

III

'O eyes long laid in happy sleep!'
'O happy sleep, that lightly fled!'
'O happy kiss, that woke thy sleep!'
'O love, thy kiss would wake the dead!'
And o'er them many a flowing range
Of vapour buoy'd the crescent-bark,
And, rapt thro' many a rosy change,
The twilight died into the dark.
'A hundred summers! can it be?
And whither goest thou, tell me where?'
'O seek my father's court with me,

For there are greater wonders there.'
And o'er the hills, and far away
Beyond their utmost purple rim,
Beyond the night, across the day
Thro' all the world she follow'd him.

Moral

I

So, Lady Flora, take my lay,
And if you find no moral there,
Go, look in any glass and say,
What moral is in being fair.
Oh, to what uses shall we put
The wildweed-flower that simply blows?
And is there any moral shut
Within the bosom of the rose?

II

But any man that walks the mead
In bud or blade, or bloom, may find,
According as his humours lead
A meaning suited to his mind.
And liberal applications lie
In Art like Nature, dearest friend;
So 'twere to cramp its use, if I

Should hook it to some useful end.

L'Envoi

I

You shake your head. A random string
  Your finer female sense offends.
Well — were it not a pleasant thing
  To fall asleep with all one's friends;
To pass with all our social ties
  To silence from the paths of men;
And every hundred years to rise
  And learn the world, and sleep again;
To sleep thro' terms of mighty wars,
  And wake on science grown to more,
On secrets of the brain, the stars,
  As wild as aught of fairy lore;
And all that else the years will show,
  The Poet-forms of stronger hours,
The vast Republics that may grow,
  The Federations and the Powers;
Titanic forces taking birth
  In divers seasons, divers climes;
For we are Ancients of the earth,
  And in the morning of the times.

II

So sleeping, so aroused from sleep
  Thro' sunny decads new and strange,
Or gay quinquenniads would we reap
  The flower and quintessence of change.

III

Ah, yet would I — and would I might!
  So much your eyes my fancy take —
Be still the first to leap to light
  That I might kiss those eyes awake!
For, am I right or am I wrong,
  To choose your own you did not care;
You'd have *my* moral from the song,
  And I will take my pleasure there:
And, am I right or am I wrong,
  My fancy, ranging thro' and thro',
To search a meaning for the song,
  Perforce will still revert to you;
Nor finds a closer truth than this
  All-graceful head, so richly curl'd,
And evermore a costly kiss
  The prelude to some brighter world.

IV

For since the time when Adam first
  Embraced his Eve in happy hour,
And every bird of Eden burst
  In carol, every bud to flower,
What eyes, like thine, have waken'd hopes?
  What lips, like thine, so sweetly join'd?
Where on the double rosebud droops
  The fullness of the pensive mind;
Which all too dearly self-involved,
  Yet sleeps a dreamless sleep to me;
A sleep by kisses undissolved,
  That lets thee neither hear nor see:
But break it. In the name of wife,
  And in the rights that name may give,
Are clasp'd the moral of thy life,
  And that for which I care to live.

Epilogue

So, Lady Flora, take my lay,
  And, if you find a meaning there,
O whisper to your glass, and say,
  'What wonder, if he thinks me fair?'
What wonder I was all unwise,
  To shape the song for your delight
Like long-tail'd birds of Paradise,
  That float thro' Heaven, and cannot light?

Or old-world trains, upheld at court
  By Cupid-boys of blooming hue —
But take it — earnest wed with sport,
  And either sacred unto you.

Amphion

My father left a park to me,
  But it is wild and barren,
A garden too with scarce a tree
  And waster than a warren:
Yet say the neighbours when they call,
  It is not bad but good land,
And in it is the germ of all
  That grows within the woodland.

O had I lived when song was great
  In days of old Amphion,
And ta'en my fiddle to the gate,
  Nor cared for seed or scion!
And had I lived when song was great,
  And legs of trees were limber,
And ta'en my fiddle to the gate,
  And fiddled in the timber!

'Tis said he had a tuneful tongue,
  Such happy intonation,
Wherever he sat down and sung
  He left a small plantation;

Wherever in a lonely grove
  He set up his forlorn pipes,
The gouty oak began to move,
  And flounder into hornpipes.

The mountain stirr'd its bushy crown,
  And, as tradition teaches,
Young ashes pirouetted down
  Coquetting with young beeches;
And briony-vine and ivy-wreath
  Ran forward to his rhyming,
And from the valleys underneath
  Came little copses climbing.

The linden broke her ranks and rent
  The woodbine wreaths that bind her,
And down the middle, buzz! she went
  With all her bees behind her.
The poplars, in long order due,
  With cypress promenaded,
The shock-head willows two and two
  By rivers gallopaded.

Came wet-shod alder from the wave,
  Came yews, a dismal coterie;
Each pluck'd his one foot from the grave,
  Poussetting with a sloe-tree:
Old elms came breaking from the vine,
  The vine stream'd out to follow,
And, sweating rosin, plump'd the pine

From many a cloudy hollow.

And wasn't it a sight to see,
When, ere his song was ended,
Like some great landslip, tree by tree,
The country-side descended;
And shepherds from the mountain-eaves
Look'd down, half-pleased, half
frighten'd
As dash'd about the drunken leaves
The random sunshine lighten'd!

Oh, nature first was fresh to men
And wanton without measure;
So youthful and so flexile then,
You moved her at your pleasure.
Twang out, my fiddle! shake the twigs!
And make her dance attendance
Blow, flute, and stir the stiff-set sprigs,
And scirrhous roots and tendons.
'Tis vain! in such a brassy age
I could not move a thistle;
The very sparrows in the hedge
Scarce answer to my whistle;
Or at the most, when three-parts-sick
With strumming and with scraping,
A jackass heehaws from the rick,
The passive oxen gaping.

But what is that I hear? a sound

Like sleepy counsel pleading:
OLord! — 'tis in my neighbour's ground,
The modern Muses reading.
They read Botanic Treatises,
And Works on Gardening thro' there,
And Methods of transplanting trees,
To look as if they grew there.

The wither'd Misses! how they prose
O'er books of travell'd seamen,
And show you slips of all that grows
From England to Van Diemen.
They read in arbours clipt and cut,
And alleys, faded places,
By squares of tropic summer shut
And warm'd in crystal cases.

But these, tho' fed with careful dirt,
Are neither green nor sappy;
Half-conscious of the garden-squirt,
The spindlings look unhappy.
Better to me the meanest weed
That blows upon its mountain,
The vilest herb that runs to seed
Beside its native fountain.

And I must work thro' months of toil,
And years of cultivation,
Upon my proper patch of soil
To grow my own plantation.

I'll take the showers as they fall,
  I will not vex my bosom:
Enough if at the end of all
  A little garden blossom.

Sir Galahad

My good blade carves the casques of men,
  My tough lance thrusteth sure,
My strength is as the strength of ten,
  Because my heart is pure.
The shattering trumpet shrilleth high,
  The hard brands shiver on the steel,
The splinter'd spear-shafts crack and fly,
  The horse and rider reel:
They reel, they roll in clanging lists,
  And when the tide of combat stands,
Perfume and flowers fall in showers,
  That lightly rain from ladies' hands.
How sweet are looks that ladies bend
  On whom their favours fall!
For them I battle till the end,
  To save from shame and thrall:
But all my heart is drawn above,
  My knees are bow'd in crypt and shrine:
I never felt the kiss of love,
  Nor maiden's hand in mine.
More bounteous aspects on me beam,
  Me mightier transports move and thrill;

So keep I fair thro' faith and prayer
  A virgin heart in work and will.

When down the stormy crescent goes,
  A light before me swims,
Between dark stems the forest glows,
  I hear a noise of hymns:
Then by some secret shrine I ride;
  I hear a voice, but none are there;
The stalls are void, the doors are wide,
  The tapers burning fair.
Fair gleams the snowy altar-cloth,
  The silver vessels sparkle clean,
The shrill bell rings, the censer swings,
  And solemn chaunts resound between.

Sometimes on lonely mountain-meres
  I find a magic bark;
I leap on board: no helmsman steers:
  I float till all is dark.
A gentle sound, an awful light!
  Three angels bear the holy Grail:
With folded feet, in stoles of white,
  On sleeping wings they sail.
Ah, blessed vision! blood of God!
  My spirit beats her mortal bars,
As down dark tides the glory slides,
  And star-like mingles with the stars.

When on my goodly charger borne

Thro' dreaming towns I go,
The cock crows ere the Christmas morn,
The streets are dumb with snow.
The tempest crackles on the leads,
And, ringing, springs from brand and
mail;
But o'er the dark a glory spreads,
And gilds the driving hail.
I leave the plain, I climb the height;
No branchy thicket shelter yields;
But blessed forms in whistling storms
Fly o'er waste fens and windy fields.

A maiden knight — to me is given
Such hope, I know not fear;
I yearn to breathe the airs of heaven
That often meet me here.
I muse on joy that will not cease,
Pure spaces clothed in living beams,
Pure lilies of eternal peace,
Whose odours haunt my dreams;
And, stricken by an angel's hand
This mortal armour that I wear,
This weight and size, this heart and eyes,
Are touch'd, are turn'd to finest air.

The clouds are broken in the sky,
And thro' the mountain-walls
A rolling organ harmony
Swells up, and shakes and falls.

Then move the trees, the copses nod,
  Wings flutter, voices hover clear
'O just and faithful knight of God!
  Ride on! the prize is near.'
So pass I hostel, hall, and grange;
  By bridge and ford, by park and pale,
All-arm'd I ride, whate'er betide,
  Until I find the holy Grail.

Edward Gray

Sweet Emma Moreland of yonder town
  Met me walking on yonder way,
'And have you lost your heart?' she said;
  'And are you married yet, Edward Gray?'

Sweet Emma Moreland spoke to me:
  Bitterly weeping I turn'd away:
'Sweet Emma Moreland, love no more
  Can touch the heart of Edward Gray

'Ellen Adair she loved me well,
  Against her father's and mother's will:
To-day I sat for an hour and wept,
  By Ellen's grave, on the windy hill

'Shy she was, and I thought her cold;
  Thought her proud, and fled over the sea;
Fill'd I was with folly and spite,

When Ellen Adair was dying for me.

'Cruel, cruel the words I said!
Cruelly came they back to-day
"You're too slight and fickle," I said,
"To trouble the heart of Edward Gray"

'There I put my face in the grass —
Whisper'd, "Listen to my despair:
I repent me of all I did:
Speak a little, Ellen Adair!"

'Then I took a pencil, and wrote
On the messy stone, as I lay,
"Here lies the body of Ellen Adair;
And here the heart of Edward Gray!"

'Love may come, and love may go,
And fly, like a bird, from tree to tree
But I will love no more, no more,
Till Ellen Adair come back to me.

'Bitterly wept I over the stone:
Bitterly weeping I turn'd away:
There lies the body of Ellen Adair!
And there the heart of Edward Gray!'

Will Waterproof's Lyrical Monologue

Made at the Cock

O plump head-waiter at The Cock,
  To which I most resort,
How goes the time? 'Tis five o'clock.
  Go fetch a pint of port:
But let it not be such as that
  You set before chance-corners,
But such whose father-grape grew fat
  On Lusitanian summers.

No vain libation to the Muse,
  But may she still be kind,
And whisper lovely words, and use
  Her influence on the mind,
To make me write my random rhymes,
  Ere they be half-forgotten;
Nor add and alter, many times,
  Till all be ripe and rotten,

I pledge her, and she comes and dips
  Her laurel in the wine,
And lays it thrice upon my lips,
  These favour'd lips of mine;
Until the charm have power to make
  New lifeblood warm the bosom
And barren commonplaces break
  In full and kindly blossom.

I pledge her silent at the board;
  Her gradual fingers steal
And touch upon the master-chord
  Of all I felt and feel.
Old wishes, ghosts of broken plans,
  And phantom hopes assemble;
And that child's heart within the man's
  Begins to move and tremble.

Thro' many an hour of summer suns.
  By many pleasant ways,
Against its fountain upward runs
  The current of my days:
I kiss the lips I once have kiss'd;
  The gas-light wavers dimmer;
And softly, thro' a vinous mist,
  My college friendships glimmer.

I grow in worth, and wit, and sense,
  Unboding critic-pen,
Or that eternal want of pence,
  Which vexes public men,
Who hold their hands to all, and cry
  For that which all deny them —
Who sweep the crossings, wet or dry,
  And all the world go by them.

Ah yet, tho' all the world forsake,
  Tho' fortune clip my wings,
I will not cramp my heart, nor take

Half-views of men and things.
Let Whig and Tory stir their blood;
There must be stormy weather;
But for some true result of good
All parties work together.

Let there be thistles, there are grapes;
If old things, there are new;
Ten thousand broken lights and shapes,
Yet glimpses of the true.
Let raffs be rife in prose and rhyme,
We lack not rhymes and reasons,
As on this whirligig of Time
We circle with the seasons.

This earth is rich in man and maid;
With fair horizons bound:
This whole wide earth of light and shade
Comes out, a perfect round.
High over roaring Temple-bar,
And, set in Heaven's third story,
I look at all things as they are,
But thro' a kind of glory.

*

Head-waiter, honour'd by the guest
Half-mused, or reeling-ripe,
The pint, you brought me, was the best
That ever came from pipe.

But tho' the port surpasses praise,
  My nerves have dealt with stiffer
Is there some magic in the place?
  Or do my peptics differ?

For since I came to live and learn,
  No pint of white or red
Had ever half the power to turn
  This wheel within my head,
Which bears a season'd brain about,
  Unsubject to confusion,
Tho' soak'd and saturate, out and out,
  Thro' every convolution.

For I am of a numerous house,
  With many kinsmen gay,
Where long and largely we carouse
  As who shall say me nay:
Each month, a birth-day coming on,
  We drink defying trouble,
Or sometimes two would meet in one,
  And then we drank it double;

Whether the vintage, yet unkept,
  Had relish fiery-new,
Or, elbow-deep in sawdust, slept,
  As old as Waterloo;
Or stow'd (when classic Canning died)
  In musty bins and chambers,
Had cast upon its crusty side

The gloom of ten Decembers.

The Muse, the jolly Muse, it is!
She answer'd to my call,
She changes with that mood or this,
Is all-in-all to all:
She lit the spark within my throat,
To make my blood run quicker,
Used all her fiery will, and smote
Her life into the liquor.

And hence this halo lives about
The waiter's hands, that reach
To each his perfect pint of stout,
His proper chop to each.
He looks not like the common breed
That with the napkin dally;
I think he came like Ganymede,
From some delightful valley.

The Cock was of a larger egg
Than modern poultry drop,
Stept forward on a firmer leg,
And cramm'd a plumper crop;
Upon an ampler dunghill trod,
Crow'd lustier late and early,
Sipt wine from silver, praising God,
And raked in golden barley.

A private life was all his joy,

Till in a court he saw
A something-pottle-bodied boy,
That knuckled at the taw:
He stoop'd and clutch'd him, fair and good,
Flew over roof and casement:
His brothers of the weather stood
Stock-still for sheer amazement.

But he, by farmstead, thorpe and spire,
And follow'd with acclaims,
A sign to many a staring shire,
Came crowing over Thames.
Right down by smoky Paul's they bore,
Till, where the street grows straiter,
One fix'd for ever at the door,
And one became head-waiter.

⋆

But whither would my fancy go?
How out of place she makes
The violet of a legend blow
Among the chops and steaks!
'Tis but a steward of the can
One shade more plump than common;
As just and mere a serving-man
As any, born of woman.

I ranged too high: what draws me down
Into the common day?

Is it the weight of that half-crown,
   Which I shall have to pay?
For, something duller than at first,
   Nor wholly comfortable,
I sit (my empty glass reversed),
   And thrumming on the table:

Half fearful that, with self at strife,
   I take myself to task;
Lest of the fullness of my life
   I leave an empty flask:
For I had hope, by something rare,
   To prove myself a poet;
But, while I plan and plan, my hair
   Is grey before I know it.

So fares it since the years began,
   Till they be gather'd up;
The truth, that flies the flowing can,
   Will haunt the vacant cup:
And others' follies teach us not,
   Nor much their wisdom teaches;
And most, of sterling worth, is what
   Our own experience preaches.

Ah, let the rusty theme alone!
   We know not what we know.
But for my pleasant hour, 'tis gone,
   'Tis gone, and let it go.
'Tis gone: a thousand such have slipt

Away from my embraces,
And fall'n into the dusty crypt
Of darken'd forms and faces.

Go, therefore, thou! thy betters went
Long since, and came no more;
With peals of genial clamour sent
From many a tavern-door,
With twisted quirks and happy hits,
From misty men of letters;
The tavern-hours of mighty wits —
Thine elders and thy betters.

Hours, when the Poet's words and looks
Had yet their native glow:
Nor yet the fear of little books
Had made him talk-for show;
But, all his vast heart sherris-warm'd,
He flash'd his random speeches;
Ere days, that deal in ana, swarm'd
His literary leeches.

So mix for ever with the past,
Like all good things on earth!
For should I prize thee, couldst thou last,
At half thy real worth?
I hold it good, good things should pass:
With time I will not quarrel:
It is but yonder empty glass
That makes me maudlin-moral.

*

Head-waiter of the chop-house here,
  To which I most resort,
I too must part: I hold thee dear
  For this good pint of port,
For this, thou shalt from all things suck
  Marrow of mirth and laughter;
And, wheresoe'er thou move, good luck
  Shall fling her old shoe after.

But thou wilt never move from hence,
  The sphere thy fate allots:
Thy latter days increased with pence
  Go down among the pots:
Thou battenest by the greasy gleam
  In haunts of hungry sinners,
Old boxes, larded with the steam
  Of thirty thousand dinners.

We fret, *we* fume, would shift our skins,
  Would quarrel with our lot;
Thy care is, under polish'd tins,
  To serve the hot-and-hot;
To come and go, and come again,
  Returning like the pewit,
And watch'd by silent gentlemen,
  That trifle with the cruet.

Live long, ere from thy topmost head

The thick-set hazel dies;
Long, ere the hateful crow shall tread
The corners of thine eyes:
Live long, nor feel in head or chest
Our changeful equinoxes,
Till mellow Death, like some late guest,
Shall call thee from the boxes.

But when he calls, and thou shalt cease
To pace the gritted floor,
And, laying down an unctuous lease
Of life, shalt earn no more;
No carved cross-bones, the types of Death,
Shall show thee past to Heaven
But carved cross-pipes, and, underneath,
A pint-pot, neatly graven.

Lady Clare

It was the time when lilies blow,
And clouds are highest up in air,
Lord Ronald brought a lily-white doe
To give his cousin, Lady Clare.

I trow they did not part in scorn:
Lovers long-betroth'd were they:
They two will wed the morrow morn:
God's blessing on the day!

‘He does not love me for my birth,
  Nor for my lands so broad and fair;
He loves me for my own true worth,
  And that is well,’ said Lady Clare.

In there came old Alice the nurse,
  Said, ‘Who was this that went from thee?’
‘It was my cousin,’ said Lady Clare,
  ‘To-morrow he weds with me.’

‘O God be thank’d!’ said Alice the nurse,
  ‘That all comes round so just and fair:
Lord Ronald is heir of all your lands,
  And you are not the Lady Clare.’

‘Are ye out of your mind, my nurse,
    my nurse?’
  Said Lady Clare, ‘that ye speak so wild?’
‘As God’s above,’ said Alice the nurse,
  ‘I speak the truth: you are my child.

‘The old Earl’s daughter died at my breast;
  I speak the truth, as I live by bread!
I buried her like my own sweet child,
  And put my child in her stead.’

‘Falsely, falsely have ye done,
  O mother,’ she said, ‘if this be true,
To keep the best man under the sun
  So many years from his due.’

'Nay now, my child,' said Alice the nurse,
'But keep the secret for your life,
And all you have will be Lord Ronald's
When you are man and wife.'

'If I'm a beggar born,' she said,
'I will speak out, for I dare not lie.
Pull off, pull off, the brooch of gold,
And fling the diamond necklace by.'

'Nay now, my child,' said Alice the nurse,
'But keep the secret all ye can.'
She said 'Not so: but I will know
If there be any faith in man.'

'Nay now, what faith?' said Alice the nurse,
'The man will cleave unto his right.'
'And he shall have it,' the lady replied,
'Tho' I should die to-night.'

'Yet give one kiss to your mother dear!
Alas, my child, I sinn'd for thee.'
'O mother, mother, mother,' she said,
'So strange it seems to me.

'Yet here's a kiss for my mother dear,
My mother dear, if this be so,
And lay your hand upon my head,
And bless me, mother, ere I go.'

She clad herself in a russet gown,
  She was no longer Lady Clare:
She went by dale, and she went by down,
  With a single rose in her hair.

The lily-white doe Lord Ronald had brought
  Leapt up from where she lay,
Dropt her head in the maiden's hand,
  And follow'd her all the way.

Down stept Lord Ronald from his tower:
  'O Lady Clare, you shame your worth!
Why come you drest like a village maid,
  That are the flower of the earth?'

'If I come drest like a village maid,
  I am but as my fortunes are:
I am a beggar born,' she said,
  'And not the Lady Clare.'

'Play me no tricks,' said Lord Ronald
  'For I am yours in word and in deed.
Play me no tricks,' said Lord Ronald,
  'Your riddle is hard to read.'
O and proudly stood she up!
  Her heart within her did not fail:
She look'd into Lord Ronald's eyes,
  And told him all her nurse's tale.

He laugh'd a laugh of merry scorn:
  He turn'd and kiss'd her where she stood
'If you are not the heiress born,
  And I,' said he, 'the next in blood —

'If you are not the heiress born,
  And I,' said he, 'the lawful heir,
We two will wed to-morrow morn,
  And you shall still be Lady Clare.'

The Lord Burleigh

In her ear he whispers gaily,
  'If my heart by signs can tell,
Maiden, I have watch'd thee daily,
  And I think thou lov'st me well.'
She replies, in accents fainter,
  'There is none I love like thee.'
He is but a landscape-painter,
  And a village maiden she.
He to lips, that fondly falter,
  Presses his without reproof:
Leads her to the village altar,
  And they leave her father's roof.
'I can make no marriage present:
  Little can I give my wife.
Love will make our cottage pleasant,
  And I love thee more than life.'
They by parks and lodges going

See the lordly castles stand:
Summer woods, about them blowing,
Made a murmur in the land.
From deep thought himself he rouses,
Says to her that loves him well,
'Let us see these handsome houses
Where the wealthy nobles dwell.'
So she goes by him attended,
Hears him lovingly converse,
Sees whatever fair and splendid
Lay betwixt his home and hers;
Parks with oak and chestnut shady,
Parks and order'd gardens great,
Ancient homes of lord and lady,
Built for pleasure and for state.
All he shows her makes him dearer:
Evermore she seems to gaze
On that cottage growing nearer,
Where they twain will spend their days.
O but she will love him truly!
He shall have a cheerful home;
She will order all things duly,
When beneath his roof they come.
Thus her heart rejoices greatly,
Till a gateway she discerns
With armorial bearings stately,
And beneath the gate she turns;
Sees a mansion more majestic
Than all those she saw before:
Many a gallant gay domestic

Bows before him at the door.
And they speak in gentle murmur,
When they answer to his call,
While he treads with footstep firmer,
Leading on from hall to hall.
And, while now she wonders blindly,
Nor the meaning can divine,
Proudly turns he round and kindly,
'All of this is mine and thine.'
Here he lives in state and bounty,
Lord of Burleigh, fair and free,
Not a lord in all the county
Is so great a lord as he.
All at once the colour flushes
Her sweet face from brow to chin:
As it were with shame she blushes,
And her spirit changed within.
Then her countenance all over
Pale again as death did prove:
But he clasp'd her like a lover,
And he cheer'd her soul with love.
So she strove against her weakness,
Tho' at times her spirit sank:
Shaped her heart with woman's meekness
To all duties of her rank:
And a gentle consort made he,
And her gentle mind was such
That she grew a noble lady,
And the people loved her much.
But a trouble weigh'd upon her,

And perplex'd her, night and morn,
With the burthen of an honour
Unto which she was not born.
Faint she grew, and ever fainter,
As she murmur'd, 'Oh, that he
Were once more that landscape-painter,
Which did win my heart from me!'
So she droop'd and droop'd before him,
Fading slowly from his side:
Three fair children first she bore him,
Then before her time she died.
Weeping, weeping late and early,
Walking up and pacing down,
Deeply mourn'd the Lord of Burleigh,
Burleigh-house by Stamford-town.
And he came to look upon her,
And he look'd at her and said,
'Bring the dress and put it on her,
That she wore when she was wed.'
Then her people, softly treading,
Bore to earth her body, drest
In the dress that she was wed in,
That her spirit might have rest.

Sir Launcelot and Queen Guinevere

A Fragment

Like souls that balance joy and pain,

With tears and smiles from heaven again
The maiden Spring upon the plain
Came in a sun-lit fall of rain.
  In crystal vapour everywhere
Blue isles of heaven laugh'd between,
And, far in forest-deeps unseen,
The topmost elm-tree gather'd green
  From draughts of balmy air.

Sometimes the linnet piped his song:
Sometimes the throstle whistled strong:
Sometimes the sparhawk, wheel'd along,
Hush'd all the groves from fear of wrong:
  By grassy capes with fuller sound
In curves the yellowing river ran,
And drooping chestnut-buds began
To spread into the perfect fan,
  Above the teeming ground.

Then, in the boyhood of the year,
Sir Launcelot and Queen Guinevere
Rode thro' the coverts of the deer,
With blissful treble ringing clear.
  She seem'd a part of joyous Spring:
A gown of grass-green silk she wore,
Buckled with golden clasps before;
A light-green tuft of plumes she bore
  Closed in a golden ring.

Now on some twisted ivy-net,

Now by some tinkling rivulet,
In mosses mixt with violet
Her cream-white mule his pastern set:
  And fleeter now she skimm'd the plains
Than she whose elfin prancer springs
By night to eery warblings,
When all the glimmering moorland rings
  With jingling bridle-reins.

As she fled fast thro' sun and shade,
The happy winds upon her play'd,
Blowing the ringlet from the braid:
She look'd so lovely, as she sway'd
  The rein with dainty finger-tips,
A man had given all other bliss,
And all his worldly worth for this
To waste his whole heart in one kiss
  Upon her perfect lips.

A Farewell

Flow down, cold rivulet, to the sea,
  Thy tribute wave deliver:
No more by thee my steps shall be,
  For ever and for ever.

Flow, softly flow, by lawn and lea,
  A rivulet then a river:
No where by thee my stops shall be,

For ever and for ever.

But here will sigh thine alder tree,
And here thine aspen shiver;
And here by thee will hum the bee,
For ever and for ever.

A thousand suns will stream on thee,
A thousand moons will quiver;
But not by thee my steps shall be,
For ever and for ever.

The Beggar Maid

Her arms across her breast she laid;
She was more fair than words can say:
Bare-footed came the beggar maid
Before the king Cophetua.
In robe and crown the king stept down,
To meet and greet her on her way;
'It is no wonder,' said the lords,
'She is more beautiful than day.'

As shines the moon in clouded skies,
She in her poor attire was seen:
One praised her ankles, one her eyes,
One her dark hair and lovesome mien.
So sweet a face, such angel grace,
In all that land had never been:

Cophetua sware a royal oath:
  'This beggar maid shall be my queen!'

The Vision of Sin

I

I had a vision when the night was late:
A youth came riding toward a palace-gate.
He rode a horse with wings, that would have
    flown,
But that his heavy rider kept him down.
And from the palace came a child of sin,
And took him by the curls, and led him in,
Where sat a company with heated eyes,
Expecting when a fountain should arise:
A sleepy light upon their brows and lips —
As when the sun, a crescent of eclipse,
Dreams over lake and lawn, and isles and
    capes —
Suffused them, sitting, lying, languid
    shapes,
By heaps of gourds, and skins of wine,
    and piles of grapes.

II

Then methought I heard a mellow sound,
Gathering up from all the lower ground;

Narrowing in to where they sat assembled
Low voluptuous music winding trembled,
Wov'n in circles: they that heard it sigh'd,
Panted hand in hand with faces pale,
Swung themselves, and in low tones replied;
Till the fountain spouted, showering wide
Sleet of diamond-drift and pearly hail;
Then the music touch'd the gates and died;
Rose again from where it seem'd to fail,
Storm'd in orbs of song, a growing gale;
Till thronging in and in, to where they
waited,
As 'twere a hundred-throated nightingale,
The strong tempestuous treble throbb'd
and palpitated;
Ran into its giddiest whirl of sound,
Caught the sparkles, and in circles,
Purple gauzes, golden hazes, liquid mazes,
Flung the torrent rainbow round:
Then they started from their places,
Moved with violence, changed in hue,
Caught each other with wild grimaces,
Half-invisible to the view,
Wheeling with precipitate paces

To the melody, till they flew,
Hair, and eyes, and limbs, and faces,
Twisted hard in fierce embraces,
Like to Furies, like to Graces,
Dash'd together in blinding dew:

Till, kill'd with some luxurious agony,
The nerve-dissolving melody
Flutter'd headlong from the sky.

III

And then I look'd up toward a
mountain-tract,
That girt the region with high cliff and
lawn:
I saw that every morning, far withdrawn
Beyond the darkness and the cataract,
God made Himself an awful rose of dawn,
Unheeded: and detaching, fold by fold,
From those still heights, and,
slowly drawing near,
A vapour heavy, hueless, formless, cold,
Came floating on for many a month and
year,
Unheeded: and I thought I would have
spoken,
And warn'd that madman ere it grew too
late:
But, as in dreams, I could not.
Mine was broken,
When that cold vapour touch'd
the palace-gate,
And link'd again, I saw within my head
A grey and gap-tooth'd man as lean as death,

Who slowly rode across a wither'd heath,
And lighted at a ruin'd inn, and said:

IV

'Wrinkled ostler, grim and thin!
  Here is custom come your way;
Take my brute, and lead him in,
  Stuff his ribs with mouldy hay.

'Bitter barmaid, waning fast!
  See that sheets are on my bed;
What! the flower of life is past.
  It is long before you wed.

'Slip-shod waiter, lank and sour,
  At the Dragon on the heath!
Let us have a quiet hour,
  Let us hob-and-nob with Death.

'I am old, but let me drink;
  Bring me spices, bring me wine;
I remember, when I think,
  That my youth was half divine.

'Wine is good for shrivell'd lips,
  When a blanket wraps the day,
When the rotten woodland drips,
  And the leaf is stamp'd in clay.

'Sit thee down, and have no shame,
  Cheek by jowl, and knee by knee:
What care I for any name?
  What for order or degree?

'Let me screw thee up a peg:
  Let me loose thy tongue with wine:
Callest thou that thing a leg?
  Which is thinnest? thine or mine

'Thou shalt not be saved by works:
  Thou hast been a sinner too:
Ruin'd trunks on wither'd forks,
  Empty scarecrows, I and you!

'Fill the cup, and fill the can:
  Have a rouse before the morn:
Every moment dies a man,
  Every moment one is born.

'We are men of ruin'd blood;
  Therefore comes it we are wise.
Fish are we that love the mud,
  Rising to no fancy-flies.

'Name and fame! to fly sublime
  Thro' the courts, the camps, the schools,
Is to be the ball of Time,
  Bandied by the hands of fools.

‘Friendship! — to be two in one —
  Let the canting liar pack!
Well I know, when I am gone,
  How she mouths behind my back

‘Virtue! — to be good and just —
  Every heart, when sifted well,
Is a clot of warmer dust,
  Mix’d with cunning sparks of hell.

‘O! we two as well can look
  Whited thought and cleanly life
As the priest, above his book
  Leering at his neighbour’s wife.

‘Fill the cup, and fill the can:
  Have a rouse before the morn:
Every moment dies a man,
  Every moment one is born.

‘Drink, and let the parties rave:
  They are fill’d with idle spleen;
Rising, falling, like a wave,
  For they know not what they mean.

‘He that roars for liberty
  Faster binds a tyrant’s power;
And the tyrant’s cruel glee
  Forces on the freer hour.

‘Fill the can, and fill the cup:
  All the windy ways of men
Are but dust that rises up,
  And is lightly laid again.

‘Greet her with applausive breath,
  Freedom, gaily doth she tread;
In her right a civic wreath,
  In her left a human head.

‘No, I love not what is new;
  She is of an ancient house:
And I think we know the hue
  Of that cap upon her brows.

‘Let her go! her thirst she slakes
  Where the bloody conduit runs:
Then her sweetest meal she makes
  On the first-born of her sons.

‘Drink to lofty hopes that cool —
  Visions of a perfect State:
Drink we, last, the public fool,
  Frantic love and frantic hate.

‘Chant me now some wicked stave,
  Till thy drooping courage rise,
And the glow-worm of the grave
  Glimmer in thy rheumy eyes.

'Fear not thou to loose thy tongue;
  Set thy hoary fancies free;
What is loathsome to the young
  Savours well to thee and me.

'Change, reverting to the years,
  When thy nerves could understand
What there is in loving tears,
  And the warmth of hand in hand.

'Tell me tales of thy first love —
  April hopes, the fools of chance;
Till the graves begin to move,
  And the dead begin to dance.

'Fill the can, and fill the cup:
  All the windy ways of men
Are but dust that rises up,
  And is lightly laid again.

'Trooping from their mouldy dens
  The chap-fallen circle spreads:
Welcome, fellow-citizens,
  Hollow hearts and empty heads!

'You are bones, and what of that?
  Every face, however full,
Padded round with flesh and fat,
  Is but modell'd on a skull.

'Death is king, and Vivat Rex!
  Tread a measure on the stones,
Madam — if I know your sex,
  From the fashion of your bones.

'No, I cannot praise the fire
  In your eye — nor yet your lip:
All the more do I admire
  Joints of cunning workmanship.

'Lo! God's likeness — the ground-plan —
  Neither modell'd, glazed, or framed:
Buss me, thou rough sketch of man,
  Far too naked to be shamed!

'Drink to Fortune, drink to Chance,
  While we keep a little breath!
Drink to heavy Ignorance!
  Hob-and-nob with brother Death!

'Thou art mazed, the night is long,
  And the longer night is near:
What! I am not all as wrong
  As a bitter jest is dear.

'Youthful hopes, by scores, to all,
  When the locks are crisp and curl'd:
Unto me my maudlin gall
  And my mockeries of the world.

'Fill the cup, and fill the can!
  Mingle madness, mingle scorn!
Dregs of life, and lees of man:
  Yet we will not die forlorn.'

V

The voice grew faint: there came a further change:
Once more uprose the mystic mountain-range:
Below were men and horses pierced with worms,
And slowly quickening into lower forms;
By shards and scurf of salt, and scum of dross,
Old plash of rains, and refuse patch'd with moss.
Then some one spake: 'Behold! it was a crime
Of sense avenged by sense that wore with time.'
Another answer'd 'But a crime of sense
Give him new nerves with old experience.'
Another said: 'The crime of sense became
The crime of malice, and is equal blame.'
And one: 'He had not wholly quench'd his power;
A little grain of conscience made him sour.'

At last I heard a voice upon the slope
Cry to the summit, 'Is there any hope?'
To which an answer peal'd from that high
    land,
But in a tongue no man could understand;
And on the glimmering limit far withdrawn
God made Himself an awful rose of dawn.

Move Eastward, Happy Earth

Move eastward, happy earth, and leave
  Yon orange sunset waning slow:
From fringes of the faded eve,
  O, happy planet, eastward go;
Till over thy dark shoulder glow
  Thy silver sister-world, and rise
To glass herself in dewy eyes
  That watch me from the glen below.

Ah, bear me with thee, smoothly borne,
  Dip forward under starry light,
And move me to my marriage-morn,
  And round again to happy night.

Break, Break, Break

Break, break, break,
  On thy cold grey stones, O Sea!

And I would that my tongue could utter
  The thoughts that arise in me.

O well for the fisherman's boy,
  That he shouts with his sister at play!
O well for the sailor lad,
  That he sings in his boat on the bay!

And the stately ships go on
  To their haven under the hill;
But O for the touch of a vanish'd hand,
  And the sound of a voice that is still!

Break, break, break,
  At the foot of thy crags, O Sea!
But the tender grace of a day that is dead
  Will never come back to me.

The Poet's Song

The rain had fallen, the Poet arose,
He pass'd by the town and out of the street,
A light wind blew from the gates of the sun,
And waves of shadow went over the wheat,
And he sat him down in a lonely place,
And chanted a melody loud and sweet,
That made the wild-swan pause in her
    cloud,
And the lark drop down at his feet.

The swallow stopt as he hunted the bee,
The snake slipt under a spray,
The wild hawk stood with the down on his beak,
And stared, with his foot on the prey,
And the nightingale thought, 'I have sung many songs,
But never a one so gay,
For he sings of what the world will be
When the years have died away.'

The Golden Year

Well, you shall have that song which Leonard wrote:
It was last summer on a tour in Wales:
Old James was with me: we that day had been
Up Snowdon; and I wish'd for Leonard there,
And found him in Llanberis: then we crost
Between the lakes, and clamber'd halfway up
The counter side; and that same song of his
He told me; for I banter'd him, and swore
They said he lived shut up within himself,
A tongue-tied Poet in the feverous days,
That, setting the *how much* before the *how*,
Cry, like the daughters of the

horseleech, 'Give,
Cram us with all,' but count not me the herd!
To which 'They call me what they will,' he said:
'But I was born too late: the fair new forms,
That float about the threshold of an age,
Like truths of Science waiting to be caught —
Catch me who can, and make the catcher crown'd —
Are taken by the forelock. Let it be.
But if you care indeed to listen, hear.
These measured words, my work of yestermorn.
'We sleep and wake and sleep, but all things move
The Sun flies forward to his brother Sun;
The dark Earth follows wheel'd in her ellipse;
And human things returning on themselves
Move onward, leading up the golden year.
'Ah, tho' the times, when some new' thought can bud,
Are but as poets' seasons when they flower,
Yet seas, that daily gain upon the shore,
Have ebb and flow conditioning their march,
And slow and sure comes up the golden year.

'When wealth no more shall rest in mounded heaps,
But smit with freër light shall slowly melt
In many streams to fatten lower lands,
And light shall spread, and man be liker man
Thro' all the season of the golden year.
'Shall eagles not be eagles? wrens be wrens?
If all the world were falcons, what of that?
The wonder of the eagle were the less,
But he not less the eagle. Happy days
Roll onward, leading up the golden year.
'Fly, happy happy sails and bear the Press;
Fly happy with the mission of the Cross;
Knit land to land, and blowing havenward
With silks, and fruits, and spices, clear of toll,
Enrich the markets of the golden year.
'But we grow old. Ah! when shall all men's good
Be each man's rule, and universal Peace
Lie like a shaft of light across the land,
And like a lane of beams athwart the sea,
Thro' all the circle of the golden year?'
Thus far he flow'd, and ended; where upon
'Ah, folly!' in mimic cadence answer'd James —
'Ah, folly! for it lies so far away,

Not in our time, nor in our children's time,
'Tis like the second world to us that live;
'Twere all as one to fix our hopes on Heaven
As on this vision of the golden year.'
With that he struck his staff against the rocks
And broke it, — James, — you know him, — old, but full
Of force and choler, and firm upon his feet,
And like an oaken stock in winter woods,
O'erflourish'd with the hoary clematis:
Then added, all in heat:
'What stuff is this!
Old writers push'd the happy season back, —
The more fools they, — we forward: dreamers both:
You most, that in an age, when every hour
Must sweat her sixty minutes to the death
Live on, God love us, as if the seedsman, rapt
Upon the teeming harvest, should not plunge
His hand into the bag: but well I know
That unto him who works, and feels he works,
This same grand year is ever at the doors.'
He spoke; and, high above I heard them blast

The steep slate-quarry, and the great echo flap
And buffet round the hills from bluff to bluff.

After-Thought

Ah, God! the petty fools of rhyme,
  That shriek and sweat in pigmy wars
Before the stony face of Time
  And look'd at by the silent stars; —

That hate each other for a song,
  And do their little best to bite,
That pinch their brothers in the throng,
  And scratch the very dead for spite; —

And strain to make an inch of room
  For their sweet selves, and cannot hear
The sullen Lethe rolling doom
  On them and theirs, and all things here

When one small touch of Charity
  Could lift them nearer Godlike State,
Than if the crowded Orb should cry
  Like those that cried Diana great:

And *I* too talk, and lose the touch
  I talk of. Surely, after all,

The noblest answer unto such
  Is kindly silence when they brawl.

THE PRINCESS

A Medley

Prologue

Sir Walter Vivian all a summer's day
Gave his broad lawns until the set of sun
Up to the people: thither flock'd at noon
His tenants, wife and child, and thither
    half
The neighbouring borough with their
    Institute
Of which he was the patron. I was there
From college, visiting the son, — the son
A Walter too, — with others of our set,
Five others: we were seven at Vivian-place.

  And me that morning Walter show'd the
    house,
Greek, set with busts: from vases in the hail
Flowers of all heavens, and lovelier than
    their names,
Grew side by side; and on the pavement lay
Carved stones of the Abbey-ruin in
    the park,

Huge Ammonites, and the first bones of
Time
And on the tables every clime and age
Jumbled together; celts and calumets,
Claymore and snowshoe, toys in lava, fans
Of sandal, amber, ancient rosaries,
Laborious orient ivory sphere in sphere,
The cursed Malayan crease,
and battle-clubs
From the isles of palm: and higher on the
walls,
Betwixt the monstrous horns of elk and
deer,
His own forefathers' arms and armour
hung.

And 'this' he said 'was Hugh's
at Agincourt;
And that was old Sir Ralph's at Ascalon:
A good knight he! we keep a chronicle
With all about him' — which he brought,
and I
Dived in a hoard of tales that dealt with
knights,
Half-legend, half-historic, counts and kings
Who laid about them at their wills and died;
And mixt with these, a lady, one that arm'd
Her own fair head, and sallying thro' the gate,
Had beat her foes with slaughter from her
walls.

‘O miracle of women,’ said the book,
‘O noble heart who, being strait-besieged
By this wild king to force her to his wish,
Nor bent, nor broke, nor shunn’d a soldier’s death,
But now when all was lost or seem’d as lost —
Her stature more than mortal in the burst
Of sunrise, her arm lifted, eyes on fire —
Brake with a blast of trumpets from the gate,
And, falling on them like a thunderbolt,
She trampled some beneath her horses’ heels,
And some were whelm’d with missiles of the wall,
And some were push’d with lances from the rock,
And part were drown’d within the whirling brook:
O miracle of noble womanhood!’

So sang the gallant glorious chronicle;
And, I all rapt in this, ‘Come out,’ he said,
‘To the Abbey: there is Aunt Elizabeth
And sister Lilia with the rest.’ We went
(I kept the book and had my finger in it)
Down thro’ the park: strange was the sight to me;
For all the sloping pasture murmur’d, sown

With happy faces and with holiday.
There moved the multitude,
a thousand heads:
The patient leaders of their Institute
Taught them with facts. One rear'd a font
of stone
And drew, from butts of water on the slope,
The fountain of the moment, playing now
A twisted snake, and now a rain of pearls,
Or steep-up spout whereon the gilded ball
Danced like a wisp: and somewhat lower
down
A man with knobs and wires and vials fired
A cannon: Echo answer'd in her sleep
From hollow fields: and here were
telescopes
For azure views; and there a group of girls
In circle waited, whom the electric shock
Dislink'd with shrieks and laughter: round
the lake
A little clock-work steamer paddling plied
And shook the lilies: perch'd about the
knolls
A dozen angry models jetted steam:
A petty railway ran: a fire-balloon
Rose gem-like up before the dusky
groves
And dropt a fairy parachute and past:
And there thro' twenty posts of telegraph
They flash'd a saucy message to and fro

Between the mimic stations; so that sport
Went hand in hand with Science; otherwhere
Pure sport: a herd of boys with clamour bowl'd
And stump'd the wicket; babies roll'd about
Like tumbled fruit in grass; and men and maids
Arranged a country dance, and flew thro' light
And shadow, while the twangling violin
Struck up with Soldier-laddie, and overhead
The broad ambrosial aisles of lofty lime
Made noise with bees and breeze from end to end.

Strange was the sight and smacking of the time;
And long we gazed, but satiated at length
Came to the ruins. High-arch'd and ivy-claspt,
Of finest Gothic lighter than a fire,
Thro' one wide chasm of time and frost they gave
The park, the crowd, the house; but all within
The sward was trim as any garden lawn:
And here we lit on Aunt Elizabeth,

And Lilia with the rest, and lady friends
From neighbour seats: and there was Ralph himself,
A broken statue propt against the wall,
As gay as any. Lilia, wild with sport,
Half child half woman as she was, had wound
A scarf of orange round the stony helm,
And robed the shoulders in a rosy silk,
That made the old warrior from his ivied nook
Glow like a sunbeam: near his tomb a feast
Shone, silver-set; about it lay the guests,
And there we join'd them: then the maiden Aunt
Took this fair day for text, and from it preach'd
An universal culture for the crowd,
And all things great; but we, unworthier, told
Of college: he had climb'd across the spikes,
And he had squeezed himself betwixt the bars,
And he had breath'd the Proctor's dogs; and one
Discuss'd his tutor, rough to common men,
But honeying at the whisper of a lord;
And one the Master, as a rogue in grain
Veneer'd with sanctimonious theory.

But while they talk'd, above their heads I saw
The feudal warrior lady-clad; which brought
My book to mind: and opening this I read
Of old Sir Ralph a page or two that rang
With tilt and tourney; then the tale of her
That drove her foes with slaughter from her walls,
And much I praised her nobleness, and 'Where,'
Ask'd Walter, patting Lilia's head (she lay
Beside him) 'lives there such a woman now?'

Quick answer'd Lilia 'There are thousands now
Such women, but convention beats them down:
It is but bringing up; no more than that:
You men have done it: how I hate you all!
Ah, were I something great! I wish I were
Some mighty poetess, I would shame you then,
That love to keep us children! O I wish
That I were some great Princess, I would build
Far off from men a college like a man's,
And I would teach them all that men are taught;

We are twice as quick!' And here she shook aside
The hand that play'd the patron with her curls.

And one said smiling, 'Pretty were the sight
If our old halls could change their sex, and flaunt
With prudes for proctors, dowagers for deans,
And sweet girl-graduates in their golden hair.
I think they should not wear our rusty gowns,
But move as rich as Emperor-moths, or Ralph
Who shines so in the corner; yet I fear,
If there were many Lilias in the brood,
However deep you might embower the nest,
Some boy would spy it.'
At this upon the sward
She tapt her tiny silken-sandal'd foot:
'That's your light way; but I would make it death
For any male thing but to peep at us.'

Petulant she spoke, and at herself she laugh'd;
A rosebud set with little wilful thorns,

And sweet as English air could make her,
she:
But Walter hail'd a score of names upon her
And 'petty Ogress,' and 'ungrateful Puss,'
And swore he long'd at college, only long'd,
All else was well, for she-society.
They boated and they cricketed; they talk'd
At wine, in clubs, of art, of politics;
They lost their weeks; they vext the souls of
deans;
They rode; they betted; made a hundred
friends
And caught the blossom of the flying terms,
But miss'd the mignonette of Vivian-place
The little hearth-flower Lilia. Thus he spoke,
Part banter, part affection.
'True,' she said,
'We doubt not that. O yes, you miss'd us
much.
I'll stake my ruby ring upon it you did.'
She held it out; and as a parrot turns
Up thro' gilt wires a crafty loving eye,
And takes a lady's finger with all care,
And bites it for true heart and not for harm,
So he with Lilia's. Daintily she shriek'd
And wrung it. 'Doubt my word again!'
he said.
'Come, listen! here is proof that you were
miss'd:
We seven stay'd at Christmas up to read;

And there we took one tutor as to read:
The hard-grain'd Muses of the cube and
 square
Were out of season: never man, I think,
So moulder'd in a sinecure as he:
For while our cloisters echo'd frosty feet,
And our long walks were stnpt as bare as
 brooms,
We did but talk you over, pledge you all
In wassail; often, like as many girls —
Sick for the hollies and the yews of home —
As many little trifling Lilias — play'd
Charades and riddles as at Christmas here,
And *what's my thought* and *when* and
 where and *how,*
And often told a tale from mouth to mouth
As here at Christmas.'
 She remember'd that:
A pleasant game, she thought:
 she liked it more
Than magic music, forfeits, all the rest.
But these — what kind of tales did men tell
 men,
She wonder'd, by themselves?
 A half-disdain
Perch'd on the pouted blossom of her lips:
And Walter nodded at me; '*He* began,
The rest would follow, each in turn; and so
We forged a sevenfold story. Kind?
 what kind?

Chimeras, crotchets, Christmas solecisms,
Seven-headed monsters only made to kill
Time by the fire in winter.'
'Kill him now
The tyrant! kill him in the summer too.'
Said Lilia; 'Why not now?'
the maiden Aunt.
'Why not a summer's as a winter's tale?
A tale for summer as befits the time,
And something it should be to suit
the place,
Heroic, for a hero lies beneath,
Grave, solemn!'
Walter warp'd his mouth at this
To something so mock-solemn,
that I laugh'd
And Lilia woke with sudden-shrilling mirth
An echo like a ghostly woodpecker,
Hid in the ruins; till the maiden Aunt
(A little sense of wrong had touch'd her face
With colour) turn'd to me with 'As you will;
Heroic if you will, or what you will
Or be yourself your hero if you will.'

'Take Lilia, then, for heroine,'
clamour'd he,
'And make her some great Princess,
six feet high,
Grand, epic, homicidal; and be you The
Prince to win her!'

'Then follow me, the Prince,'
I answer'd, 'each be hero in his turn!
Seven and yet one, like shadows in
a dream. —
Heroic seems our Princess as required —
But something made to suit with Time and
place,
A Gothic ruin and a Grecian house,
A talk of college and of ladies' rights,
A feudal knight in silken masquerade,
And, yonder, shrieks and strange
experiments
For which the good Sir Ralph had burnt
them all —
This *were* a medley! we should have him
back
Who told the 'Winter's tale' to do it for us.
No matter: we will say whatever comes.
And let the ladies sing us, if they will,
From time to time, some ballad or a song
To give us breathing-space.'
So I began,
And the rest follow'd: and the women sang
Between the rougher voices of the men,
Like linnets in the pauses of the wind:
And here I give the story and the songs.

I

A Prince I was, blue-eyed, and fair in face,
Of temper amorous as the first of May,
With lengths of yellow ringlets, like a girl,
For on my cradle shone the Northern star.

There lived an ancient legend in our house.
Some sorcerer, whom a far-off grandsire burnt
Because he cast no shadow, had foretold,
Dying, that none of all our blood should know
The shadow from the substance, and that one
Should come to fight with shadows and to fall.
For so, my mother said, the story ran.
And, truly, waking dreams were, more or less,
An old and strange affection of the house.
Myself too had weird seizures, Heaven knows what:
On a sudden in the midst of men and day,
And while I walk'd and talk'd as heretofore,
I seem'd to move among a world of ghosts,
And feel myself the shadow of a dream.
Our great court-Galen poised his gilt-head cane,

And paw'd his beard, and mutter'd
'catalepsy.'
My mother pitying made a thousand
prayers;
My mother was as mild as any saint,
Half-canonized by all that look'd on her,
So gracious was her tact and tenderness:
But my good father thought a king a king;
He cared not for the affection of the
house;
He held his sceptre like a pedant's wand
To lash offence, and with long arms and
hands
Reach'd out, and pick'd offenders from the
mass
For judgement.
Now it chanced that I had been,
While life was yet in bud and blade,
betroth'd
To one, a neighbouring Princess: she to me
Was proxy-wedded with a bootless calf
At eight years old; and still from time to time
Came murmurs of her beauty from the
South,
And of her brethren, youths of puissance;
And still I wore her picture by my heart,
And one dark tress; and all around them
both
Sweet thoughts would swarm as bees about
their queen.

But when the days drew nigh that I should
wed,
My father sent ambassadors with furs
And jewels, gifts, to fetch her: these brought
back
A present, a great labour of the loom
And therewithal an answer vague as wind:
Besides, they saw the king; he took the gifts;
He said there was a compact; that was true:
But then she had a will; was he to blame?
And maiden fancies; loved to live alone
Among her women; certain, would not wed.

That morning in the presence room I
stood
With Cyril and with Florian, my two
friends:
The first, a gentleman of broken means
(His father's fault) but given to starts and
bursts
Of revel; and the last, my other heart,
And almost my half-self, for still we moved
Together, twinn'd as horse's ear and eye.

Now, while they spake, I saw my father's
face
Grow long and troubled like a rising moon,
Inflamed with wrath: he started on his feet,
Tore the king's letter, snow'd it down,
and rent

The wonder of the loom thro' warp and
woof
From skirt to skirt; and at the last he sware
That he would send a hundred thousand
men,
And bring her in a whirlwind: then he
chew'd
The thrice-turn'd cud of wrath, and cook'd
his spleen,
Communing with his captains of the war.

At last I spoke. 'My father, let me go.
It cannot be but some gross error lies
In this report, this answer of a king,
Whom all men rate as kind and hospitable:
Or, maybe, I myself, my bride once seen,
Whate'er my grief to find her less than
fame,
May rue the bargain made.' And Florian
said:
'I have a sister at the foreign court,
Who moves about the Princess; she,
you know,
Who wedded with a nobleman from thence:
He, dying lately, left her, as I hear,
The lady of three castles in that land:
Thro' her this matter might be sifted clean.
And Cyril whisper'd: 'Take me with you too.'
Then laughing 'what, if these weird seizures
come

Upon you in those lands, and no one near
To point you out the shadow from the truth!
Take me: I'll serve you better in a strait;
I grate on rusty hinges here:' but 'No!'
Roar'd the rough king, 'you shall not; we ourself
Will crush her pretty maiden fancies dead
In iron gauntlets: break the council up.'

But when the council broke, I rose and past
Thro' the wild woods that hung about the town;
Found a still place, and pluck'd her likeness out;
Laid it on flowers, and watch'd it lying bathed
In the green gleam of dewy-tassell'd trees:
What were those fancies? wherefore break her troth?
Proud look'd the lips: but while I meditated
A wind arose and rush'd upon the South,
And shook the songs, the whispers, and the shrieks
Of the wild woods together; and a Voice
Went with it, 'Follow, follow, thou shalt win.'
Then, ere the silver sickle of that month
Became her golden shield, I stole from court
With Cyril and with Florian, unperceived,

Cat-footed thro' the town and half in dread
To hear my father's clamour at our backs
With Ho! from some bay-window shake the
night;
But all was quiet: from the basnon'd walls
Like threaded spiders, one by one, we dropt,
And flying reach'd the frontier:
then we crost
To a livelier land; and so by tilth and grange,
And vines, and blowing bosks of wilderness.
We gain'd the mother-city thick with towers,
And in the imperial palace found the king.

His name was Gama; crack'd and small
his voice
But bland the smile that like a wrinkling
wind
On glassy water drove his cheek in lines;
A little dry old man, without a star,
Not like a king: three days he feasted us,
And on the fourth I spake of why we came,
And my betroth'd. 'You do us, Prince,'
he said,
Airing a snowy hand and signet gem,
'All honour. We remember love ourselves
In our sweet youth: there did a compact pass
Long summers back, a kind of ceremony —
I think the year in which our olives fail'd.
I would you had her, Prince, with all
my heart,

With my full heart: but there were widows here,
Two widows, Lady Psyche, Lady Blanche;
They fed her theories, in and out of place
Maintaining that with equal husbandry
The woman were an equal to the man.
They harp'd on this; with this our banquets rang;
Our dances broke and buzz'd in knots of talk;
Nothing but this; my very ears were hot
To hear them: knowledge, so my daughter held,
Was all in all: they had but been, she thought,
As children; they must lose the child, assume
The woman: then, Sir, awful odes she wrote,
Too awful, sure, for what they treated of,
But all she is and does is awful; odes
About this losing of the child; and rhymes
And dismal lyrics, prophesying change
Beyond all reason: these the women sang;
And they that know such things —
I sought but peace;
No critic I — would call them masterpieces:
They master'd me. At last she begg'd a boon,
A certain summer-palace which I have
Hard by your father's frontier: I said no,

Yet being an easy man, gave it: and there,
All wild to found an University
For maidens, on the spur she fled; and more
We know not, — only this: they see no men
Not ev'n her brother Arac, nor the twins
Her brethren, tho' they love her,
    look upon her
As on a kind of paragon; and I
(Pardon me saying it) were much loath to
    breed
Dispute betwixt myself and mine: but since
(And I confess with right) you think me
    bound
In some sort, I can give you letters to her;
And yet, to speak the truth, I rate your
    chance
Almost at naked nothing.'
                    Thus the king;
And I, tho' nettled that he seem'd to slur
With garrulous ease and oily courtesies
Our formal compact, yet, not less (all frets
But chafing me on fire to find my bride)
Went forth again with both my friends.
    We rode
Many a long league back to the North.
    At last
From hills, that look'd across a land
    of hope,
We dropt with evening on a rustic town
Set in a gleaming river's crescent-curve,

Close at the boundary of the liberties;
There, enter'd an old hostel,
    call'd mine host
To council, plied him with his richest wines,
And show'd the late-writ letters of the king.

He with a long low sibilation, stared
As blank as death in marble; then exclaim'd
Averring it was clear against all rules
For any man to go: but as his brain
Began to mellow, 'If the king,' he said,
'Had given us letters, was he bound to
    speak?
The king would bear him out;' and at the
    last —
The summer of the vine in all his veins —
'No doubt that we might make it worth his
    while
She once had past that way; he heard her
    speak
She scared him; life! he never saw the like;
She look'd as grand as doomsday and as
    grave:
And he, he reverenced his liege-lady there;
He always made a point to post with mares;
His daughter and his housemaid were the
    boys:
The land, he understood, for miles about
Was till'd by women; all the swine were
    sows,

And all the dogs' —
But while he jested thus,
A thought flash'd thro' me which I clothed in act,
Remembering how we three presented Maid,
Or Nymph, or Goddess, at high tide of feast,
In masque or pageant at my father's court,
We sent mine host to purchase female gear;
He brought it, and himself, a sight to shake
The midriff of despair with laughter, holp
To lace us up, till, each, in maiden plumes
We rustled: him we gave a costly bribe
To guerdon silence, mounted our good steeds,
And boldly ventured on the liberties.

We follow'd up the river as we rode,
And rode till midnight when the college lights
Began to glitter firefly-like in copse
And linden alley: then we past an arch,
Whereon a woman-statue rose with wings
From four wing'd horses dark against the stars;
And some inscription ran along the front,
But deep in shadow: further on we gain'd
A little street half garden and half house;
But scarce could hear each other speak for noise

Of clocks and chimes, like silver hammers
falling
On silver anvils, and the splash and stir
Of fountains spouted up and showering
down
In meshes of the jasmine and the rose:
And all about us peal'd the nightingale,
Rapt in her song, and careless of the
snare.

There stood a bust of Pallas for a sign,
By two sphere lamps blazon'd like Heaven
and Earth
With constellation and with continent,
Above an entry: riding in, we call'd;
A plump-arm'd Ostleress and a stable wench
Came running at the call, and help'd us
down.
Then stept a buxom hostess forth,
and sail'd,
Full-blown, before us into rooms which
gave
Upon a pillar'd porch, the bases lost
In laurel: her we ask'd of that and this
And who were tutors. 'Lady Blanche'
she said,
'And Lady Psyche.' 'Which was prettiest
Best-natured?' 'Lady Psyche.' 'Hers are we,'
One voice, we cried; and I sat down and
wrote

In such a hand as when a field of corn
Bows all its ears before the roaring East;

'Three ladies of the Northern empire pray
Your Highness would enroll them with your
    own,
As Lady Psyche's pupils.'
                    This I seal'd:
The seal was Cupid bent above a scroll,
And o'er his head Uranian Venus hung,
And raised the blinding bandage from his
    eyes:
I gave the letter to be sent with dawn;
And then to bed, where half in doze I seem'd
To float about a glimmering night, and
    watch
A full sea glazed with muffled moonlight,
    swell
On some dark shore just seen that it was
    rich.

*

As thro' the land at eve we went,
  And pluck'd the ripen'd ears,
We fell out, my wife and I
O we fell out I know not why,
  And kiss'd again with tears.
And blessings on the falling out
  That all the more endears,

When we fall out with those we love
And kiss again with tears!
For when we came where lies the child
We lost in other years,
There above the little grave,
O there above the little grave,
We kiss'd again with tears.

II

At break of day the College Portress came:
She brought us Academic silks, in hue
The lilac, with a silken hood to each,
And zoned with gold; and now when these were on,
And we as rich as moths from dusk cocoons,
She, curtseying her obeisance, let us know
The Princess Ida waited: out we paced,
I first, and following thro' the porch that sang
All round with laurel, issued in a court
Compact with lucid marbles, boss'd with lengths
Of classic frieze, with ample awnings gay
Betwixt the pillars, and with great urns of flowers.
The Muses and the Graces, group'd in threes,
Enring'd a billowing fountain in the midst;

And here and there on lattice edges lay
Or book or lute; but hastily we past,
And up a flight of stairs into the hall.

There at a board by tome and paper sat,
With two tame leopards couch'd beside her throne,
All beauty compass'd in a female form,
The Princess; liker to the inhabitant
Of some clear planet close upon the Sun,
Than our man's earth; such eyes were in her head,
And so much grace and power, breathing down
From over her arch'd brows, with every turn
Lived thro' her to the tips of her long hands,
And to her feet. She rose her height, and said:

'We give you welcome: not without redound
Of use and glory to yourselves ye come,
The first-fruits of the stranger: aftertime,
And that full voice which circles round the grave,
Will rank you nobly, mingled up with me.
What! are the ladies of your land so tall?'
'We of the court' said Cyril. 'From the court'
She answer'd, 'then ye know the Prince?' and he:

'The climax of his age! as tho' there were
One rose in all the world, your Highness
    that,
He worships your ideal:' she replied:
'We scarcely thought in our own hall to hear
This barren verbiage, current among men,
Light coin, the tinsel clink of compliment.
Your flight from out your bookless wilds
    would seem
As arguing love of knowledge and of power;
Your language proves you still the child.
    Indeed,
We dream not of him: when we set our hand
To this great work, we purposed with ourself
Never to wed. You likewise will do well,
Ladies, in entering here, to cast and fling
The tricks, which make us toys of men,
    that so,
Some future time, if so indeed you will,
You may with those self-styled our lords ally
Your fortunes, justlier balanced,
    scale with scale.'

At those high words, we conscious of
    ourselves,
Perused the matting; then an officer
Rose up, and read the statutes,
    such as these:
Not for three years to correspond
    with home;

Not for three years to cross the liberties;
Not for three years to speak with any men;
And many more, which hastily subscribed,
We enter'd on the boards: and 'Now'
she cried,
'Ye are green wood, see ye warp not.
Look, our hall!
Our statues! — not of those that men desire,
Sleek Odalisques, or oracles of mode
Nor stunted squaws of West or East; but she
That taught the Sabine how to rule and she
The foundress of the Babylonian wail,
The Carian Artemisia strong in war,
The Rhodope, that built the pyramid,
Clelia, Cornelia, with the Palmyrene
That fought Aurelian, and the Roman
brows
Of Agrippina. Dwell with these, and lose
Convention, since to look on noble forms
Makes noble thro' the sensuous organism
That which is higher. O lift your natures up:
Embrace our aims: work out your freedom.
Girls,
Knowledge is now no more a fountain
seal'd:
Drink deep, until the habits of the slave,
The sins of emptiness, gossip and spite
And slander, die. Better not be at all
Than not be noble. Leave us: you may go:
To-day the Lady Psyche will harangue

The fresh arrivals of the week before;
For they press in from all the provinces,
And fill the hive.'
She spoke, and bowing waved
Dismissal: back again we crost the court
To Lady Psyche's: as we enter'd in,
There sat along the forms, like morning
doves
That sun their milky bosoms on the thatch,
A patient range of pupils; she herself
Erect behind a desk of satin-wood,
A quick brunette, well-moulded,
falcon-eyed,
And on the hither side, or so she look'd,
Of twenty summers. At her left, a child,
In shining draperies, headed like a star,
Her maiden babe, a double April old,
Aglaïa slept. We sat: the Lady glanced:
Then Florian, but no livelier than the dame
That whisper'd 'Asses' ears' among the sedge,
'My sister.' 'Comely, too, by all that's fair,'
Said Cyril. 'O hush, hush!' and she began.

'This world was once a fluid haze of
light,
Till toward the centre set the starry tides,
And eddied into suns, that wheeling cast
The planets: then the monster,
then the man;
Tattoo'd or woaded, winter-clad in skins,

Raw from the prime, and crushing down his
mate;
As yet we find in barbarous isles, and here
Among the lowest.'
Thereupon she took
A bird's-eye-view of all the ungracious past;
Glanced at the legendary Amazon
As emblematic of a nobler age;
Appraised the Lycian custom,
spoke of those
That lay at wine with Lar and Lucumo;
Ran down the Persian, Grecian,
Roman lines
Of empire, and the woman's state in each,
How far from just; till warming with her
theme
She fulmined out her scorn of laws Salique
And little-footed China, touch'd on
Mahomet
With much contempt, and came to chivalry:
When some respect, however slight, was
paid
To woman, superstition all awry:
However then commenced the dawn:
a beam
Had slanted forward, falling in a land
Of promise; fruit would follow.
Deep, indeed,
Their debt of thanks to her who first had
dared

To leap the rotten pales of prejudice,
Disyoke their necks from custom, and assert
None lordlier than themselves but that
which made
Woman and man. She had founded;
they must build.
Here might they learn whatever men were
taught:
Let them not fear: some said their heads
were less:
Some men's were small; not they the least of
men;
For often fineness compensated size:
Besides the brain was like the hand,
and grew
With using; thence the man's, if more was
more;
He took advantage of his strength to be
First in the field: some ages had been lost;
But woman ripen'd earlier, and her life
Was longer; and albeit their glorious names
Were fewer, scatter'd stars, yet since in truth
The highest is the measure of the man,
And not the Kaffir, Hottentot, Malay,
Nor those horn-handed breakers of the
glebe,
But Homer, Plato, Verulam; even so
With woman: and in arts of government
Elizabeth and others; arts of war
The peasant Joan and others; arts of grace

Sappho and others vied with any man:
And, last not least, she who had left her
place
And bow'd her state to them, that they
might grow
To use and power on this Oasis, lapt
In the arms of leisure, sacred from the
blight
Of ancient influence and scorn.
At last
She rose upon a wind of prophecy
Dilating on the future; 'everywhere
Two heads in council, two beside the hearth
Two in the tangled business of the world,
Two in the liberal offices of life,
Two plummets dropt for one to sound the
abyss
Of science, and the secrets of the mind:
Musician, painter, sculptor, critic, more:
And everywhere the broad and bounteous
Earth
Should bear a double growth of those rare
souls,
Poets, whose thoughts enrich the blood of
the world.'

She ended here, and beckon'd us: the rest
Parted; and, glowing full-faced welcome,
she
Began to address us, and was moving on

In gratulation, till as when a boat
Tacks, and the slacken'd sail flaps,
all her voice
Faltering and fluttering in her throat,
she cried,
'My brother!' 'Well, my sister.' 'O,' she said,
'What do you here? and in this dress?
and these?
Why who are these? a wolf within the fold!
A pack of wolves! the Lord be gracious
to me!
A plot, a plot, a plot, to ruin all!'
'No plot, no plot,' he answer'd. 'Wretched
boy,
How saw you not the inscription on the
gate,
LET NO MAN ENTER IN ON PAIN OF
DEATH?'
'And if I had,' he answer'd, 'who could think
The softer Adams of your Academe,
O sister,
Sirens tho' they be, were such
As chanted on the blanching bones of men?'
'But you will find it otherwise' she said.
'You jest: ill jesting with edge-tools! my vow
Binds me to speak, and O that iron will,
That axelike edge unrurnable, our Head,
The Princess.' 'Well then, Psyche,
take my life,
And nail me like a weasel on a grange

For warning: bury me beside the gate,
And cut this epitaph above my bones;
Here lies a brother by a sister slain
All for the common good of womankind.'
'Let me die too,' said Cyril, 'having seen
And heard the Lady Psyche.'
I struck in:
'Albeit so mask'd, Madam, I love the truth;
Receive it; and in me behold the Prince
Your countryman, affianced years ago
To the Lady Ida: here, for here she was,
And thus (what other way was left) I came.'
'O Sir, O Prince, I have no country; none;
If any, this; but none. Whate'er I was
Disrooted, what I am is grafted here.
Affianced, Sir? love-whispers may not breathe
Within this vestal limit, and how should I,
Who am not mine, say, live: the thunderbolt
Hangs silent; out prepare: I speak; it falls.'
'Yet pause,' I said: 'for that inscription there,
I think no more of deadly lurks therein,
Than in a clapper clapping in a garth,
To scare the fowl from fruit: if more there be,
If more and acted on, what follows? war;
Your own work marr'd: for this your Academe,
Whichever side be Victor, in the halloo

Will topple to the trumpet down, and pass
With all fair theories only made to gild
A stormless summer.' 'Let the Princess judge
Of that' she said: 'farewell, Sir — and to you.
I shudder at the sequel, but I go.'

'Are you that Lady Psyche,' I rejoin'd,
'The fifth in line from that old Florian,
Yet hangs his portrait in my father's hall
(The gaunt old Baron with his beetle brow
Sun-shaded in the heat of dusty fights)
As he bestrode my Grandsire, when he fell,
And all else fled? we point to it, and we say,
The loyal warmth of Florian is not cold,
But branches current yet in kindred veins.'
'Are you that Psyche,' Florian added, 'she
With whom I sang about the morning hills,
Flung ball, flew kite, and raced the purple fly,
And snared the squirrel of the glen? are you
That Psyche, wont to bind my throbbing brow,
To smoothe my pillow, mix the foaming draught
Of fever, tell me pleasant tales, and read
My sickness down to happy dreams? are you
That brother-sister Psyche, both in one?
You were that Psyche, but what are you now?'

'You are that Psyche,' Cyril said, 'for whom
I would be that for ever which I seem,
Woman, if I might sit beside your feet,
And glean your scatter'd sapience.'
Then once more
'Are you that Lady Psyche,' I began,
'That on her bridal morn before she past
From all her old companions, when the king
Kiss'd her pale cheek, declared that ancient
ties
Would still be dear beyond the southern
hills;
That were there any of our people there
In want or peril, there was one to hear
And help them? look! for such are these
and I.'
'Are you that Psyche,' Florian ask'd,
'to whom,
In gentler days, your arrow-wounded fawn
Came flying while you sat beside the well?
The creature laid his muzzle on your lap,
And sobb'd, and you sobb'd with it, and the
blood
Was sprinkled on your kirtle, and you wept.
That was fawn's blood, not brother's,
yet you wept.
O by the bright head of my little niece,
You were that Psyche, and what are you
now?
'You are that Psyche,' Cyril said again,

'The mother of the sweetest little maid
That ever crow'd for kisses.'
'Out upon it!'
She answer'd, 'peace! and why should I not play
The Spartan Mother with emotion, be
The Lucius Junius Brutus of my kind?
Him you call great: he for the common weal,
The fading politics of mortal Rome,
As I might slay this child, if good need were,
Slew both his sons: and I, shall I, on whom
The secular emancipation turns
Of half this world, be swerved from right to save
A prince, a brother? a little will I yield.
Best so, perchance, for us, and well for you.
O hard, when love and duty clash! I fear
My conscience will not count me fleckless; yet —
Hear my conditions: promise (otherwise
You perish) as you came, to slip away,
To-day, to-morrow, soon: it shall be said,
These women were too barbarous, would not learn
They fled, who might have shamed us: promise, all.

What could we else, we promised each; and she,

Like some wild creature newly-caged,
commenced
A to-and-fro, so pacing till she paused
By Florian; holding out her lily arms
Took both his hands, and smiling faintly
said:
'I knew you at the first: tho' you have grown
You scarce have alter'd: I am sad and glad
To see you, Florian. I give thee to death
My brother! it was duty spoke, not I.
My needful seeming harshness, pardon it.
Our mother, is she well?'
With that she kiss'd
His forehead, then, a moment after, clung
About him, and betwixt them blossom'd up
From out a common vein of memory
Sweet household talk, and phrases of the
hearth,
And far allusion, till the gracious dews
Began to glisten and to fall: and while
They stood, so rapt, we gazing,
came a voice,
'I brought a message here from Lady
Blanche.'
Back started she, and turning round we saw
The Lady Blanche's daughter where she
stood,
Melissa, with her hand upon the lock,
A rosy blonde, and in a college gown,
That clad her like an April daffodilly

(Her mother's colour) with her lips apart,
And all her thoughts as fair within her eyes,
As bottom agates seen to wave and float
In crystal currents of clear morning seas.

So stood that same fair creature at the door.
Then Lady Psyche, 'Ah — Melissa — you!
You heard us?' and Melissa, 'O pardon me!
I heard, I could not help it, did not wish:
But, dearest Lady, pray you fear me not,
Nor think I bear that heart within my breast,
To give three gallant gentlemen to death.'
'I trust you,' said the other, 'for we two
Were always friends, none closer, elm and vine:
But yet your mother's jealous temperament —
Let not your prudence, dearest, drowse, or prove
The Danaid of a leaky vase, for fear
This whole foundation ruin, and I lose
My honour, these their lives.' 'Ah, fear me not'
Replied Melissa; 'no — I would not tell,
No, not for all Aspasia's cleverness,
No, not to answer, Madam, all those hard things
That Sheba came to ask of Solomon.'
'Be it so' the other, 'that we still may lead

The new light up, and culminate in
peace,
For Solomon may come to Sheba yet.'
Said Cyril, 'Madam, he the wisest man
Feasted the woman wisest then, in halls
Of Lebanonian cedar: nor should you
(Tho', madam, *you* should answer,
we would ask)
Less welcome find among us, if you came
Among us, debtors for our lives to you,
Myself for something more.' He said not
what,
But 'Thanks,' she answer'd 'Go: we have
been too long
Together: keep your hoods about the face;
They do so that affect abstraction here.
Speak little; mix not with the rest; and hold
Your promise: all, I trust, may yet be well.'

We turn'd to go, but Cyril took the child,
And held her round the knees against his
waist,
And blew the swoll'n cheek of a trumpeter,
While Psyche watch'd them, smiling,
and the child
Push'd her flat hand against his face and
laugh'd
And thus our conference closed.
And then we stroll'd
For half the day thro' stately theatres

Bench'd crescent-wise. In each we sat,
we heard
The grave Professor. On the lecture slate
The circle rounded under female hands
With flawless demonstration: follow'd then
A classic lecture, rich in sentiment,
With scraps of thundrous Epic lilted out
By violet-hooded Doctors, elegies
And quoted odes, and jewels
five-words-long
That on the stretch'd forefinger of all Time
Sparkle for ever: then we dipt in all
That treats of whatsoever is, the state
The total chronicles of man, the mind,
The morals, something of the frame,
the rock,
The star, the bird, the fish, the shell,
the flower,
Electric, chemic laws, and all the rest,
And whatsoever can be taught and known;
Till like three horses that have broken fence,
And glutted all night long breast-deep in
corn,
We issued gorged with knowledge,
and I spoke:
'Why, Sirs, they do all this as well as we.'
'They hunt old trails' said Cyril 'very well;
But when did woman ever yet invent?'
'Ungracious!' answer'd Florian, 'have you
learnt

No more from Psyche's lecture, you that talk'd
The trash that made me sick, and almost sad?'
'O trash' he said, 'but with a kernel in it.
Should I not call her wise, who made me wise?
And learnt? I learnt more from her in a flash,
Than if my brainpan were an empty hull,
And every Muse tumbled a science in.
A thousand hearts lie fallow in these halls,
And round these halls a thousand baby loves
Fly twanging headless arrows at the hearts
Whence follows many a vacant pang; but O
With me, Sir, enter'd in the bigger boy,
The Head of all the golden-shafted firm,
The long-limb'd lad that had a Psyche too;
He cleft me thro' the stomacher; and now
What think you of it, Florian? do I chase
The substance or the shadow? will it hold?
I have no sorcerer's malison on me,
No ghostly hauntings like his Highness. I
Flatter myself that always everywhere
I know the substance when I see it. Well,
Are castles shadows? Three of them? Is she
The sweet proprietress a shadow? If not,
Shall those three castles patch my tatter'd coat?

For dear are those three castles to my wants,
And dear is sister Psyche to my heart,
And two dear things are one of double
worth,
And much I might have said, but that my
zone
Unmann'd me: then the Doctors! O to hear
The Doctors! O to watch the thirsty plants
Imbibing! once or twice I thought to roar,
To break my chain, to shake my mane: but
thou,
Modulate me, Soul of mincing mimicry!
Make liquid treble of that bassoon, my
throat;
Abase those eyes that ever loved to meet
Star-sisters answering under crescent
brows;
Abate the stride, which speaks of man,
and loose
A flying charm of blushes o'er this cheek,
Where they like swallows coming out of
time
Will wonder why they came: but hark the
bell
For dinner, let us go!'
And in we stream'd
Among the columns, pacing staid and still
By twos and threes, till all from end to end
With beauties every shade of brown and fair
In colours gayer than the morning mist,

The long hall glitter'd like a bed of flowers.
How might a man not wander from his wits
Pierced thro' with eyes, but that I kept mine
own
Intent on her, who rapt in glorious dreams,
The second-sight of some Astraean age,
Sat compass'd with professors: they,
the while,
Discuss'd a doubt and tost it to and fro:
A clamour thicken'd, mixt with inmost
terms
Of art and science: Lady Blanche alone
Of faded form and haughtiest lineaments,
With all her autumn tresses falsely brown,
Shot sidelong daggers at us, a tiger-cat
In act to spring.
At last a solemn grace
Concluded, and we sought the gardens:
there
One walk'd reciting by herself, and one
In this hand held a volume as to read,
And smoothed a petted peacock down with
that:
Some to a low song oar'd a shallop by,
Or under arches of the marble bridge
Hung, shadow'd from the heat:
some hid and sought
In the orange thickets: others tost a ball
Above the fountain-jets, and back again
With laughter: others lay about the lawns,

Of the older sort, and murmur'd that their
May
Was passing: what was learning unto
them?
They wish'd to marry; they could rule a
house
Men hated learned women: but we three
Sat muffled like the Fates; and often came
Melissa hitting all we saw with shafts
Of gentle satire, kin to charity,
That harm'd not: then day droopt;
the chapel bells
Call'd us: we left the walks; we mixt with
those
Six hundred maidens clad in purest white,
Before two streams of light from wall to
wall,
While the great organ almost burst his
pipes,
Groaning for power, and rolling thro' the
court
A long melodious thunder to the sound
Of solemn psalms, and silver litanies
The work of Ida, to call down from Heaven
A blessing on her labours for the world.

⋆

Sweet and low, sweet and low,
Wind of the western sea,

Low, low, breathe and blow,
Wind of the western sea!
Over the rolling waters go
Come from the dying moon, and blow,
Blow him again to me;
While my little one, while my pretty one,
sleeps.

Sleep and rest, sleep and rest,
Father will come to thee soon;
Rest, rest, on mother's breast,
Father will come to thee soon;
Father will come to his babe in the nest,
Silver sails all out of the west
Under the silver moon:
Sleep, my little one, sleep, my pretty one,
sleep.

III

Morn in the white wake of the morning star
Came furrowing all the orient into gold.
We rose, and each by other drest with care
Descended to the court that lay three parts
In shadow, but the Muses' heads were
touch'd
Above the darkness from their native East.

There while we stood beside the fount,
and watch'd

Or seem'd to watch the dancing bubble, approach'd
Melissa, tinged with wan from lack of sleep,
Or grief, and glowing round her dewy eyes
The circled Iris of a night of tears;
'And fly,' she cried, 'O fly, while yet you may!
My mother knows:' and when I ask'd her 'how'
'My fault' she wept 'my fault! and yet not mine;
Yet mine in part. O hear me, pardon me.
My mother, 'tis her wont from night to night
To rail at Lady Psyche and her side.
She says the Princess should have been the Head,
Herself and Lady Psyche the two arms;
And so it was agreed when first they came;
But Lady Psyche was the right hand now,
And she the left, or not, or seldom used;
Hers more than half the students, all the love.
And so last night she fell to canvass you:
Her countrywomen! she did not envy her.
"Who ever saw such wild barbarians?
Girls? — more like men!" and at these words the snake,
My secret, seem'd to stir within my breast;
And oh, Sirs, could I help it, but my cheek

Began to burn and burn, and her lynx eye
To fix and make me hotter, till she laugh'd:
"O marvellously modest maiden, you!
Men! girls, like men! why, if they had been men
You need not set your thoughts in rubric thus
For wholesale comment." Pardon, I am shamed
That I must needs repeat for my excuse
What looks so little graceful: "men" (for still
My mother went revolving on the word)
"And so they are, — very like men indeed —
And with that woman closeted for hours!"
Then came these dreadful words out one by one,
"Why — these — are — men:" I shudder'd: "and you know it."
"O ask me nothing," I said: "And she knows too,
And she conceals it." So my mother clutch'd
The truth at once, but with no word from me;
And now thus early risen she goes to inform
The Princess: Lady Psyche will be crush'd;
But you may yet be saved, and therefore fly:
But heal me with your pardon ere you go.'

'What pardon, sweet Melissa, for a blush?'

Said Cyril: 'Pale one, blush again: than wear
Those lilies, better blush our lives away.
Yet let us breathe for one hour more in
Heaven'
He added, 'lest some classic Angel speak
In scorn of us, "They mounted,
Ganymedes,
To tumble, Vulcans, on the second morn."
But I will melt this marble into wax
To yield us farther furlough:' and he went.

Melissa shook her doubtful curls, and
thought
He scarce would prosper. 'Tell us,' Florian
ask'd,
'How grew this feud betwixt the right and
left,'
'O long ago,' she said, 'betwixt these two
Division smoulders hidden; 'tis my mother,
Too jealous, often fretful as the wind
Pent in a crevice: much I bear with her:
I never knew my father, but she says
(God help her) she was wedded to a fool;
And still she rail'd against the state of
things.
She had the care of Lady Ida's youth,
And from the Queen's decease she brought
her up.
But when your sister came she won the
heart

Of Ida: they were still together, grew
(For so they said themselves) inosculated;
Consonant chords that shiver to one note;
One mind in all things: yet my mother still
Affirms your Psyche thieved her theories,
And angled with them for her pupil's love:
She calls her plagiarist; I know not what:
But I must go: I dare not tarry' and light,
As flies the shadow of a bird, she fled.

Then murmur'd Florian gazing after her:
'An open-hearted maiden, true and pure.
If I could love, why this were she: how pretty
Her blushing was, and how she blush'd
again,
As if to close with Cyril's random wish:
Not like your Princess cramm'd with erring
pride,
Nor like poor Psyche whom she drags in
tow.'

'The crane,' I said, 'may chatter of the
crane,
The dove may murmur of the dove, but I
An eagle clang an eagle to the sphere.
My princess, O my princess! true she errs,
But in her own grand way: being herself
Three times more noble than three score of
men,
She sees herself in every woman else,

And so she wears her error like a crown
To blind the truth and me: for her, and her,
Hebes are they to hand ambrosia mix
The nectar; but — ah she — whene'er she moves
The Samian Here rises and she speaks
A Memnon smitten with the morning Sun.'

So saying from the court we paced, and gain'd
The terrace ranged along the Northern front,
And leaning there on those balusters, high
Above the empurpled champaign, drank the gale
That blown about the foliage underneath,
And sated with the innumerable rose,
Beat balm upon our eyelids. Hither came
Cyril, and yawning 'O hard task,' he cried;
'No fighting shadows here! I forced a way
Thro' solid opposition crabb'd and gnarl'd.
Better to clear prime forests, heave and thump
A league of street in summer solstice down,
Than hammer at this reverend gentlewoman.
I knock'd and, bidden, enter'd; found her there
At point to move, and settled in her eyes
The green malignant light of coming storm.

Sir, I was courteous, every phrase well-oil'd,
As man's could be; yet maiden-meek I pray'd
Concealment:she demanded who we were,
And why we came? I fabled nothing fair,
But, your example pilot, told her all.
Up went the hush'd amaze of hand and eye.
But when I dwelt upon your old affiance,
She answer'd sharply that I talk'd astray.
I urged the fierce inscription on the gate,
And our three lives. True — we had limed ourselves
With open eyes, and we must take the chance.
But such extremes, I told her, well might harm
The woman's cause. "Not more than now," she said
"So puddled as it is with favouritism."
I tried the mother's heart. Shame might befall
Melissa, knowing, saying not she knew:
Her answer was "Leave me to deal with that."
I spoke of war to come and many deaths,
And she replied, her duty was to speak,
And duty duty, clear of consequences.
I grew discouraged, Sir; but since I knew
No rock so hard but that a little wave
May beat admission in a thousand years,
I recommenced; "Decide not ere you pause.

I find you here but in the second place,
Some say the third — the authentic
foundress you.
I offer boldly: we will seat you highest:
Wink at our advent: help my prince to gain
His rightful bride, and here I promise you
Some palace in our land, where you shall
reign
The head and heart of all our fair she-world,
And your great name flow on with
broadening time
For ever." Well, she balanced this a little,
And told me she would answer us to-day
Meantime be mute: thus much, nor more I
gain'd.'
He ceasing, came a message from the
Head.
'That afternoon the Princess rode to take
The dip of certain strata to the North.
Would we go with her? we should find the
land
Worth seeing; and the river made a fall
Out yonder:' then she pointed on to where
A double hill ran up his furrowy forks
Beyond the thick-leaved platans of the vale.

Agreed to, this, the day fled on thro' all
Its range of duties to the appointed hour.
Then summon'd to the porch we went.
She stood

Among her maidens, higher by the head,
Her back against a pillar, her foot on one
Of those tame leopards. Kittenlike he roll'd
And paw'd about her sandal. I drew near;
I gazed. On a sudden my strange seizure
came
Upon me, the weird vision of our house:
The Princess Ida seem'd a hollow show,
Her gay-furr'd cats a painted fantasy,
Her college and her maidens, empty masks,
And I myself the shadow of a dream
For all things were and were not. Yet I felt
My heart beat thick with passion and with
awe;
Then from my breast the involuntary sigh
Brake, as she smote me with the light of eyes
That lent my knee desire to kneel,
and shook
My pulses, till to horse we got, and so
Went forth in long retinue following up
The river as it narrow'd to the hills.

I rode beside her and to me she said:
'O friend, we trust that you esteem'd us not
Too harsh to your companion yestermorn;
Unwillingly we spake.' 'No — not to her,'
I answer'd, 'but to one of whom we spake
Your Highness might have seem'd the thing
you say.'
'Again?' she cried, 'are you ambassadresses

From him to me? we give you, being strange,
A licence: speak, and let the topic die.'

I stammer'd that I knew him — could have wish'd —
'Our king expects — was there no precontract?
There is no truer-hearted — ah, you seem
All he prefigured, and he could not see
The bird of passage flying south but long'd
To follow: surely, if your Highness keep
Your purport, you will shock him ev'n to death.
Or baser courses, children of despair.'
'Poor boy,' she said, 'can he not read — no books?
Quoit, tennis, ball — no games? nor deals in that
Which men delight in, martial exercise?
To nurse a blind ideal like a girl;
Methinks he seems no better than a girl;
As girls were once, as we ourself have been:
We had our dreams; perhaps he mixt with them:
We touch on our dead self, nor shun to do it
Being other — since we learnt our meaning here,
To lift the woman's fall'n divinity
Upon an even pedestal with man.'

She paused, and added with a haughtier
smile
'And as to precontracts, we move,
my friend,
At no man's beck, but know ourself and
thee,
O Vashti, noble Vashti! Summon'd out
She kept her state, and left the drunken king
To brawl at Shushan underneath the palms.'

'Alas your Highness breathes full East,' I
said,
'On that which leans to you. I know the
Prince,
I prize his truth: and then how vast a work
To assail this grey preeminence of man!
You grant me licence; might I use it? think;
Ere half be done perchance your life may
fail;
Then comes the feebler heiress of your plan,
And takes and ruins all; and thus your pains
May only make that footprint upon sand
Which old-recurring waves of prejudice
Resmooth to nothing: might I dread that
you,
With only Fame for spouse and your great
deeds
For issue, yet may live in vain, and miss,
Meanwhile, what every woman counts her
due,

Love, children, happiness?'
And she exclaim'd
'Peace, you young savage of the Northern wild!
What! tho' your Prince's love were like a God's,
Have we not made ourself the sacrifice?
You are bold indeed: we are not talk'd to thus:
Yet will we say for children, would they grew
Like field-flowers everywhere! we like them well:
But children die; and let me tell you, girl,
Howe'er you babble, great deeds cannot die;
They with the sun and moon renew their light
For ever, blessing those that look on them.
Children — that men may pluck them from our hearts
Kill us with pity, break us with ourselves
O — children — there is nothing upon earth
More miserable than she that has a son
And sees him err: nor would we work for fame;
Tho' she perhaps might reap the applause of Great,
Who learns the one POU STO whence after-hands
May move the world, tho' she herself effect

But little: wherefore up and act, nor shrink
For fear our solid aim be dissipated
By frail successors. Would, indeed,
we had been,
In lieu of many mortal flies, a race
Of giants living, each, a thousand years,
That we might see our own work out,
and watch
The sandy footprint harden into stone.'

I answer'd nothing, doubtful in myself
If that strange Poet-princess with her grand
Imaginations might at all be won.
And she broke out interpreting my
thoughts:

'No doubt we seem a kind of monster to
you;
We are used to that: for women, up till this
Cramp'd under worse than South-sea-isle
taboo,
Dwarfs of the gynaeceum, fail so far
In high desire, they know not, cannot
guess
How much their welfare is a passion to us.
If we could give them surer, quicker
proof —
Oh if our end were less achievable
By slow approaches, than by single act
Of immolation, any phase of death,

We were as prompt to spring against the
pikes,
Or down the fiery gulf as talk of it,
To compass our dear sisters' liberties.'

She bow'd as if to veil a noble tear;
And up we came to where the river sloped
To plunge in cataract, shattering on black
blocks
A breadth of thunder. O'er it shook the
woods,
And danced the colour, and, below,
stuck out
The bones of some vast bulk that lived and
roar'd
Before man was. She gazed awhile and said,
'As these rude bones to us, are we to her
That will be.' 'Dare we dream of that,'
I ask'd,
'Which wrought us, as the workman and his
work
That practice betters?' 'How,' she cried,
'you love
The metaphysics! read and earn our prize,
A golden brooch: beneath an emerald plane
Sits Diotima, teaching him that died
Of hemlock; our devices wrought to the life,
She rapt upon her subject, he on her:
For there are schools for all.' 'And yet' I said
'Methinks I have not found among them all

One anatomic.' 'Nay, we thought of that,'
She answer'd, 'but it pleased us not: in truth
We shudder but to dream our maids should ape
Those monstrous males that carve the living hound,
And cram him with the fragments of the grave,
Or in the dark dissolving human heart,
And holy secrets of this microcosm,
Dabbling a shameless hand with shameful jest,
Encarnalize their spirits: yet we know
Knowledge is knowledge, and this matter hangs:
Howbeit ourself, foreseeing casualty,
Nor willing men should come among us, learnt,
For many weary moons before we came
This craft of healing, Were you sick, ourself
Would tend upon you. To your question now,
Which touches on the workman and his work.
Let there be light and there was light: 'tis so:
For was, and is, and will be, are but is;
And all creation is one act at once,
The birth of light: but we that are not all,

As parts, can see but parts, now this,
now that,
And live, perforce, from thought to thought,
and make
One act a phantom of succession: thus
Our weakness somehow shapes the shadow,
Time;
But in the shadow will we work, and mould
The woman to the fuller day.'
She spake
With kindled eyes: we rode a league beyond,
And, o'er a bridge of pinewood crossing,
came
On flowery levels underneath the crag,
Full of all beauty. 'O how sweet' I said
(For I was half-oblivious of my mask)
'To linger here with one that loved us.'
'Yea,'
She answer'd, 'or with fair philosophies
That lift the fancy; for indeed these fields
Are lovely, lovelier not the Elysian lawns,
Where paced the Demigods of old, and saw
The soft white vapour streak the crowned
towers
Built to the Sun:' then, turning to her
maids,
'Pitch our pavilion here upon the sward;
Lay out the viands.' At the word, they raised
A tent of satin, elaborately wrought
With fair Corinna's triumph; here she stood,

Engirt with many a florid maiden-cheek,
The woman-conqueror; woman-conquer'd
there
The bearded Victor of ten-thousand hymns,
And all the men mourn'd at his side:
but we
Set forth to climb; then, climbing,
Cyril kept
With Psyche, with Melissa Florian, I
With mine affianced. Many a little hand
Glanced like a touch of sunshine on the
rocks,
Many a light foot shone like a jewel set
In the dark crag: and then we turn'd,
we wound
About the cliffs, the copses, out and in,
Hammering and clinking, chattering stony
names
Of shale and hornblende, rag and trap and
tuff,
Amygdaloid and trachyte, till the Sun
Grew broader toward his death and fell,
and all
The rosy heights came out above the
lawns.

★

The splendour falls on castle walls
And snowy summits old in story:

The long light shakes across the lakes,
And the wild cataract leaps in glory.
Blow, bugle, blow, set the wild echoes flying,
Blow, bugle; answer, echoes, dying, dying, dying.

O hark, O hear! how thin and clear,
And thinner, clearer, farther going!
O sweet and far from cliff and scar
The horns of Elfland faintly blowing!
Blow, let we hear the purple glens replying:
Blow, bugle; answer, echoes, dying, dying, dying.

O love, they die in yon rich sky.
They faint on hill or field or river:
Our echoes roll from soul to soul,
And grow for ever and for ever.
Blow, bugle, blow, set the wild echoes flying,
And answer, echoes, answer, dying, dying, dying.

IV

'There sinks the nebulous star we call the Sun
If that hypothesis of theirs be sound'

Said Ida; 'let us down and rest;' and we
Down from the lean and wrinkled
    precipices
By every coppice-feather'd chasm and cleft
Dropt thro' the ambrosial gloom to where
    below
No bigger than a glow-worm shone the tent
Lamp-lit from the inner. Once she lean'd
    on me,
Descending; once or twice she lent her hand
And blissful palpitations in the blood,
Stirring a sudden transport rose and fell.
  But when we planted level feet, and dipt
Beneath the satin dome and enter'd in,
There leaning deep in broider'd down we
    sank
Our elbows: on a tripod in the midst
A fragrant flame rose, and before us glow'd:
Fruit, blossom, viand, amber wine,
    and gold.

  Then she, 'Let some one sing to us:
      lightlier move
The minutes fledged with music:' and a
    maid,
Of those beside her, smote her harp,
    and sang.

Tears, idle tears, I know not what they
    mean,

Tears from the depth of some divine despair
Rise in the heart, and gather to the eyes,
In looking on the happy Autumn-fields,
And thinking of the days that are no more.

Fresh as the first beam glittering on a sail,
That brings our friends up from the underworld,
Sad as the last which reddens over one
That sinks with all we love below the verge;
So sad, so fresh, the days that are no more.
Ah, sad and strange as in dark summer dawns
The earliest pipe of half-awaken'd birds
To dying ears, when unto dying eyes
The casement slowly grows a glimmering square
So sad, so strange, the days that are no more.

Dear as remember'd kisses after death,
And sweet as those by hopeless fancy feign'd
On lips that are for others; deep as love,
Deep as first love, and wild with all regret;
O Death in Life, the days that are no more.

She ended with such passion that the tear,
She sang of, shook and fell, an erring pearl

Lost in her bosom: but with some disdain
Answer'd the Princess, 'If indeed there haunt
About the mouldered lodges of the Past
So sweet a voice and vague, fatal to men,
Well needs it we should cram our ears with wool
And so pace by: but thine, are fancies hatch'd
In silken-folded idleness; nor is it
Wiser to weep a true occasion lost,
But trim our sails, and let old bygones be,
While down the streams that float us each and all
To the issue, goes, like glittering bergs of ice,
Throne after throne, and molten on the waste
Becomes a cloud: for all things serve their time
Toward that great year of equal mights and rights,
Nor would I fight with iron laws, in the end
Found golden: let the past be past; let be
Their cancell'd Babels: tho' the rough kex break
The starr'd mosaic, and the beard-blown goat
Hang on the shaft, and the wild figtree split
Their monstrous idols, care not while we hear

A trumpet in the distance pealing news
Of better, and Hope, a poising eagle, burns
Above the unrisen morrow:' then to me;
'Know you no song of your own land,'
she said,
'Not such as moans about the retrospect,
But deals with the other distance and the
hues
Of promise; not a death's-head at the wine.'

Then I remember'd one myself had
made,
What time I watch'd the swallow winging
south
From mine own land, part made long since,
and part
Now while I sang, and maidenlike as far
As I could ape their treble, did I sing.

O Swallow, Swallow, flying, flying South,
Fly to her, and fall upon her gilded eaves,
And tell her, tell her, what I tell to thee.

O tell her, Swallow, thou that knowest each,
That bright and fierce and fickle is the
South,
And dark and true and tender is the North.

O Swallow, Swallow, if I could follow,
and light

Upon her lattice, I would pipe and trill,
And cheep and twitter twenty million loves.

O were I thou that the might take me in,
And lay me on her bosom, and her heart
Would rock the snowy cradle till I died.

Why lingereth she to clothe her heart with
love,
Delaying as the tender ash delays
To clothe herself when all the woods are
green?
O tell her, Swallow, that thy brood is flown:
Say to her, I do but wanton in the South,
But in the North long since my nest is
made.

O tell her, brief is life but love is long
And brief the sun of summer in the North
And brief the moon of beauty in the South.

O Swallow, flying from the golden woods
Fly to her, and pipe and woo her, and make
her mine,
And tell her, tell her, that I follow thee.

I ceased, and all the ladies, each at each,
Like the Ithacensian suitors in old time,
Stared with great eyes, and laugh'd with
alien lips,

And knew not what they meant; for still my
voice
Rang false: but smiling 'Not for thee,'
she said,
'O Bulbul, any rose of Gulistan
Shall burst her veil: marsh-divers, rather
maid
Shall croak thee sister, or the meadow-crake
Grate her harsh kindred in the grass:
and this
A mere love-poem! O for such,
my friend
We hold them slight: they mind us of the
time
When we made bricks in Egypt. Knaves are
men,
That lute and flute fantastic tenderness,
And dress the victim to the offering up
And paint the gates of Hell with Paradise,
And play the slave to gain the tyranny.
Poor soul! I had a maid of honour once;
She wept her true eyes blind for such a one,
A rogue of canzonets and serenades.
I loved her. Peace be with her. She is dead.
So they blaspheme the muse! But great is
song
Used to great ends: ourself have often tried
Valkyrian hymns, or into rhythm have
dash'd
The passion of the prophetess; for song

Is duer unto freedom, force and growth
Of spirit than to junketing and love.
Love is it? Would this same mock-love,
and this
Mock-Hymen were laid up like winter bats,
Till all men grew to rate us at our worth,
Not vassals to be beat, nor pretty babes
To be dandled, no, but living wills,
and sphered
Whole in ourselves and owed to none.
Enough!
But now to leaven play with profit, you,
Know you no song, the true growth of your
soil,
That gives the manners of your
countrywomen?'

She spoke and turn'd her sumptuous bead
with eyes
Of shining expectation fixt on mine.
Then while I dragg'd my brains for such a
song,
Cyril, with whom the bell-mouth'd glass
had wrought,
Or master'd by the sense of sport, began
To troll a careless, careless tavern-catch
Of Moll and Meg, and strange experiences
Unmeet for ladies. Florian nodded at him,
I frowning; Psyche flush'd and wann'd and
shook;

The lilylike Melissa droop'd her brows
'Forbear,' the Princess cried; 'Forbear,
    Sir' I;
And heated thro' and thro' with wrath and
    love,
I smote him on the breast; he started up;
There rose a shriek as of a city sack'd;
Melissa clamour'd 'Flee the death;'
    'To horse,'
Said Ida; 'home! to horse!' and fled,
    as flies
A troop of snowy doves athwart the dusk,
When some one batters at the
    dovecote-doors,
Disorderly the women. Alone I stood
With Florian, cursing Cyril, vext at heart,
In the pavilion: there like parting hopes
I heard them passing from me: hoof by hoof,
And every hoof a knell to my desires,
Clang'd on the bridge; and then another
    shriek,
'The Head, the Head, the Princess,
    O the Head!'
For blind with rage she miss'd the plank,
    and roll'd
In the river. Out I sprang from glow to
    gloom:
There whirl'd her white robe like a
    blossom'd branch
Rapt to the horrible fall: a glance I gave,

No more; but woman-vested as I was
Plunged; and the flood drew; yet I caught
her; then
Oaring one arm, and bearing in my left
The weight of all the hopes of half the world,
Strove to buffet to land in vain. A tree
Was half-disrooted from his place and
stoop'd
To drench his dark locks in tile gurgling wave
Mid channel. Right on this we drove and
caught,
And grasping down the boughs I gain'd
the shore.

There stood her maidens glimmeringly
group'd
In the hollow bank. One reaching forward
drew
My burthen from mine arms; they cried
'she lives:'
They bore her back into the tent: but I
So much a kind of shame within me
wrought,
Not yet endured to meet her opening eyes,
Nor found my friends; but push'd alone on
foot
(For since her horse was lost I left her mine)
Across the woods, and less from lndian craft
Than beelike instinct hiveward, found at
length

The garden portals. Two great statues,
Art
And Science, Caryatids, lifted up
A weight of emblem, and betwixt were
valves
Of open-work in which the hunter rued
His rash intrusion, manlike, but his brows
Had sprouted, and the branches thereupon
Spread out at top, and grimly spiked
the gates.

A little space was left between the horns,
Thro' which I clamber'd o'er at top with
pain,
Dropt on the sward, and up the linden
walks,
And, tost on thoughts that changed from
hue to hue,
Now poring on the glowworm, now the star,
I paced the terrace, till the Bear had wheel'd
Thro' a great arc his seven slow suns.
A step
Of lightest echo, then a loftier form
Than female, moving thro' the uncertain
gloom,
Disturb'd me with the doubt 'if this were
she,'
But it was Florian. 'Hist O Hist,' he said,
'They seek us: out so late is out of rules.
Moreover "seize the strangers" is the cry.

How came you here?' I told him: 'I' said he,
'Last of the train, a moral leper, I,
To whom none spake, half-sick at heart,
return'd.
Arriving all confused among the rest
With hooded brows I crept into the hall,
And couch'd behind a Judith, underneath
The head of Holofernes peep'd and saw.
Girl after girl was call'd to trial: each
Disclaim'd all knowledge of us: last of all,
Melissa: trust me, Sir, I pitied her.
She, question'd if she knew us men, at first
Was silent; closer prest, denied it not:
And then, demanded if her mother knew,
Or Psyche, she affirm'd not, or denied:
From whence the Royal mind, familiar with
her,
Easily gather'd either guilt. She sent
For Psyche, but she was not there; she call'd
For Psyche's child to cast it from the doors;
She sent for Blanche to accuse her face to
face;
And I slipt out: but whither will you now?
And where are Psyche, Cyril? both are fled:
What, if together? that were not so well.
Would rather we had never come! I dread
His wildness, and the chances of the dark.'

'And yet,' I said, 'you wrong him more
than I

That struck him: this is proper to the clown,
Tho' smock'd, or furr'd and purpled, still
the clown,
To harm the thing that trusts him,
and to shame
That which he says he loves: for Cyril,
howe'er
He deal in frolic, as to-night — the song
Might have been worse and sinn'd in grosser
lips
Beyond all pardon — as it is, I hold
These flashes on the surface are not he.
He has a solid base of temperament:
But as the waterlily starts and slides
Upon the level in little puffs of wind,
Tho' anchor'd to the bottom, such is he.

Scarce had I ceased when from a tamarisk
near
Two Proctors leapt upon us, crying,
'Names:'
He, standing still, was clutch'd; but I began
To thrid the musky-circled mazes, wind
And double in and out the boles, and race
By all the fountains: fleet I was of foot;
Before me shower'd the rose in flakes;
behind
I heard the puff'd pursuer, at mine ear
Bubbled the nightingale and heeded not
And secret laughter tickled all my soul.

At last I hook'd my ankle in a vine,
That claspt the feet of a Mnemosyne,
And falling on my face was caught and
known.

They haled us to the Princess where she
sat
High in the hall: above her droop'd a lamp,
And made the single jewel on her brow
Burn like the mystic fire on a mast-head
Prophet of storm: a handmaid on each side
Bow'd toward her, combing out her long
black hair
Damp from the river; and close behind her
stood
Eight daughters of the plough, stronger
than men,
Huge women blowzed with health,
and wind, and rain,
And labour. Each was like a Druid rock;
Or like a spire of land that stands apart
Cleft from the main, and wail'd about with
mews.

Then, as we came, the crowd dividing
clove
An advent to the throne: and there beside,
Half-naked as if caught at once from bed
And tumbled on the purple footcloth, lay
The lily-shining child; and on the left,

Bow'd on her palms and folded up from
wrong,
Her round white shoulder shaken with her
sobs
Melissa knelt; but Lady Blanche erect
Stood up and spake, an affluent orator.

'It was not thus, O Princess, in old days:
You prized my counsel, lived upon my lips:
I led you then to all the Castalies;
I fed you with the milk of every Muse;
I loved you like this kneeler, and you me
Your second mother: those were gracious
times.
Then came your new friend: you began to
change —
I saw it and grieved — to slacken and to
cool;
Till taken with her seeming openness
You turn'd your warmer currents all to her,
To me you froze: this was my meed for all.
Yet I bore up in part from ancient love,
And partly that I hoped to win you back,
And partly conscious of my own deserts,
And partly that you were my civil head,
And chiefly you were born for something
great,
In which I might your fellow-worker be,
When time should serve; and thus a noble
scheme

Grew up from seed we two long since had sown;
In us true growth, in her a Jonah's gourd,
Up in one night and due to sudden sun:
We took this palace; but even from the first
You stood in your own light and darken'd mine.
What student came but that you planed her path
To Lady Psyche, younger, not so wise,
A foreigner, and I your countrywoman
I your old friend and tried, she new in all?
But still her lists were swell'd and mine were lean;
Yet I bore up in hope she would be known:
Then came these wolves: *they* knew her: *they* endured,
Long-closeted with her the yestermorn,
To tell her what they were, and she to hear:
And me none told: not less to an eye like mine,
A lidless watcher of the public weal,
Last night, their mask was patent, and my foot
Was to you: but I thought again: I fear'd
To meet a cold "We thank you, we shall hear of it
From Lady Psyche:" you had gone to her,
She told, perforce; and winning easy grace,

No doubt, for slight delay, remain'd
among us
In our young nursery still unknown, the stem
Less grain than touchwood, while my
honest heat
Were all miscounted as malignant haste
To push my rival out of place and power.
But public use required she should be
known;
And since my oath was ta'en for public use,
I broke the letter of it to keep the sense.
I spoke not then at first, but watch'd them
well,
Saw that they kept apart, no mischief done;
And yet this day (tho' you should hate me
for it)
I came to tell you, found that you had gone,
Ridd'n to the hills she likewise: now,
I thought,
That surely she will speak, if not, then I:
Did she? These monsters blazon'd what
they were,
According to the coarseness of their kind,
For thus I hear; and known at last (my work)
And full of cowardice and guilty shame,
I grant in her some sense of shame, she flies;
And I remain on whom to wreak your rage,
I, that have lent my life to build up yours,
I that have wasted here health, wealth, and
time,

And talents, I — you know it — I will not boast:
Dismiss me, and I prophesy your plan,
Divorced from my experience, will be chaff
For every gust of chance, and men will say
We did not know the real light, but chased
The wisp that flickers where no foot can tread.'

She ceased: the Princess answer'd coldly, 'Good:
Your oath is broken: we dismiss you: go.
For this lost lamb (she pointed to the child)
Our mind is changed: we take it to ourself.'

Thereat the Lady stretch'd a vulture throat.
And shot from crooked lips a haggard smile.
'The plan was mine. I built the nest' she said,
'To hatch the cuckoo. Rise!' and stoop'd to updrag
Melissa: she, half on her mother propt,
Half-drooping from her, turn'd her face, and cast
A liquid look on Ida, full of prayer,
Which melted Florian's fancy as she hung,
A Niobean daughter, one arm out,
Appealing to the bolts of Heaven; and while

We gazed upon her came a little stir
About the doors, and on a sudden rush'd
Among us, out of breath, as one pursued,
A woman-post in flying raiment. Fear
Stared in her eyes, and chalk'd her face,
and wing'd
Her transit to the throne, whereby she fell
Delivering seal'd dispatches which the Head
Took half-amazed, and in her lion's mood
Tore open, silent we with blind surmise
Regarding, while she read, till over brow
And cheek and bosom brake the wrathful
bloom
As of some fire against a stormy cloud,
When the wild peasant rights himself,
the rick
Flames, and his anger reddens in the heavens;
For anger most it seem'd, while now her
breast,
Beaten with some great passion at her heart,
Palpitated, her hand shook, and we heard
In the dead hush the papers that she held
Rustle: at once the lost lamb at her feet
Sent out a bitter bleating for its dam;
The plaintive cry jarr'd on her ire;
she crush'd
The scrolls together, made a sudden turn
As if to speak, but, utterance failing her,
She whirl'd them on to me, as who should
say

'Read,' and I read — two letters — one her sire's.

'Fair daughter, when we sent the Prince your way
We knew not your ungracious laws, which learnt,
We, conscious of what temper you are built,
Came all in haste to hinder wrong, but fell
Into his father's hands, who has this night,
You lying close upon his territory,
Slipt round and in the dark invested you,
And here he keeps me hostage for his son.'

The second was my father's running thus:
'You have our son: touch not a hair of his head:
Render him up unscathed: give him your hand:
Cleave to your contract: tho' indeed we hear
You hold the woman is the better man;
A rampant heresy, such as if it spread
Would make all women kick against their Lords
Thro' all the world, and which might well deserve
That we this night should pluck your palace down;
And we will do it, unless you send us back
Our son, on the instant, whole.'

So far I read;
And then stood up and spoke impetuously.

'O not to pry and peer on your reserve,
But led by golden wishes, and a hope
The child of regal compact, did I break
Your precinct; not a scorner of your sex
But venerator, zealous it should be
All that it might be: hear me, for I bear,
Tho' man, yet human, whatsoe'er your wrongs,
From the flaxen curl to the grey lock a life
Less mine than yours: my nurse would tell me of you;
I babbled for you, as babies for the moon,
Vague brightness; when a boy, you stoop'd to me
From all high places, lived in all fair lights,
Came in long breezes rapt from inmost south
And blown to inmost north; at eve and dawn
With Ida, Ida, Ida, rang the woods;
The leader wildswan in among the stars
Would clang it, and lapt in wreaths of glowworm light
The mellow breaker murmur'd Ida. Now,
Because I would have reach'd you, had you been
Sphered up with Cassiopëia, or the enthroned

Persephone in Hades, now at length,
Those winters of abeyance all worn out,
A man I came to see you: but, indeed,
Not in this frequence can I lend full tongue,
O noble Ida, to those thoughts that wait
On you, their centre: let me say but this,
That many a famous man and woman, town
And landskip, have I heard of, after seen
The dwarfs of presage: tho' when known, there grew
Another kind of beauty in detail
Made them worth knowing; but in you I found
My boyish dream involved and dazzled down
And master'd, while that after-beauty makes
Such head from act to act, from hour to hour,
Within me, that except you slay me here,
According to your bitter statute-book,
I cannot cease to follow you, as they say
The seal does music; who desire you more
Than growing boys their manhood; dying lips,
With many thousand matters left to do,
The breath of life; O more than poor men wealth,
Than sick men health — yours, yours, not mine — but half

Without you; with you, whole; and of those
halves
You worthiest; and howe'er you block and
bar
Your heart with system out from mine,
I hold
That it becomes no man to nurse despair,
But in the teeth of clench'd antagonisms
To follow up the worthiest till he die:
Yet that I came not all unauthorized
Behold your father's letter.'
On one knee
Kneeling, I gave it, which she caught,
and dash'd
Unopen'd at her feet: a tide of fierce
Invective seem'd to wait behind her lips,
As waits a river level with the dam
Ready to burst and flood the wodd with
foam:
And so she would have spoken,
but there rose
A hubbub in the court of half the maids
Gather'd together: from the illumined hall
Long lanes of splendour slanted o'er a press
Of snowy shoulders, thick as herded ewes,
And rainbow robes, and gems and gemlike
eyes,
And gold and golden heads, they to and fro
Fluctuated, as flowers in storm, some red,
some pale,

All open-mouth'd, all gazing to the light,
Some crying there was an army in the land,
And some that men were in the very walls,
And some they cared not; till a clamour
grew
As of a new-world Babel, woman-built,
And worse-confounded: high above them
stood
The placid marble Muses, looking peace.
Not peace she look'd, the Head:
but rising up
Robed in the long night of her deep hair, so
To the open window moved, remaining
there
Fixt like a beacon-tower above the waves
Of tempest, when the crimson-rolling eye
Glares ruin, and the wild birds on the light
Dash themselves dead. She stretch'd her
arms and call'd
Across the tumult and the tumult fell.

'What fear ye, brawlers? am not I your
Head?
On me, me, me, the storm first breaks: I dare
All these male thunderbolts: what is it ye
fear?
Peace! there are those to avenge us and they
come:
If not, — myself were like enough, O girls,
To urfurl the maiden banner of our rights,

And clad in iron burst the ranks of war,
Or, falling, protomartyr of our cause,
Die: yet I blame you not so much for fear;
Six thousand years of fear have made you that
From which I would redeem you: but for those
That stir this hubbub — you and you — I know
Your faces there in the crowd — to-morrow morn
We hold a great convention: then shall they
That love their voices more than duty, learn
With whom they deal, dismiss'd in shame to live
No wiser than their mothers, household stuff,
Live chattels, mincers of each other's fame,
Full of weak poison, turnspits for the clown,
The drunkard's football, laughing-stocks of Time,
Whose brains are in their hands and in their heels,
But fit to flaunt, to dress, to dance, to thrum,
To tramp, to scream, to burnish, and to scour,
For ever slaves at home and fools abroad.'

She, ending, waved her hands: thereat the crowd
Muttering, dissolved: then with a smile, that look'd
A stroke of cruel sunshine on the cliff,
When all the glens are drown'd in azure gloom
Of thunder-shower, she floated to us and said:

'You have done well and like a gentleman,
And like a prince: you have our thanks for all:
And you look well too in your woman's dress:
Well have you done and like a gentleman.
You saved our life: we owe you bitter thanks:
Better have died and spilt our bones in the flood —
Then men had said — but now —
What hinders me
To take such bloody vengeance on you both? —
Yet since our father — Wasps in our good hive,
You would-be quenchers of the light to be,
Barbarians, grosser than your native bears —
O would I had his sceptre for one hour!
You that have dared to break our bound, and gull'd

Our servants, wrong'd and lied and
thwarted us —
I wed with thee! *I* bound by precontract
Your bride, your bondslave! not tho' all the
gold
That veins the world were pack'd to make
your crown,
And every spoken tongue should lord you.
Sir,
Your falsehood and yourself are hateful
to us:
I trample on your offers and on you:
Begone: we will not look upon you more.
Here, push them out at gates.'
In wrath she spake
Then those eight mighty daughters of the
plough
Bent their broad faces toward us and
address'd
Their motion: twice I sought to plead my
cause,
But on my shoulder hung their heavy hands,
The weight of destiny: so from her face
They push'd us, down the steps, and thro'
the court,
And with grim laughter thrust us out at
gates.

We cross'd the street and gain'd a petty
mound

Beyond it, whence we saw the lights and
heard
The voices murmuring. While I listen'd,
came
On a sudden the weird seizure and the
doubt:
I seem'd to move among a world of ghosts;
The Princess with her monstrous
woman-guard,
The jest and earnest working side by side,
The cataract and the tumult and the kings
Were shadows; and the long fantastic night
With all its doings had and had not been,
And all things were and were not.
This went by
As strangely as it came, and on my spirits
Settled a gentle cloud of melancholy
Not long; I shook it off; for spite of doubts
And sudden ghostly shadowings I was one
To whom the touch of all mischance but
came
As night to him that sitting on a hill
Sees the midsummer, midnight,
Norway sun
Set into sunrise; then we moved away.

★

Thy voice is heard thro' rolling drums,
That beat to battle where he stands;

Thy face across his fancy comes,
And gives the battle to his hands:
A moment, while the trumpets blow,
He sees his brood about thy knee;
The next, like fire he meets the foe,
And strikes him dead for thine and thee.

So Lilia sang: we thought her half-possess'd,
She struck such warbling fury thro' the words
And, after, feigning pique at what she call'd
The raillery, or grotesque, or false sublime —
Like one that wishes at a dance to change
The music — clapt her hands and cried for war,
Or some grand fight to kill and make an end:
And he that next inherited the tale
Half turning to the broken statue, said,
'Sir Ralph has got your colours: if I prove
Your knight, and fight your battle, what for me?'
It chanced, her empty glove upon the tomb
Lay by her like a model of her liand,
She took it and she flung it. 'Fight' she said
'And make us all we would be, great and good.'
He knightlike in his cap instead of casque,

A cap of Tyrol borrow'd from the hall,
Arranged the favour, and assumed the
  Prince.

V

Now, scarce three paces measured from the
  mound,
We stumbled on a stationary voice,
And 'Stand, who goes?' 'Two from the
  palace' I.
'The second two: they wait,' he said,
  'pass on;
His Highness wakes:' and one, that clash'd
  in arms,
By glimmering lanes and walls of canvas, led
Threading the soldier-city, till we heard
The drowsy folds of our great ensign shake
From blazon'd lions o'er the imperial tent
Whispers of war.
          Entering, the sudden light
Dazed me half-blind: I stood and seem'd to
  hear,
As in a poplar grove when a light wind
  wakes
A lisping of the innumerous leaf and dies,
Each hissing in his neighbour's ear;
  and then
A strangled titter, out of which there brake

On all sides, clamouring etiquette to
death,
Unmeasured mirth; while now the two old
kings
Began to wag their baldness up and down,
The fresh young captains flash'd their
glittering teeth,
The huge bush-bearded Barons heaved and
blew,
And slain with laughter roll'd the gilded
Squire.

At length my Sire, his rough cheek wet
with tears,
Panted from weary sides 'King, you are free!
We did but keep you surety for our son,
If this be he, — or a draggled mawkin, thou,
That tends her bristled grunters in the
sludge: '
For I was drench'd with ooze, and torn with
briers,
More crumpled than a poppy from the
sheath,
And all one rag, disprinced from head to
heel.
Then some one sent beneath his vaulted
palm
A whisper'd jest to some one near him,
'Look,
He has been among his shadows.'

'Satan take
The old women and their shadows!
(thus the King
Roar'd) make yourself a man to fight with
men.
Go: Cyril told us all.'
As boys that slink
From ferule and the trespass-chiding eye,
Away we stole, and transient in a trice
From what was left of faded woman-slough
To sheathing splendours and the golden
scale
Of harness, issued in the sun, that now
Leapt from the dewy shoulders of the Earth,
And hit the Northern hills. Here Cyril
met us,
A little shy at first, but by and by
We twain, with mutual pardon ask'd and
given
For stroke and song, resolder'd peace,
whereon
Follow'd his tale. Amazed he fled away
Thro' the dark land, and later in the night
Had come on Psyche weeping: 'then we fell
Into your father's hand, and there she lies,
But will not speak, nor stir.'
He show'd a tent
A stone-shot off: we enter'd in, and there
Among piled arms and rough
accoutrements,

Pitiful sight, wrapp'd in a soldier's cloak,
Like some sweet sculpture draped from
head to foot,
And push'd by rude hands from its pedestal,
All her fair length upon the ground she lay:
And at her head a follower of the camp,
A charr'd and wrinkled piece of
womanhood,
Sat watching like a watcher by the dead.

Then Florian knelt, and 'Come' he
whisper'd to her,
'Lift up your head, sweet sister: lie not thus.
What have you done but right? you could
not slay
Me, nor your prince: look up: be comforted:
Sweet is it to have done the thing one ought,
When fall'n in darker ways.' And likewise I:
'Be comforted: have I not lost her too,
In whose least act abides the nameless
charm
That none has else for me?' She heard,
she moved,
She moan'd, a folded voice; and up she sat,
And raised the cloak from brows as pale and
smooth
As those that mourn half-shrouded over
death
In deathless marble. 'Her,' she said,
'my friend —

Parted from her — betray'd her cause and
mine —
Where shall I breathe? why kept ye not your
faith?
O base and bad! what comfort? none
for me!'
To whom remorseful Cyril, 'Yet I pray
Take comfort: live, dear lady, for your child!'
At which she lifted up her voice and cried.

'Ah me, my babe, my blossom, ah my
child,
May one sweet child, whom I shall see no
more!
For now will cruel Ida keep her back;
And either she will die from want of care,
Or sicken with ill-usage, when they say
The child is hers — for every little fault,
The child is hers; and they will beat my girl
Remembering her mother: O my flower!
Or they will take her, they will make her
hard,
And she will pass me by in after-life
With some cold reverence worse than were
she dead.
Ill mother that I was to leave her there,
To lag behind, scared by the cry they made,
The horror of the shame among them all:
But I will go and sit beside the doors,
And make a wild petition night and day,

Until they hate to hear me like a wind
Wailing for ever, till they open to me,
And lay my little blossom at my feet,
My babe, my sweet Aglama, my one child:
And I will take her up and go my way,
And satisfy my soul with kissing her:
Ah! what might that man not deserve of me,
Who gave me back my child?' 'Be
comforted,'
Said Cyril, 'you shall have it:' but again
She veil'd her brows, and prone she sank,
and so
Like tender things that being caught feign
death,
Spoke not, nor stirr'd.
By this a murmur ran
Thro' all the camp and inward raced the
scouts
With rumour of Prince Arac hard at hand.
We left her by the woman, and without
Found the grey kings at parle:
and 'Look you' cried
My father 'that our compact be fulfill'd:
You have spoilt this child; she laughs at you
and man:
She wrongs herself, her sex, and me,
and him:
But red-faced war has rods of steel and
fire;
She yields, or war.'

Then Gama turn'd to me:
'We fear, indeed, you spent a stormy time
With our strange girl: and yet they say that
still
You love her. Give us, then, your mind at
large:
How say you, war or not?'
'Not war, if possible,
O king,' I said, 'lest from the abuse of war,
The desecrated shrine, the trampled year,
The smouldering homestead, and the
household flower
Torn from the lintel — all the common
wrong —
A smoke go up thro' which I loom to her
Three times a monster: now she lightens
scorn
At him that mars her plan, but then would
hate
(And every voice she talk'd with ratify it,
And every face she look'd on justify it)
The general foe. More soluble is this knot,
By gentleness than war. I want her love.
What were I nigher this altho' we dash'd
Your cities into shards with catapults,
She would not love; — or brought her
chain'd, a slave,
The lifting of whose eyelash is my lord,
Not ever would she love; but brooding turn
The book of scorn, till all my little chance

Were caught within the record of her wrongs
And crush'd to death: and rather, Sire, than this
I would the old God of war himself were dead,
Forgotten, rusting on his iron hills,
Rotting on some wild shore with ribs of wreck,
Or like an old-world mammoth bulk'd in ice,
Not to be molten out.'
And roughly spake
My father, 'Tut, you know them not, the girls.
Boy, when I hear you prate I almost think
That idiot legend credible. Look you, Sir!
Man is the hunter; woman is his game:
The sleek and shining creatures of the chase,
We hunt them for the beauty of their skins;
They love us for it, and we ride them down.
Wheedling and siding with them! Out! for shame!
Boy, there's no rose that's half so dear to them
As he that does the thing they dare not do,
Breathing and sounding beauteous battle, comes
With the air of the trumpet round him, and leaps in

Among the women, snares them by the
    score
Flatter'd and fluster'd, wins, tho' dash'd
    with death
He reddens what he kisses: thus I won
Your mother, a good mother, a good wife,
Worth winning; but this firebrand —
    gentleness
To such as her! if Cyril spake her true,
To catch a dragon in a cherry net,
To trip a tigress with a gossamer,
Were wisdom to it.'
                    'Yea but Sire,' I cried,
'Wild natures need wise curbs. The soldier?
    No:
What dares not Ida do that she should prize
The soldier? I beheld her, when she rose
The yesternight, and storming in extremes
Stood for her cause, and flung defiance
    down
Gagelike to man, and had not shunn'd the
    death,
No, not the soldier's: yet I hold her, king,
True woman: but you clash them all in one,
That have as many differences as we.
The violet varies from the lily as far
As oak from elm: one loves the soldier, one
The silken priest of peace, one this, one
    that,
And some unworthily; their sinless faith,

A maiden moon that sparkles on a sty,
Glorifying clown and satyr; whence they
    need
More breadth of culture: is not Ida right?
They worth it? truer to the law within?
Severer in the logic of a life?
Twice as magnetic to sweet influences
Of earth and heaven? and she of whom
    you speak,
My mother, looks as whole as some serene
Creation minted in the golden moods
Of sovereign artists; not a thought, a touch,
But pure as lines of green that streak the
    white
Of the first snowdrop's inner leaves; I say,
Not like the piebald miscellany, man,
Bursts of great heart and slips in sensual
    mire,
But whole and one: and take them all-in-all,
Were we ourselves but half as good, as kind,
As truthful, much that Ida claims as right
Had ne'er been mooted, but as frankly
    theirs
As dues of Nature. To our point: not war:
Lest I lose all.'
                'Nay, nay, you spake but sense,'
Said Gama. 'We remember love ourself
In our sweet youth; we did not rate him then
This red-hot iron to be shaped with blows.
You talk almost like Ida: she can talk;

And there is something in it as you say:
But you talk kindlier: we esteem you
for it. —
He seems a gracious and a gallant Prince,
I would he had our daughter: for the rest,
Our own detention, why, the causes
weigh'd,
Fatherly fears — you used us courteously —
We would do much to gratify your Prince —
We pardon it; and for your ingress here
Upon the skirt and fringe of our fair land,
You did but come as goblins in the night,
Nor in the furrow broke the ploughman's
head,
Nor burnt the grange, nor buss'd the
milking-maid,
Nor robb'd the farmer of his bowl of cream:
But let your Prince (our royal word upon it,
He comes back safe) ride with us to our lines,
And speak with Arac: Arac's word is thrice
As ours with Ida: something may be done —
I know not what — and ours shall see us
friends.
You, likewise, our late guests, if so you will,
Follow us: who knows? we four may build
some plan
Foursquare to opposition.'
Here he reach'd
White hands of farewell to my sire,
who growl'd

An answer which, half-muffled in his beard,
Let so much out as gave us leave to go.

Then rode we with the old king across the lawns
Beneath huge trees, a thousand rings of Spring
In every bole, a song on every spray
Of birds that piped their Valentines, and woke
Desire in me to infuse my tale of love
In the old king's ears, who promised help, and oozed
All o'er with honey'd answer as we rode;
And blossom-fragrant slipt the heavy dews
Gather'd by night and peace, with each light air
On our mail'd heads: but other thoughts than Peace
Burnt in us, when we saw the embattled squares,
And squadrons of the Prince, trampling the flowers
With clamour: for among them rose a cry
As if to greet the king; they made a halt;
The horses yell'd; they clash'd their arms; the drum
Beat; merrily-blowing shrill'd the martial fife;

And in the blast and bray of the long horn
And serpent-throated bugle, undulated
The banner: anon to meet us lightly
    pranced
Three captains out; nor ever had I seen
Such thews of men: the midmost and the
    highest
Was Arac: all about his motion clung
The shadow of his sister, as the beam
Of the East, that play'd upon them,
    made them glance
Like those three stars of the airy Giant's
    zone,
That glitter burnish'd by the frosty dark;
And as the fiery Sirius alters hue,
And bickers into red and emerald, shone
Their morions, wash'd with morning, as
    they came

And I that prated peace, when first I heard
War-music, felt the blind wildbeast of force,
Whose home is in the sinews of a man
Stir in me as to strike: then took the king
His three broad sons; with now a wandering
    hand
And now a pointed finger, told them all:
A common light of smiles at our disguise
Broke from their lips, and, ere the windy jest
Had labour'd down within his ample lungs,
The genial giant, Arac, roll'd himself

Thrice in the saddle, then burst out in words.

'Our land invaded, 'sdeath! and he himself
Your captive, yet my father wills not war:
And, 'sdeath! myself, what care I, war or no?
But then this question of your troth remains:
And there's a downright honest meaning in her;
She flies too high, she flies too high! and yet
She ask'd but space and fairplay for her scheme;
She prest and prest it on me — I myself,
What know I of these things? but, life and soul!
I thought her half-right talking of her wrongs;
I say she flies too high, 'sdeath! what of that?
I take her for the flower of womankind,
And so I often told her, right or wrong,
And, Prince, she can be sweet to those she loves,
And, right or wrong, I care not: this is all,
I stand upon her side: she made me swear it —
'Sdeath — and with solemn rites by candle-light —
Swear by St. something — I forget her name —

Her that talk'd down the fifty wisest men;
She was a princess too; and so I swore.
Come, this is all; she will not: waive your
claim:
If not, the foughten field, what else, at once
Decides it, 'sdeath! against my father's will.'

I lagg'd in answer loath to render up
My precontract, and loath by brainless war
To cleave the rift of difference deeper yet;
Till one of those two brothers, half aside
And fingering at the hair about his lip,
To prick us on to combat 'Like to like!
The woman's garment hid the woman's
heart.'
A taunt that clench'd his purpose like a
blow!
For fiery-short was Cyril's counter-scoff,
And sharp I answer'd, touch'd upon the
point
Where idle boys are cowards to their shame,
'Decide it here: why not? we are three to
three.

Then spake the third 'But three to three?
no more?
No more, and in our noble sister's cause?
More, more, for honour: every captain waits
Hungry for honour, angry for his king.
More, more, some fifty on a side, that each

May breathe himself, and quick! by
overthrow
Of these or those, the question settled die.'

'Yea,' answer'd I, 'for this wild wreath of
air,
This flake of rainbow flying on the highest
Foam of men's deeds — this honour,
if ye will.
It needs must be for honour if at all:
Since, what decision? if we fail, we fail,
And if we win, we fail: she would not keep
Her compact. ' 'Sdeath! but we will send
to her,'
Said Arac, 'worthy reasons why she should
Bide by this issue: let our missive thro',
And you shall have her answer by the word.'

'Boys!' shriek'd the old king, but vainlier
than a hen
To her false daughters in the pool; for none
Regarded; neither seem'd there more to say:
Back rode we to my father's camp, and found
He thrice had sent a herald to the gates,
To learn if Ida yet would cede our claim,
Or by denial flush her babbling wells
With her own people's life: three times he
went:
The first, he blew and blew, but none
appear'd:

He batter'd at the doors; none came: the next,
An awful voice within had warn'd him thence:
The third, and those eight daughters of the plough
Came sallying thro' the gates, and caught his hair,
And so belabour'd him on rib and cheek
They made him wild: not less one glance he caught
Thro' open doors of Ida station'd there
Unshaken, clinging to her purpose, firm
Tho' compass'd by two armies and the noise
Of arms; and standing like a stately Pine
Set in a cataract on an island-crag,
When storm is on the heights, and right and left
Suck'd from the dark heart of the long hills roll
The torrents, dash'd to the vale: and yet her will
Bred will in me to overcome it or fall.

But when I told the king that I was pledged
To fight in tourney for my bride, he clash'd
His iron palms together with a cry;
Himself would tilt it out among the lads:
But overborne by all his bearded lords

With reasons drawn from age and state,
perforce
He yielded, wroth and red, with fierce
demur:
And many a bold knight started up in heat,
And sware to combat for my claim till death.

All on this side the palace ran the field
Flat to the garden-wall: and likewise here,
Above the garden's glowing blossom-belts,
A column'd entry shone and marble stairs,
And great bronze valves, emboss'd with
Tomyris
And what she did to Cyrus after fight,
But now fast barr'd: so here upon the flat
All that long morn the lists were
hammer'd up,
And all that morn the heralds to and fro,
With message and defiance, went and came;
Last, Ida's answer, in a royal hand,
But shaken here and there, and rolling
words
Oration-like. I kiss'd it and I read.

'O brother, you have known the pangs we
felt,
What heats of indignation when we heard
Of those that iron-cramp'd their women's
feet;
Of lands in which at the altar the poor bride

Gives her harsh groom for bridal-gift a scourge;
Of living hearts that crack within the fire
Where smoulder their dead despots; and of those, —
Mothers, — that, all prophetic pity, fling
Their pretty maids in the running flood, and swoops
The vulture, beak and talon, at the heart
Made for all noble motion: and I saw
That equal baseness lived in sleeker times
With smoother men: the old leaven leaven'd all:
Millions of throats would bawl for civil rights,
No woman named therefore I set my face
Against all men, and lived but for mine own.
Far off from men I built a fold for them
I stored it full of rich memorial:
I fenced it round with gallant institutes,
And biting laws to scare the beasts of prey,
And prosper'd; till a rout of saucy boys
Brake on us at our books, and marr'd our peace,
Mask'd like our maids, blustering I know not what
Of insolence and love, some pretext held
Of baby troth, invalid, since my will
Seal'd not the bond — the striplings! — for their sport! —

I tamed my leopards shall I not tame these?
Or you? or I? for since you think me touch'd
In honour — what, I would not aught of
false —
Is not our cause pure? and whereas I know
Your prowess, Arac, and what mother's
blood
You draw from, fight; you failing, I abide
What end soever: fail you will not. Still
Take not his life: he risk'd it for my own;
His mother lives: yet whatsoe'er you do,
Fight and fight well; strike and strike home
O dear Brothers, the woman's Angel guards
you, you
The sole men to be mingled with our cause,
The sole men we shall prize in the
after-time,
Your very armour hallow'd, and your statues
Rear'd, sung to, when, this gad-fly brush'd
aside,
We plant a solid foot into the Time,
And mould a generation strong to move
With claim on claim from right to right,
till she
Whose name is yoked with children's,
know herself;
And Knowledge in our own land make her
free,
And, ever following those two crowned
twins,

Commerce and conquest, shower the fiery grain
Of freedom broadcast over all that orbs
Between the Northern and the Southern morn.'

Then came a postscript dash'd across the rest.
See that there be no traitors in your camp:
We seem a nest of traitors — none to trust
Since our arms fail'd — this Egypt-plague of men!
Almost our maids were better at their homes
Than thus man-girdled here: indeed I think
Our chiefest comfort is the little child
Of one unworthy mother; which she left:
She shall not have it back: the child shall grow
To prize the authentic mother of her mind.
I took it for an hour in mine own bed
This morning: there the tender orphan hands
Felt at my heart, and seemed to charm from thence
The wrath I nursed against the world: farewell.'

I ceased; he said: 'Stubborn, but she may sit
Upon a king's right hand in thunder-storms,

And breed up warriors! See now, tho' yourself
Be dazzled by the wildfire Love to sloughs
That swallow common sense, the spindling king,
This Gama swamp'd in lazy tolerance.
When the man wants weight, the woman takes it up,
And topples down the scales; but this is fixt
As are the roots of earth and base of all;
Man for the field and woman for the hearth:
Man for the sword and for the needle she:
Man with the head and woman with the heart:
Man to command and woman to obey;
All else confusion. Look you! the grey mare
Is ill to live with, when her whinny shrills
From tile to scullery, and her small goodman
Shrinks in his arm-chair while the fires of Hell
Mix with his hearth: but you — she's yet a colt —
Take, break her: strongly groom'd and straitly curb'd
She might not rank with those detestable
That let the bantling scald at home, and brawl
Their rights or wrongs like potherbs in the street.

They says she's comely; there's the fairer
chance:
I like her none the less for rating at her!
Besides, the woman wed is not as we,
But suffers change of frame. A lusty brace
Of twins may weed her of her folly. Boy,
The bearing and the training of a child
Is woman's wisdom.'
Thus the hard old king:
I took my leave, for it was nearly noon:
I pored upon her letter which I held,
And on the little clause 'take not his life:'
I mused on that wild morning in the woods,
And on the 'Follow, follow, thou shalt win:'
I thought on all the wrathful king had said,
And how the strange betrothment was to
end:
Then I remember'd that burnt sorcerer's
curse
That one should fight with shadows and
should fall;
And like a flash the weird affection came:
King, camp and college turn'd to hollow
shows;
I seem'd to move in old memorial tilts,
And doing battle with forgotten ghosts,
To dream myself the shadow of a dream:
And ere I woke it was the point of noon,
The lists were ready. Empanoplied and
plumed

We enter'd in, and waited, fifty there
Opposed to fifty, till the trumpet blared
At the barrier like a wild horn in a land
Of echoes, and a moment, and once more
The trumpet, and again: at which the storm
Of galloping hoofs bare on the ridge of spears
And riders front to front, until they closed
In conflict with the crash of shivering points,
And thunder. Yet it seem'd a dream, I dream'd
Of fighting. On his haunches rose the steed,
And into fiery splinters leapt the lance,
And out of stricken helmets sprang the fire.
Part sat like rocks: part reel'd but kept their seats:
Part roll'd on the earth and rose again and drew:
Part stumbled mixt with floundering horses. Down
From those two bulks at Arac's side, and down
From Arac's arm, as from a giant's flail,
The large blows rain'd, as here and everywhere
He rode the mellay, lord of the ringing lists,
And all the plain, — brand, mace. and shaft, and shield —
Shock'd, like an iron-clanging anvil bang'd

With hammers; till I thought, can this be he
From Gama's dwarfish loins? if this be so,
The mother makes us most — and in my dream
I glanced aside, and saw the palace-front
Alive with fluttering scarfs and ladies' eyes,
And highest, among the statues, statue-like,
Between a cymbal'd Miriam and a Jael,
With Psyche's babe, was Ida watching us,
A single band of gold about her hair,
Like a Saint's glory up in heaven: but she
No saint — inexorable — no tenderness —
Too hard, too cruel: yet she sees me fight,
Yea, let her see me fall! with that I drave
Among the thickest and bore down a Prince,
And Cyril, one. Yea, let me make my dream
All that I would. But that large-moulded man,
His visage all agrin as at a wake,
Made at me thro' the press, and, staggering back
With stroke on stroke the horse and horseman, came
As comes a pillar of electric cloud,
Flaying the roofs and sucking up the drains,
And shadowing down the champaign till it strikes
On a wood, and takes, and breaks, and cracks, and splits

And twists the grain with such a roar that
Earth
Reels, and the herdsmen cry; for everything
Cave way before him: only Florian, he
That loved me closer than his own right eye,
Thrust in between; but Arac rode him
down:
And Cyril seeing it, push'd against the
Prince,
With Psyche's colour round his helmet,
tough,
Strong, supple, sinew-corded, apt at arms;
But tougher, heavier, stronger, he that smote
And threw him: last I spurr'd; I felt my veins
Stretch with fierce heat; a moment hand to
hand,
And sword to sword, and horse to horse we
hung,
Till I struck out and shouted; the blade
glanced;
I did but shear a feather, and dream and truth
Flow'd from me; darkness closed me;
and I fell.

★

Home they brought her warrior dead:
She nor swoon'd, nor utter'd cry:
All her maidens, watching, said,
'She must weep or she will die.'

Then they praised him, soft and low,
Call'd him worthy to be loved,
Truest friend and noblest foe;
Yet she neither spoke nor moved.

Stole a maiden from her place,
Lightly to the warrior stept,
Took the face cloth from the face:
Yet she neither moved nor wept.

Rose a nurse of ninety years,
Set his child upon her knee —
Like summer tempest came her tears —
'Sweet my child, I live for thee.'

VI

My dream had never died or lived again.
As in some mystic middle state I lay;
Seeing I saw not, hearing not I heard:
Tho', if I saw not, yet they told me all
So often that I speak as having seen.

For so it seem'd, or so they said to me,
That all things grew more tragic and more strange;
That when our side was vanquish'd and my cause
For ever lost, there went up a great cry,

The Prince is slain. My father heard and ran
In on the lists, and there unlaced my casque
And grovell'd on my body, and after him
Came Psyche, sorrowing for Aglaïa.

But high upon the palace Ida stood
With Psyche's babe in arm: there on the roofs
Like that great dame of Lapidoth she sang.

'Our enemies have fall'n, have fall'n: the seed,
The little seed they laugh'd at in the dark,
Has risen and cleft the soil, and grown a bulk
Of spanless girth, that lays on every side
A thousand arms and rushes to the Sun.

'Our enemies have fall'n, have fall'n: they came;
The leaves were wet with women's tears: they heard
A noise of songs they would not understand:
They mark'd it with the red cross to the fall,
And would have strown it, and are fall'n themselves.

'Our enemies have fall'n, have fall'n: they came,
The woodmen with their axes: lo the tree!

But we will make it faggots for the hearth,
And shape it plank and beam for roof and floor,
And boats and bridges for the use of men.

'Our enemies have fall'n, have fall'n: they struck;
With their own blows they hurt themselves, nor knew
There dwelt an iron nature in the grain:
The glittering axe was broken in their arms
Their arms were shatter'd to the shoulder blade.

'Our enemies have fall'n, but this shall grow
A night of Summer from the heat, a breadth
Of Autumn, dropping fruits of power; and roll'd
With music in the growing breeze of Time,
The tops shall strike from star to star, the fangs
Shall move the stony bases of the world.

'And now, O maids, behold our sanctuary
Is violate, our laws broken: fear we not
To break them more in their behoof, whose arms
Champion'd our cause and won it with a day

Blanch'd in our annals, and perpetual feast,
When dames and heroines of the golden year
Shall strip a hundred hollows bare of
Spring,
To rain an April of ovation round
Their statues, borne aloft, the three:
but come,
We will be liberal, since our rights are won.
Let them not lie in the tents with coarse
mankind,
Ill nurses; but descend, and proffer these
The brethren of our blood and cause,
that there
Lie bruised and maim'd, the tender
ministries
Of female hands and hospitality.'

She spoke, and with the babe yet in her
arms,
Descending, burst the great bronze valves,
and led
A hundred maids in train across the Park.
Some cowl'd, and some bare-headed,
on they came,
Their feet in flowers, her loveliest:
by them went
The enamour'd air sighing, and on their curls
From the high tree the blossom wavering
fell,
And over them the tremulous isles of light

Slided, they moving under shade:
but Blanche
At distance follow'd: so they came: anon
Thro' open field into the lists they wound
Timorously; and as the leader of the herd
That holds a stately fretwork to the Sun,
And follow'd up by a hundred airy does,
Steps with a tender foot, light as on air,
The lovely, lordly creature floated on
To where her wounded brethren lay;
there stay'd;
Knelt on one knee, — the child on one, —
and prest
Their hands, and call'd them dear
deliverers,
And happy warriors, and immortal names,
And said 'You shall not lie in the tents
but here,
And nursed by those for whom you fought,
and served
With female hands and hospitality.'

Then, whether moved by this, or was it
chance,
She past my way. Up started from my side
The old lion, glaring with his whelpless eye,
Silent; but when she saw me lying stark,
Dishelm'd and mute, and motionlessly pale,
Cold ev'n to her, she sigh'd; and when she
saw

The haggard father's face and reverend
beard
Of grisly twine, all dabbled with the blood
Of his own son, shudder'd, a twitch of pain
Tortured her mouth, and o'er her forehead
past
A shadow, and her hue changed,
and she said:
'He saved my life: my brother slew him
for it.'
No more: at which the king in bitter scorn
Drew from my neck the painting and the
tress
And held them up: she saw them, and a day
Rose from the distance on her memory,
When the good Queen, her mother,
shore the tress
With kisses, ere the days of Lady Blanche:
And then once more she looked at my pale
face:
Till understanding all the foolish work
Of Fancy, and the bitter close of all,
Her iron will was broken in her mind;
Her noble heart was molten in her breast;
She bow'd, she set the child on the earth;
she laid
A feeling finger on my brows, and presently
'O Sire,' she said, 'he lives: he is not dead:
O let me have him with my brethren here
In our own palace: we will tend on him

Like one of these; if so, by any means,
To lighten this great clog of thanks,
that make
Our progress falter to the woman's goal.'

She said: but at the happy word 'he lives'
My father stoop'd, re-father'd o'er my
wounds.
So those two foes above my fallen life,
With brow to brow like night and evening
mixt
Their dark and grey, while Psyche ever stole
A little nearer, till the babe that by us
Half-lapt in glowing gauze and golden
brede,
Lay like a new-fall'n meteor on the grass,
Uncared for, spied its mother and began
A blind and babbling laughter, and to dance
Its body, and reach its fatling innocent arms
And lazy lingering fingers. She the appeal
Brook'd not, but clamouring out 'Mine —
mine — not yours,
It is not yours, but mine: give me the child'
Ceased all on tremble: piteous was the cry:
So stood the unhappy mother
open-mouth'd,
And turn'd each face her way: wan was her
cheek
With hollow watch, her blooming mantle
torn,

Red grief and mother's hunger in her eye,
And down dead-heavy sank her curls,
and half
The sacred mother's bosom, panting, burst
The laces toward her babe; but she nor cared
Nor knew it, clamouring on, till Ida heard,
Look'd up, and rising slowly from me, stood
Erect and silent, striking with her glance
The mother, me, the child; but he that lay
Beside us, Cyril, batter'd as he was,
Trail'd himself up on one knee:
then he drew
Her robe to meet his lips, and down
she look'd
At the arm'd man sideways, pitying,
as it seem'd,
Or self-involved; but when she learnt his
face,
Remembering his ill-omen'd song, arose
Once more thro' all her height, and o'er him
grew
Tall as a figure lengthen'd on the sand
When the tide ebbs in sunshine, and he said
'O fair and strong and terrible! Lioness
That with your long locks play the Lion's
mane!
But Love and Nature, these are two more
terrible
And stronger. See, your foot is on our necks,
We vanquish'd, you the Victor of your will.

That would you more? give her the child! remain
Orb'd in your isolation: he is dead,
Or all as dead: henceforth we let you be:
Win you the hearts of women; and beware
Lest, where you seek the common love of these,
The common hate with the revolving wheel
Should drag you down, and some great Nemesis
Break from a darken'd future; crown'd with fire,
And tread you out for ever: but howsoe'er
Fix'd in yourself, never in your own arms
To hold your own, deny not hers to her,
Give her the child! O if, I say, you keep
One pulse that beats true woman, if you loved
The breast that fed or arm that dandled you,
Or own one part of sense not flint to prayer,
Give her the child! or if you scorn to lay it,
Yourself, in hands so lately claspt with yours,
Or speak to her, your dearest, her one fault
The tenderness, not yours, that could not kill,
Give *me* it: *I* will give it her.'

He said:
At first her eye with slow dilation roll'd
Dry flame, she listening; after sank and sank

And, into mournful twilight mellowing,
dwelt
Full on the child; she took it: 'Pretty bud!
Lily of the vale! half open'd bell of the
woods!
Sole comfort of my dark hour, when a world
Of traitorous friend and broken system made
No purple in the distance, mystery,
Pledge of a love not to be mine, farewell;
These men are hard upon us as of old,
We two must part: and yet how fain was I
To dream thy cause embraced in mine,
to think
I might be something to thee, when I felt
Thy helpless warmth about my barren
breast
In the dead prime: but may thy mother
prove
As true to thee as false, false, false to me!
And, if thou needs must bear the yoke,
I wish it
Gentle as freedom' — here she kiss'd it:
then —
'All good go with thee! take it, Sir,' and so
Laid the soft babe in his hard-mailed hands,
Who turn'd half-round to Psyche as she
sprang
To meet it, with an eye that swum in thanks;
Then felt it sound and whole from head to
foot,

And hugg'd and never hugg'd it close
enough,
And in her hunger mouth'd and
mumbled it,
And hid her bosom with it; after that
Put on more calm and added suppliantly:

'We two were friends: I go to mine own
land
For ever: find some other: as for me
I scarce am fit for your great plans:
yet speak to me,
Say one soft word and let me part forgiven.'

But Ida spoke not, rapt upon the child.
Then Arac. 'Ida — 'sdeath! you blame the
man;
You wrong yourselves — the woman is so
hard
Upon the woman. Come, a grace to me!
I am your warrior: I and mine have fought
Your battle: kiss her; take her hand,
she weeps:
'Sdeath! I would sooner fight thrice o'er
than see it. '

But Ida spoke not, gazing on the ground,
And reddening in the furrows of his chin,
And moved beyond his custom, Gama said:

‘I’ve heard that there is iron in the blood,
And I believe it, Not one word? not one?
Whence drew you this steel temper?
not from me,
Not from your mother now a saint with
saints.
She said you had a heart — I heard her say
it —
“Our Ida has a heart” — just ere she died —
“But see that some one with authority
Be near her still” and I — I sought for one —
All people said she had authority —
The Lady Blanche: much profit! Not one
word;
No! tho’ your father sues: see how you stand
Stiff as Lot’s wife, and all the good knights
maim’d,
I trust that there is no one hurt to death,
For your wild whim: and was it then for this,
Was it for this we gave our palace up,
Where we withdrew from summer heats and
state,
And had our wine and chess beneath the
planes,
And many a pleasant hour with her that’s
gone,
Ere you were born to vex us? Is it kind?
Speak to her I say: is this not she of whom,
When first she came, all flush’d you said
to me

Now had you got a friend of your own age
Now could you share your thought;
now should men see
Two women faster welded in one love
Than pairs of wedlock; she you walk'd with,
she
You talk'd with, whole nights long,
up in the tower,
Of sine and arc, spheroid and azimuth,
And right ascension, Heaven knows what;
and now
A word, but one, one little kindly word,
Not one to spare her out upon you, flint!
You love nor her, nor me, nor any; nay,
You shame your mother's judgement too.
Not one?
You will not? well — no heart have you,
or such
As fancies like the vermin in a nut
Have fretted all to dust and bitterness.'
So said the small king moved beyond his
wont.

But Ida stood nor spoke, drain'd of her
force
By many a varying influence and so long.
Down thro' her limbs a drooping languor
wept:
Her head a little bent; and on her mouth
A doubtful smile dwelt like a clouded moon

In a still water: then brake out my sire,
Lifting his grim head from my wounds.
'O you,
Woman, whom we thought woman even
now,
And were half fool'd to let you tend our son,
Because he might have wish'd it —
but we see
The accomplice of your madness
unforgiven,
And think that you might mix his draught
with death,
When your skies change again: the rougher
hand
Is safer: on to the tents take up the Prince.'

He rose, and while each ear was prick'd to
attend
A tempest, thro' the cloud that dimm'd her
broke
A genial warmth and light once more, and
shone
Thro' glittering drops on her sad friend.
'Come hither,
O Psyche,' she cried out, 'embrace me,
come,
Quick while I melt; make reconcilement
sure
With one that cannot keep her mind an
hour:

Come to the hollow heart they slander so!
Kiss and be friends, like children being
chid!
I seem no more: *I* want forgiveness too:
I should have had to do with none but
maids,
That have no links with men. Ah false but
dear,
Dear traitor, too much loved, why? — why?
— Yet see,
Before these kings we embrace you yet once
more
With all forgiveness, all oblivion,
And trust, not love, you less.
And now, O Sire,
Grant me your son, to nurse, to wait upon
him,
Like mine own brother. For my debt to him,
This nightmare weight of gratitude,
I know it;
Taunt me no more: yourself and yours shall
have
Free adit; we will scatter all our maids
Till happier times each to her proper
hearth:
What use to keep them here — now?
grant my prayer.
Help, father, brother, help; speak to the king:
Thaw this male nature to some touch of
that

Which kills me with myself, and drags me
down
From my fixt height to mob me up
with all
The soft and milky rabble of womankind,
Poor weakling ev'n as they are.'
Passionate tears
Follow'd: the king replied not: Cyril said:
'Your brother, Lady, — Florian, —
ask for him
Of your great head — for he is wounded
too —
That you may tend upon him with the
prince.'
'Aye so,' said Ida with a bitter smile,
'Our laws are broken: let him enter too,
Then Violet, she that sang the mournful
song,
And had a cousin tumbled on the plain,
Petition'd too for him. 'Aye so,' she said,
'I stagger in the stream: I cannot keep
My heart an eddy from the brawling hour:
We break our laws with ease, but let it be.'
'Aye so?' said Blanche: 'Amazed am I to
hear
Your Highness: but your Highness breaks
with ease
The law your Highness did not make:
'twas I.
I had been wedded-wife, I knew mankind,

And block'd them out; but these men came to woo
Your Highness — verily I think to win.'

So she, and turn'd askance a wintry eye:
But Ida with a voice, that like a bell
Toll'd by an earthquake in a trembling tower,
Rang ruin, answer'd full of grief and scorn.

'Fling our doors wide! all, all, not one, but all,
Not only he, but by my mother's soul,
Whatever man lies wounded, friend or foe,
Shall enter, if he will. Let our girls flit,
Till the storm die! but had you stood by us,
The roar that breaks the Pharos from his base
Had left us rock. She fain would sting us too,
But shall not, Pass, and mingle with your likes.
We brook no further insult but are gone.

She turn'd; the very nape of her white neck
Was rosed with indignation: but the Prince
Her brother came; the king her father charm'd

Her wounded soul with words: nor did mine own
Refuse her proffer, lastly gave his hand.

Then us they lifted up, dead weights, and bare
Straight to the doors: to them the doors gave way
Groaning, and in the Vestal entry shriek'd
The virgin marble under iron heels:
And on they moved and gain'd the hall, and there
Rested: but great the crush was, and each base,
To left and right, of those tall columns drown'd
In silken fluctuation and the swarm
Of female whisperers: at the further end
Was Ida by the throne, the two great cats
Close by her, like supporters on a shield,
Bow-back'd with fear: but in the centre stood
The common men with rolling eyes; amazed
They glared upon the women, and aghast
The women stared at these, all silent, save
When armour clash'd or jingled, while the day,
Descending, struck athwart the hall, and shot
A flying splendour out of brass and steel,

That o'er the statues leapt from head to
head,
Now fired an angry Pallas on the helm,
Now set a wrathful Dian's moon on flame,
And now and then an echo started up,
And shuddering tied from room to room,
and died
Of fright in far apartments.
Then the voice
Of Ida sounded, issuing ordinance:
And me they bore up the broad stairs,
and thro'
The long-laid galleries past a hundred
doors
To one deep chamber shut from sound,
and due
To languid limbs and sickness; left me in it;
And others otherwhere they laid; and all
That afternoon a sound arose of hoof
And chariot, many a maiden passing home
Till happier times; but some were left of
those
Held sagest, and the great lords out and in,
From those two hosts that lay beside the
walls,
Walk'd at their will, and everything was
changed.

*Ask me no more: the moon may draw the
sea;*

The cloud may stoop from heaven and take the shape,
With fold to fold, of mountain or of cape;
But O too fond, when have I answer'd thee?
Ask me no more.

Ask me no more: what answer should I give?
I love not hollow cheek or faded eye:
Yet, O my friend, I will not have thee die!
Ask me no more, lest I should bid thee live;
Ask me no more.

Ask me no more: thy fate and mine are seal'd
I strove against the stream and all in vain:
Let the great river take me to the main:
No more, dear love, for at a touch I yield;
Ask me no more.

VII

So was their sanctuary violated,
So their fair college turn'd to hospital;
At first with all confusion: by and by
Sweet order lived again with other laws:
A kindlier influence reign'd; and everywhere
Low voices with the ministering hand

Hung round the sick: the maidens came, they talk'd,
They sang, they read: till she not fair, began
To gather light, and she that was, became
Her former beauty treble; and to and fro
With books, with flowers, with Angel offices,
Like creatures native unto gracious act,
And in their own clear element, they moved.

But sadness on the soul of Ida fell,
And hatred of her weakness, blent with shame.
Old studies fail'd; seldom she spoke; but oft
Clomb to the roofs, and gazed alone for hours
On that disastrous leaguer, swarms of men
Darkening her female field: void was her use;
And she as one that climbs a peak to gaze
O'er land and main, and sees a great black cloud
Drag inward from the deeps, a wall of night,
Blot out the slope of sea from verge to shore,
And suck the blinding splendour from the sand,
And quenching lake by lake and tarn by tarn
Expunge the world: so fared she gazing there;
So blacken'd all her world in secret, blank
And waste it seem'd and vain; till down she came,

And found fair peace once more among the sick.

And twilight dawn'd; and morn by morn the lark
Shot up and shrill'd in flickering gyres, but I
Lay silent in the muffled cage of life:
And, twilight gloom'd; and broader-grown the bowers
Drew the great night into themselves, and Heaven,
Star after star, arose and fell; but I,
Deeper than those weird doubts could reach me, lay
Quite sunder'd from the moving Universe,
Nor knew what eye was on me, nor the hand
That nursed me, more than infants in their sleep.

But Psyche tended Florian: with her oft,
Melissa came; for Blanche had gone, but left
Her child among us, willing she should keep
Court-favour: here and there the small bright head,
A light of healing, glanced about the cough,
Or thro' the parted silks the tender face
Peep'd, shining in upon the wounded man
With blush and smile, a medicine in themselves
To wile the length from languorous hours,

and draw
The sting from pain; nor seem'd it strange that soon
He rose up whole, and those fair charities
Join'd at her side, nor stranger seem'd that hearts
So gentle, so employ'd, should close in love,
Than when two dewdrops on the petal shake
To the same sweet air, and tremble deeper down,
And slip at once all-fragrant into one.

Less prosperously the second suit obtain'd
At first with Psyche. Not tho' Blanche had sworn
That after that dark night among the fields
She needs must wed him for her own good name;
Not tho' he built upon the babe restored;
Nor tho' she liked him, yielded she, but fear'd
To incense the Head once more; till on a day
When Cyril pleaded, Ida came behind
Seen but of Psyche: on her foot she hung
A moment, and she heard, at which her face
A little flush'd, and she past on; but each
Assumed from thence a half-consent involved

In stillness, plighted troth, and were at peace.

Nor only these: Love in the sacred halls
Held carnival at will, and flying struck
With showers of random sweet on maid and
man.
Nor did her father cease to press my claim
Nor did mine own now reconciled; nor yet
Did those twin brothers, risen again and
whole;
Nor Arac, satiate with his victory.

But I lay still, and with me oft she sat:
Then came a change; for sometimes I would
catch
Her hand in wild delirium, gripe it hard,
And fling it like a viper off, and shriek,
'You are not Ida;' clasp it once again,
And call her Ida, tho' I knew her not,
And call her sweet, as if in irony,
And call her hard and cold which seem'd a
truth:
And still she fear'd that I should lose my
mind,
And often she believed that I should die:
Till out of long frustration of her care,
And pensive tendance in the all weary
noons,
And watches in the dead, the dark,
when clocks

Throbb'd thunder thro' the palace floors, or
call'd
On flying Time from all their silver
tongues —
And out of memories of her kindlier days,
And sidelong glances at my father's grief,
And at the happy lovers heart in heart —
And out of hauntings of my spoken love,
And lonely listenings to my mutter'd dream,
And often feeling of the helpless bands,
And wordless broodings on the wasted
cheek —
From all a closer interest flourish'd up,
Tenderness touch by touch, and last,
to these,
Love, like an Alpine harebell hung with
tears
By some cold morning glacier; frail at first
And feeble, all unconscious of itself,
But such as gather'd colour day by day.

Last I woke sane, but wellnigh close to
death
For weakness: it was evening: silent light
Slept on the painted walls, wherein were
wrought
Two grand designs; for on one side arose
The women up in wild revolt, and storm'd
At the Oppian law. Titanic shapes,
they cramm'd

The forum, and half-crush'd among the rest
A dwarf-like Cato cower'd. On the other side
Hortensia spoke against the tax; behind,
A train of dames: by axe and eagle sat,
With all their foreheads drawn in Roman
 scowls,
And half the wolf's-milk curdled in their
 veins,
The fierce triumvirs; and before them paused
Hortensia, pleading: angry was her face.

I saw the forms: I knew not where I was:
They did but look like hollow shows;
 nor more
Sweet Ida: palm to palm she sat: the dew
Dwelt in her eyes, and softer all her shape
And rounder seem'd: I moved: I sigh'd:
 a touch
Came round my wrist, and tears upon my
 hand:
Then all for languor and self-pity ran
Mine down my face, and with what life
 I had,
And like a flower that cannot all unfold,
So drench'd it is with tempest, to the sun,
Yet, as it may, turns toward him, I on her
Fixt my faint eyes, and utter'd whisperingly:

'If you be, what I think you, some sweet
 dream,

I would but ask you to fulfil yourself:
But if you be that Ida whom I knew,
I ask you nothing: only, if a dream,
Sweet dream, be perfect. I shall die to-night.
Stoop down and seem to kiss me ere I die.'

I could no more, but lay like one in trance,
That hears his burial talk'd of by his friends,
And cannot speak, nor move, nor make one sign,
But lies and dreads his doom. She turn'd; she paused;
She stoop'd; and out of languor leapt a cry;
Leapt fiery Passion from the brinks of death;
And I believed that in the living world
My spirit closed with Ida's at the lips;
Till back I fell, and from mine arms she rose
Glowing all over noble shame; and all
Her falser self slipt from her like a robe,
And left her woman, lovelier in her mood
Than in her mould that other, when she came
From barren deeps to conquer all with love;
And down the streaming crystal dropt; and she
Far-fleeted by the purple island-sides,
Naked, a double light in air and wave,
To meet her Graces, where they deck'd her out

For worship without end; nor end of mine,
Stateliest, for thee! but mute she glided forth,
Nor glanced behind her, and I sank and slept,
Fill'd thro' and thro' with Love, a happy sleep.

Deep in the night I woke: she, near me, held
A volume of the Poets of her land:
There to herself, all in low tones, she read.

'Now sleeps the crimson petal now the white;
Nor waves the cypress in the palace walk;
Nor winks the gold fin in the porphyry font:
The fire-fly wakens: waken thou with me.

Now droops the milkwhite peacock like a ghost,
And like a ghost she glimmers on to me.

Now lies the earth all Danaë to the stars,
And all thy heart lies open unto me.

Now slides the silent meteor on, and leaves
A shining furrow, all thy thoughts in me.

Now folds the lily all her sweetness up,
And slips into tho bosom of the lake:
So fold thyself, my dearest, thou, and slip
Into my bosom and be lost in me.'

I heard her turn the page; she found a small
Sweet Idyl, and once more, as low, she read:

'Come down, O maid, from yonder mountain height:
What pleasure lives in height (the shepherd sang)
In height and cold, the splendour of the hills?
But cease to move so near the Heavens, and cease
To glide a sunbeam by the blasted Pine,
To sit a star upon the sparkling spire;
And come, for Love is of the valley, come,
For Love is of the valley, come thou down
And find him; by the happy threshold, he,
Or hand in hand with Plenty in the maize
Or red with spirted purple of the vats,
Or foxlike in the vine, nor cares to walk
With Death and Morning on the silver horns,
Nor wilt thou snare him in the white ravine,
Nor find him dropt upon the firths of ice,
That huddling slant in furrow-cloven falls

To roll the torrent out of dusky doors:
But follow; let the torrent dance thee down
To find him in the valley; let the wild
Lean-headed Eagles yelp alone, and leave
The monstrous ledges there to slope, and spill
Their thousand wreaths of dangling water smoke,
That like a broken purpose waste in air:
So waste not thou, but come, for all the vales
Await thee; azure pillars of the hearth
Arise to thee; the children call, and I
Thy shepherd pipe, and sweet is every sound,
Sweeter thy voice, but every sound is sweet;
Myriads of rivulets hurrying thro' the lawn,
The moan of doves in immemorial elms,
And murmuring of innumerable bees.'

So she low-toned; while with shut eyes I lay
Listening; then look'd. Pale was the perfect face;
The bosom with long sighs labour'd; and meek
Seem'd the full lips, and mild the luminous eyes,
And the voice trembled and the hand.

She said
Brokenly, that she knew it, she had fail'd
In sweet humility; had fail'd in all;
That all her labour was but as a block
Left in the quarry; but she still were loath,
She still were loath to yield herself to one
That wholly scorn'd to help their equal rights
Against the sons of men, and barbarous laws.
She pray'd me not to judge their cause from her
That wrong'd it, sought far less for truth than power
In knowledge: something wild within her breast,
A greater than all knowledge, beat her down.
And she had nursed me there from week to week:
Much had she learnt in little time. In part
It was ill counsel had misled the girl
To vex true hearts: yet was she but a girl —
'Ah fool, and made myself a Queen of farce!
When comes another such? never, I think,
Till the Sun drop dead from the signs.'
Her voice
Choked, and her forehead sank upon her hands,
And her great heart thro' all the faultful Past

Went sorrowing in a pause I dared not
break;
Till notice of a change in the dark world
Was lispt about the acacias, and a bird,
That early woke to feed her little ones,
Sent from a dewy breast a cry for light:
She moved, and at her feet the volume
fell.

'Blame not thyself too much,' I said, 'nor
blame
Too much the sons of men and barbarous
laws;
These were the rough ways of the world till
now.
Henceforth thou hast a helper, me,
that know
The woman's cause is man's: they rise or
sink
Together, dwarf'd or godlike, bond or free:
For she that out of Lethe scales with man
The shining steps of Nature, shares with
man
His nights, his days, moves with him to one
goal,
Stays all the fair young planet in her
hands —
If she be small, slight-natured, miserable,
How shall men grow? but work no more
alone!

Our place is much: as far as in us lies
We two will serve them both in aiding her —
Will clear away the parasitic forms
That seem to keep her up but drag her
down —
Will leave her space to burgeon out of all
Within her — let her make herself her own
To give or keep, to live and learn and be
All that not harms distinctive womanhood.
For woman is not undevelopt man,
But diverse: could we make her as the man,
Sweet Love were slain: his dearest bond is
this,
Not like to like, but like in difference.
Yet in the long years liker must they grow;
The man be more of woman, she of man;
He gain in sweetness and in moral height
Nor lose the wrestling thews that throw the
world;
She mental breadth, nor fail in childward
care,
Nor lose the childlike in the larger mind;
Till at the last she set herself to man,
Like perfect music unto noble words;
And so these twain, upon the skirts of Time,
Sit side by side, full-summ'd in all their
powers,
Dispensing harvest, sowing the To-be,
Self-reverent each and reverencing each,
Distinct in individualities,

But like each other ev'n as those who love.
Then comes the statelier Eden back to
men:
Then reign the world's great bridals, chaste
and calm:
Then springs the crowning race of
humankind.
May these things be!'
Sighing she spoke 'I fear
They will not.'
'Dear, but let us type them now
In our own lives, and this proud watchword
rest
Of equal; seeing either sex alone
Is half itself, and in true marriage lies
Nor equal, nor unequal: each fulfils
Defect in each, and always thought in
thought,
Purpose in purpose, will in will, they grow,
The single pure and perfect animal,
The two-cell'd heart beating,
with one full stroke,
Life.'
And again sighing she spoke: 'A dream
That once was mine! what woman taught
you this?'

'Alone,' I said, 'from earlier than I know,
Immersed in rich foreshadowings of the
world,

I loved the woman: he, that doth not, lives
A drowning life, besotted in sweet self,
Or pines in sad experience worse than death,
Or keeps his wing'd affections clipt with
    crime:
Yet was there one thro' whom I loved her,
    one
Not learned, save in gracious household
    ways,
Not perfect, nay, but full of tender wants,
No Angel, but a dearer being, all dipt
In Angel instincts, breathing Paradise,
Interpreter between the Gods and men
Who look'd all native to her place, and yet
On tiptoe seem'd to touch upon a sphere
Too gross to tread, and all male minds
    perforce
Sway'd to her from their orbits as they
    moved,
And girdled her with music. Happy he
With such a mother! faith in womankind
Beats with his blood, and trust in all things
    high
Comes easy to him, and tho' he trip and fall
He shall not blind his soul with clay.'
                                        'But I,'
Said Ida, tremulously, 'so all unlike —
It seems you love to cheat yourself with
    words:
This mother is your model. I have heard

Of your strange doubts: they well might be: I seem
A mockery to my own self. Never, Prince;
You cannot love me.'
'Nay but thee' I said
'From yearlong poring on thy pictured eyes,
Ere seen I loved, and loved thee seen, and saw
Thee woman thro' the crust of iron moods
That mask'd thee from men's reverence up, and forced
Sweet love on pranks of saucy boyhood: now,
Giv'n back to life, to life indeed, thro' thee,
Indeed I love: the new day comes, the light
Dearer for night, as dearer thou for faults
Lived over: lift thine eyes; my doubts are dead,
My haunting sense of hollow shows: the change,
This truthful change in thee has kill'd it. Dear,
Look up, and let thy nature strike on mine,
Like yonder morning on the blind half-world;
Approach and fear not; breathe upon my brows;
In that fine air I tremble, all the past
Melts mist-like into this bright hour, and this

Is morn to more, and all the rich to-come
Reels, as the golden Autumn woodland reels
Athwart the smoke of burning weeds.
Forgive me, I waste my heart in signs: let be. My bride,
My wife, my life. O we will walk this world,
Yoked in all exercise of noble end,
And so thro' those dark gates across the wild
That no man knows. Indeed I love thee: come,
Yield thyself up: my hopes and thine are one:
Accomplish thou my manhood and thyself;
Lay thy sweet hands in mine and trust to me.

Conclusion

So closed our tale, of which I give you all
The random scheme as wildly as it rose:
The words are mostly mine; for when we ceased
There came a minute's pause, and Walter said,
'I wish she had not yielded!' then to me,
'What, if you drest it up poetically!'

So pray'd the men, the women: I gave assent:
Yet how to bind the scatter'd scheme of seven
Together in one sheaf? What style could suit?
The men required that I should give throughout
The sort of mock-heroic gigantesque,
With which we banter'd little Lilia first:
The women — and perhaps they felt their power,
For something in the ballads which they sang,
Or in their silent influence as they sat
Had ever seem'd to wrestle with burlesque,
And drove us, last, to quite a solemn close —
They hated banter, wish'd for something real,
A gallant fight, a noble princess — why
Not make her true-heroic — true-sublime?
Or all, they said, as earnest as the close?
Which yet with such a framework scarce could be.
Then rose a little feud betwixt the two,
Betwixt the mockers and the realists:
And I, betwixt them both, to please them both,
And yet to give the story as it rose,

I moved as in a strange diagonal,
And maybe neither pleased myself nor them.

But Lilia pleased me, for she took no part
In our dispute: the sequel of the tale
Had touch'd her; and she sat, she pluck'd
the grass,
She flung it from her, thinking: last, she fixt
A showery glance upon her aunt, and said,
'You — tell us what we are' — who might
have told,
For she was cramm'd with theories out of
books,
But that there rose a shout: the gates were
closed
At sunset, and the crowd were swarming
now,
To take their leave, about the garden rails.

So I and some went out to these:
we climb'd
The slope to Vivian-place, and turning saw
The happy valleys, half in light, and half
Far-shadowing from the west, a land of
peace;
Grey halls alone among their massive
groves;
Trim hamlets; here and there a rustic tower
Half-lost in belts of hop and breadths of
wheat;

The shimmering glimpses of a stream;
the seas;
A red sail, or a white; and far beyond, I
Imagined more than seen, the skirts of
France,

'Look there, a garden!' said my college
friend,
The Tory member's elder son, 'and there!
God bless the narrow sea which keeps her
off,
And keeps our Britain, whole within herself,
A nation yet, the rulers and the ruled —
Some sense of duty, something of a faith,
Some reverence for the laws ourselves have
made,
Some patient force to change them when we
will,
Some civic manhood firm against the
crowd —
But yonder, whiff! there comes a sudden
heat,
The gravest citizen seems to lose his head,
The king is scared, the soldier will not fight,
The little boys begin to shoot and stab,
A kingdom topples over with a shriek
Like an old woman, and down rolls the
world
In mock heroics stranger than our own;
Revolts, republics, revolutions, most

No graver than a schoolboys' barring out;
Too comic for the solemn things they are,
Too solemn for the comic touches in them,
Like our wild Princess with as wise a dream
As some of theirs — God bless the narrow seas!
I wish they were a whole Atlantic broad.'

'Have patience,' I replied, 'ourselves are full
Of social wrong; and maybe wildest dreams
Are but the needful preludes of the truth:
For me, the genial day, the happy crowd,
The sport half-science, fill me with a faith.
This fine old world of ours is but a child
Yet in the go-cart. Patience! Give it time
To learn its limbs: there is a hand that guides.'

In such discourse we gain'd the garden rails,
And there we saw Sir Walter where he stood,
Before a tower of crimson holly-oaks,
Among six boys, head under head, and look'd
No little lily-handed Baronet he,
A great broad-shoulder'd genial Englishman,
A lord of fat prize-oxen and of sheep,
A raiser of huge melons and of pine,

A patron of some thirty charities,
A pamphleteer on guano and on grain,
A quarter-sessions chairman, abler none;
Fair-hair'd and redder than a windy
morn;
Now shaking hands with him, now him,
of those
That stood the nearest — now address'd to
speech —
Who spoke few words and pithy, such as
closed
Welcome, farewell, and welcome for the
year
To follow: a shout rose again, and made
The long line of the approaching rookery
swerve
From the elms, and shook the branches of
the deer
From slope to slope thro' distant ferns,
and rang
Beyond the bourn of sunset; O, a shout
More joyful than the city-roar that hails
Premier or king! Why should not these great
Sirs
Give up their parks some dozen times a year
To let the people breathe? So thrice they
cried
I likewise, and in groups they stream'd away.

But we went back to the Abbey, and sat on

So much the gathering darkness charm'd: we sat
But spoke not, rapt in nameless reverie,
Perchance upon the future man: the walls
Blacken'd about us, bats wheel'd, and owls whoop'd,
And gradually the powers of the night,
That range above the region of the wind,
Deepening the courts of twilight broke them up
Thro' all the silent spaces of the worlds,
Beyond all thought into the Heaven of Heavens.

Last little Lilia, rising quietly,
Disrobed the glimmering statue of Sir Ralph
From those rich silks, and home well-pleased we went.

To —

After Reading a Life and Letters

'Cursed be he that moves my bones'
Shakespeare's Epitaph

You might have won the Poet's name,
If such be worth the winning now,

And gain'd a laurel for your brow
Of sounder leaf than I can claim;

But you have made the wiser choice,
A life that moves to gracious ends
Thro' troops of unrecording friends,
A deedful life, a silent voice:

And you have miss'd the irreverent doom
Of those that wear the Poet's crown:
Hereafter, neither knave nor clown
Shall hold their orgies at your tomb.

For now the Poet cannot die,
Nor leave his music as of old,
But round him ere he scarce be cold
Begins the scandal and the cry:

'Proclaim the faults he would not show:
Break lock and seal: betray the trust:
Keep nothing sacred: 'tis but just
The many-headed beast should know.'

Ah shameless! for he did but sing
A song that pleased us from its worth;
No public life was his on earth,
No blazon'd statesman he, nor king.

He gave the people of his best:
His worst he kept, his best he gave.

My Shakespeare's curse on clown and knave
Who will not let his ashes rest!

Who make it seem more sweet to be
The little life of bank and brier,
The bird that pipes his lone desire
And dies unheard within his tree,

Than he that warbles long and loud
And drops at Glory's temple-gates,
For whom the carrion-vulture waits
To tear his heart before the crowd!

We hope you have enjoyed this Large Print book. Other Thorndike, Wheeler or Chivers Press Large Print books are available at your library or directly from the publishers.

For more information about current and upcoming titles, please call or write, without obligation, to:

Publisher
Thorndike Press
295 Kennedy Memorial Drive
Waterville, ME 04901
Tel. (800) 223-1244

Or visit our Web site at:
www.gale.com/thorndike
www.gale.com/wheeler

OR

Chivers Large Print
published by BBC Audiobooks Ltd
St James House, The Square
Lower Bristol Road
Bath BA2 3BH
England
Tel. +44(0) 800 136919
email: bbcaudiobooks@bbc.co.uk
www.bbcaudiobooks.co.uk

All our Large Print titles are designed for easy reading, and all our books are made to last.